GIVING the MINISTRY AWAY

Empowering Single Adults for Effective Leadership

TERRY HERSHEY
KAREN BUTLER • RICH HURST

NAVPRESS
A MINISTRY OF THE NAVIGATORS
P.O.BOX 35001, COLORADO SPRINGS, COLORADO 80935

Cover illustration: Tim Lewis
Those who assisted with the editing and production of this book are:
Don Burmania, Cindy Hansen, Dan Jamison, Jerry Jones, Marie
Kohlwaies, Jean Stephens, Jon Stine, Debby Weaver, Steve Webb,
Thom Westergren, and Debbie Fawcett.

Unless otherwise identified, all Scripture in this publication is from
the *Holy Bible: New International Version* (NIV). Copyright © 1973,
1978, 1984, International Bible Society. Used by permission of
Zondervan Bible Publishers. Another version used is the *Modern
Language Bible: The Berkeley Version in Modern English* (MLB),
copyright © 1945, 1959, 1969 by Zondervan Publishing House,
used by permission.

Printed in the United States of America

The Navigators is an interdenominational Christian organization.
Jesus Christ gave His followers the Great Commission to go and
make disciples (Matthew 28:19). The aim of The Navigators is to
help fulfill that commission by multiplying laborers for Christ in
every nation.

NavPress is the publishing ministry of The Navigators. NavPress
publications are tools to help Christians grow. Although publications alone cannot make disciples or change lives, they can help
believers learn biblical discipleship, and apply what they learn to
their lives and ministries.

FOR A FREE CATALOG OF
NAVPRESS BOOKS & BIBLE STUDIES,
CALL TOLL FREE 1-800-366-7788 (USA)
or 1-416-499-4615 (CANADA)

Contents

Preface

Terry Hershey

How do we find committed leaders? What do we do with the high turnover? Where are all the leadership-quality people, anyway? Why do they keep leaving so soon?

How do we help people find their niche? Then, what do we do to make sure they don't get burned out?

Leadership is the common denominator. Regardless of where I travel, no matter what the size of the church or singles group, or whether the church has a full-, part-, or no-time minister, a common quandary in single adult ministry exists—leadership. That's why we wrote *Giving the Ministry Away*. The issues addressed in this book are the issues we all have felt keenly and wrestled with over the years in our own single adult ministries.

This is a book for people who:

- find themselves overwhelmed by the busyness of singles ministry;
- often feel like the weight of the ministry is on their shoulders alone;
- wonder why it seems people do not commit;
- have a difficult time finding persons to fill leadership vacancies;
- want to build a ministry where single adults feel empowered and encouraged;
- would like practical advice on building a leadership team;
- want to learn the ingredients of leadership training and the necessary elements of a relational ministry.

ABOUT THE AUTHORS

Why are there three authors? As everyone in ministry knows, it's a lot easier to do a project alone! So why bring three authors together?

The topic makes it important to write the book as a team. Why? Because healthy ministries are built around healthy teams and relationships. Plus, each of us brings his or her own area of expertise and interest, as well as his or her own history in single adult ministry. Toward that end, we have left the personalities of each individual in his or her writing. Each chapter begins with a memo from two team members, which allows an individual response from the other.

Terry Hershey

Terry lives in Woodinville, Washington, on a wooded acreage with his wife, Norva, and two dogs and seven cats. He spends his time writing, gardening, and walking his dogs. To pay for his "hobbies," Terry spends several weekends a year lecturing at conferences, seminars, and retreats.

Terry's involvement with single adult ministry started twelve years ago with his divorce. Since that time, he has served as single adult minister at two churches in Southern California. He was a co-founder of the National Association of Single Adult Leaders and of the Leadership Training Group, a ministry specializing in training individuals in single adult and young adult ministry. His writings include *Young Adult Ministry* (step-by-step help for starting or revitalizing your ministry with people ages eighteen to thirty-five); *Beginning Again: Life After a Relationship Ends*; *Intimacy: The Longing of Every Human Heart*; and *Go Away, Come Closer*.

Karen Butler

Karen Butler, formerly Karen Fledderman, lives in Everett, Washington, where she works with churches in single adult ministry, small groups, and leadership development. She holds a M.A. from Fuller Theological Seminary and a B.A. from Willamette University.

Karen became involved in singles and young adult ministry as a lay leader at University Presbyterian Church in Seattle, where she co-founded Cornerstone Ministry for young adults. Through those experiences, Karen decided to pursue further education and professional ministry. She served on the adult education staff at University Presbyterian Church for two years and served as consultant for adult ministries at John Knox Presbyterian Church, also in Seattle.

Karen has written materials for small groups and materials that accompany Terry Hershey's tape series *Intimacy* and *Slowing Down in a Hurry-Up World*. Her newest adventures include being a wife to husband, Steve, and a step-mom to Brad and Drew.

Rich Hurst

Rich Hurst is a popular conference and seminar speaker. He has worked with churches across the United States and Canada with their single and young adult ministries. His own experience with divorce gives him special insight into being "single again."

Rich is the singles pastor at the Crystal Cathedral in Garden Grove, California, coming from the staff at University Presbyterian Church in Seattle, Washington. He was a founding board member of the National Association of Single Adult Leaders and past director of Northwest Christian Singles. Rich holds a M.Div. from Fuller Theological Seminary, where his wife, Kim, is currently pursuing graduate studies. They are the new parents of Katy Quinn, a beautiful daughter.

A SPECIAL THANKS

Having three authors is hard enough. Getting three authors to work together without a competent editor is an exercise in perseverance. Fortunately, this book had one of the best. Our hats are off to Cindy Hansen, our competent, diligent, and committed editor. And besides, we like her a lot.

How to Use
This Book

*G*iving the Ministry Away offers tools and a philosophy to equip single adult leaders. Whether your church already has a single adult ministry or wants to begin one, this book tells how to build an effective team of supportive leaders who take ownership of the ministry.

THUMB THROUGH THE BOOK

The book is divided into four sections:

"Section One: A Foundation for Effective, Relational Single Adult Ministry" addresses hindrances to effective single adult ministries and helps you show others how to own the ministry.

"Section Two: Key Ingredients for Building a Core Team of Leaders" discusses how to build a leadership core team, use the Rocket planning method (a tool to organize ministry goals), and determine where leaders prefer to serve.

"Section Three: Taking Care of Yourself" offers ideas for balancing the need for a supportive, encouraging small group of friends with the need to say no, have Sabbath, and take time to rest.

"Section Four: Ideas and Resources for Relational Single Adult Ministry" outlines one-, two-, and three-day team-building retreat agendas for your single adult ministry, as well as schedules for one-day and six-week leadership training seminars. The Role Preference Test helps single adults determine the best specific ministry roles for them. The Team-Building Assessment helps leaders evaluate how well they are doing as a team. A glossary and a bibliography of resources complete this section.

REFLECT AND REVIEW

Read *Giving the Ministry Away* with an open mind. Answer the reflection questions at the end of each chapter by yourself or with a team of leaders. See single adults for who they are. Take an honest look at your motives for single adult ministry and areas that need change at your church. Be willing to risk! Finally, apply the material to yourself and your current situation.

MEET WITH INTERESTED INDIVIDUALS—A "DREAM TEAM"

Gather a group of three to five interested people who share some of your concerns about single adult ministry—your existing singles leadership team, church staff, lay people, or anyone interested in singles ministry. (If your church already has a singles ministry, include new people in this group. New people bring new ideas.)

PLAN A TEAM-BUILDING RETREAT

Conduct a one-, two-, or three-day retreat, using the agendas in chapter 12 for you and your teammates to work through this book and build a closer team. Invite your dream team (or all interested people) to attend the retreat.

SCHEDULE A LEADERSHIP TRAINING SEMINAR

Schedule a one-day or six-week leadership training seminar as outlined in chapter 13. The seminar will cover the highlights of each chapter in this book as you and your teammates train for effective leadership. Implement the ideas listed in this book to equip your ministry team with the necessary tools to own your ministry.

TAKE THE FOLLOWING SELF-EVALUATION

How do you view single adults? How do your stereotypes and beliefs possibly affect your singles ministry? Find out in the following Self-Evaluation adapted from an inventory found in *Young Adult Ministry*.[1]

Self-Evaluation
    1. What words or phrases come to mind when you hear the phrase *single adult*?
    2. Look back over your word list. How many descriptions are negative? (For example, *lonely, irresponsible, apathetic, selfish, over-sexed, noncommittal, ingrown, materialistic*.)
    How many descriptions are positive? (For example, *potential, creative, involved, opportunities, energy, leadership, hopeful, less anxiety*.)
    3. If you are like most people who have taken the evaluation, many of your descriptions will be negative. (Note: You may object, thinking that many single adults are, in fact, irresponsible, apathetic, etc. However, there's a difference between symptoms and fundamental identity.)
    What's the lesson? Be aware of your tendency toward stereotypes, myths, and closemindedness. We program for people the way we perceive them. Learn about singles. Learn about yourself and your call to ministry. Reeducate yourself and others with positive views on single adult ministry. Think of the exciting possibilities God has for the single adults in your program. Reflect God's grace.

A FOUNDATION FOR EFFECTIVE, RELATIONAL SINGLE ADULT MINISTRY

Chapter 1: Facts and Myths About Single Adults (page 15)
This chapter highlights facts about single adult ministry, myths about common perceptions of single persons, and basic assumptions about leadership. Learn to establish a foundation for effective, relational single adult ministry.

Chapter 2: Leadership: A New Definition (page 23)
This chapter defines leadership, specifically relational leadership in which the ministry is owned by the people. Learn ways to become an effective leader as you encourage other single adults to own the ministry.

Chapter 3: Obstacles to Effective Leadership (page 33)
This chapter gives an overview of common obstacles, such as taking ourselves too seriously, assuming all problems are "fixable," misunderstanding success, assuming people are irresponsible, and having a faulty perception of leadership. Learn how these obstacles get in the way of equipping others for leadership.

Chapter 4: A Theology of Being Empowered (page 47)
This chapter lists the characteristics of an empowered leader, such as knowing to whom you belong, knowing how to play, and being patient. Learn how to better give the ministry away by being empowered.

MEMO

TO: Terry

FROM: Rich and Karen

RE: Chapter 1: Facts and Myths
    About Single Adults

We have learned from experience that just saying
the phrase "single adult ministry" does not guarantee that everyone knows what you are talking about.
Help get us started on the right foot by covering:

- The facts that form a foundation for any
  single adult ministry
- The myths we have about single persons,
  and how these myths cloud our perceptions
  and affect our ministries
- Basic assumptions about leadership that
  will set the stage for the material in this
  book

CHAPTER ONE

Facts and Myths About Single Adults

Terry Hershey

I can't wait to get started," Darrin told me, pumping my hand enthusiastically after one of my seminars on single adult ministry. "I've got some great ideas, and I know a lot of people are excited to get them off the ground," he added.

I wished him well.

One year later, he called me. "It's not working like I had hoped," he admitted. "I need some fresh ideas."

Darrin's less-than-overwhelming start in singles ministry didn't surprise me. Like a lot of us, Darrin was so enthused about new ministry ideas that he never took the time to do any homework. And he still hadn't learned that effective ministry cannot be sustained on enthusiastic willpower alone.

A task well done needs adequate preparation. That includes effective ministry and effective leadership development. If our primary task is to give the ministry away—to give single adults ownership—we need to offer more than programs that dazzle and sizzle. We need to equip single adults for leadership. We need to work as a team to build an effective ministry.

When was the last time you signed a contract (insurance, major purchase, business agreement, etc.)? Did you notice that most of the document is made up of "fine print"—the things you should probably know, but don't really have the time and energy to worry about?

After talking with Darrin, I realized he didn't want to take any time to read the fine print. He wanted to jump right in—with new ideas and programs—without preparing a foundation for effective single adult ministry.

None of us come to this task with clean slates. We're all a lot like Darrin. So, before we launch into the book, let's begin to build a foundation for effective single adult ministry. Let's look at the fine print: facts about single adult ministry, myths about single adults, and assumptions about leadership.

FACTS ABOUT SINGLE ADULT MINISTRY

Transition Is a Fact of Life

While transition is a common theme throughout our culture, it is even more so for single persons because living situations, job opportunities and financial considerations make transition more likely. As a result, even the most successful single adult programs experience as much as a 60 percent turnover rate every five or six months. That sounds drastic. But transition is normal. It comes with the turf.

If turnover and transition bother you, I recommend that you get out of single adult ministry. It won't be long before you will resent the very people with whom you are called to minister.

What does this high rate of turnover mean for our ministry? I can think of two implications.

1. *We need not take transition personally.* It's dangerous to believe that people are not staying because of something we've done. We are not personally responsible for each turnover statistic that happens in our single adult program.

2. *Build short-term alternatives for commitments.* Instead of asking for one- or two-year commitments, ask for three- or six-month commitments. Instead of planning a twelve- or thirteen-week curriculum, plan a four- to six-week (maximum) curriculum. Instead of asking for one year commitments for small groups, ask for three months. Commitments must be built slowly and in small doses. (Note: Rich further addresses this issue in chapter 6. He asks leaders for one-year commitments with an evaluation after six months.)

> *If turnover and transition bother you, I recommend that you get out of single adult ministry. It won't be long before you will resent the very people with whom you are called to minister.*

Single Adult Ministry Is Not Youth Ministry

When I was a youth minister, I assumed it was my job to keep the group busy until their hormones wore out!

Sometimes the church treats single adults the same way: They need entertainment, because they haven't quite grown up yet. This breeds a "singles-equals-youth-ministry" mentality.

Hear this loudly and clearly: It is not our job to entertain adults. It is not our job to keep adults busy. It is not our job to alleviate loneliness. It is our job, should we decide to accept it, to give the ministry away to adults—to help equip them for ministry. There is a difference . . . a big difference.

Single Adults Cannot Be "Lumped Together"

Often we find ourselves frustrated because not everyone attends our new program. Our frustrations come from the assumption that one program can meet the needs of all the single adults in our church, and that it is our job to make everyone happy. This perception (and mentality) is faulty—and leads to ulcers.

Single persons reflect a wide variety of needs and interests. Consequently, one program cannot (and must not) attempt to meet the needs of all single adults. In other words, an effective ministry is a targeted ministry. We cannot hit every need, so we must choose our aim. This gives single adults an opportunity to dream, plan, and build their own ministry based on ways to meet specific needs.

Many People in the Church Are Threatened By Single Adults

I wish it weren't so, but wishing does not take away the reality that many people act as if singleness were a contagious disease—especially as if divorce were a contagious disease.

What does this mean? That much of single adult ministry is taking opportunities to dispel myths, to provide better information to both the church leadership and the congregation as a whole.

Single Adults Are the Church

We need to be careful lest our semantics betray us. We too easily say, "The church doesn't accept single people." Meaning, of course, that certain people don't show acceptance. We are implying, however that single adults are not the church. In all likelihood, the number of single adults in many urban churches may be 50 percent or higher.

Single Adult Ministry Is Bigger Than a Program for Single Persons

Giving the ministry away is not just about finding leadership positions for a singles program. It extends beyond the confines of a program just for single persons.

When Rich Hurst went to University Presbyterian Church in Seattle, Washington, to minister with single adults, there were no single persons on the twenty-four member session (church governing body). Five years later, there were nine.

MYTHS ABOUT SINGLE ADULTS

Single People Have More Time Than Married People

Many people hold the assumption that single adults want to be involved simply because they don't have anything else to do. The result is a continued bewilderment about our difficulty and tension in soliciting involvement.

It's dangerous business to generalize about segments of the population. It's too easy to be proved wrong, and even easier to form perceptions that eventually lead to disappointment, confusion, and even resentment.

It takes only a casual observation to tell me that I have many single friends who lead far more hectic, busy, and involved lives than I do. Ironically, many single adult parents have the least amount of available time of anyone.

What does all this mean? It means that we must begin to see that responsibility can and must be given in small doses. And that our hope to find one or two tireless volunteers to carry the whole load must be abandoned. The nineties bring to all of us more options, greater workloads, and less available time. Our challenge is to build teams where several people can share the load, provide smaller doses of time, and work together toward a common goal.

Single People Are Less Committed

"You know singles," is the common lament, meaning singles are less committed, or waiting for a better offer, or unwilling to be tied down, or difficult to predict . . . or all of the above.

I wonder, is that really the case? Or do single adults merely reflect the reality of the culture in which they live? Don't all of us—married and single—suffer from an inability to commit?

Addressing this inability to commit, a recent study from the Barna Research Group tells us that people are increasingly likely to call several churches their "home" church. The individual will choose among that select group of churches which one to attend on any given Sunday.

> Recognizing that they have a breadth of needs, and recognizing that most churches are incapable of satisfying that range of needs, adults will attend several churches, visiting each on a rotating or "as needed" basis. This is a consequence of the lack of felt commitment to any single congregation, the low premium placed upon loyalty in the baby boomer mind; the heightened selfishness of perspective; and the inability of most churches to develop a ministry which addresses a wide enough range of needs, or does so with quality.[1]

I'm convinced that we treat people the way we perceive them And we minister to or program for people the way we perceive them. In other words, if we see a group of people as irresponsible and noncommitted, then we will talk to them that way. And surprise! They will never let us down! Our programs become an entertainment wheel of fortune, an extension of our presumption that those to whom we minister are not capable of commitment and require entertainment until they "grow up." The more we think single adults are irresponsible, the more we believe we have to be responsible for everything.

What does this mean? Ministry must begin with an examination of our perceptions and misconceptions. Ministry must include re-education. What stereotypes exist in our churches? In our communities? In our singles groups? How do those stereotypes affect the way we plan? The way we program? In addition, the issue is not whether there is irresponsible behavior, but what we're doing to allow single adults (or anyone) to be different.

All Single People Are Hurting

Single adulthood is full of difficult transitions. Many come to single adult ministries in pain—from loss, grief, divorce, or loneliness. Unfortunately, an accepted theory persists that singles ministry is only an "emergency room" ministry—a lonely hearts club for the socially inept.

I disagree.

Emergency room care is an important and necessary element, to be sure, but not the full picture. I see two problems. First, we assume that a singles group is only a way station for the walking wounded until they are "mainstreamed." It's a myopic picture that comes from pity (a need to "fix them"), not compassion (where we see people as whole, and we can learn from them as well). Second, we assume that wounds or hurt are not part of anyone else's experience (as if mainstreaming or marriage eliminates woundedness). This view makes pain something we talk about only in the singles group—an unfortunate perspective that turns us into a church afraid to deal with life's rough edges.

> *Singles ministry is not just a program for single adults, but the way in which single adults are given power and responsibility in the church at large.*

We must continue to have places of support for wounded persons (divorce recovery, grief support groups, single parent care groups, abused or battered women shelters, twelve-step groups for addiction issues). At the same time, we must let the church know there is more to singles ministry than first aid. Singles ministry is not just a program for single adults, but the way in which single adults are given power and responsibility in the church at large.

All Single People Are Looking for a Marriage Partner

Even though it's the nineties, we are still shadowed by the theology that says the institution of marriage is preferable to singleness. And, say some, more desirable before God. The impact of such reckless thinking is damaging to our ministry efforts. It assumes that our programming is a means to an end—namely, getting the single people married.

Granted, single adult programs are a great place to meet people. Why discourage that? Granted, many marriages will come out of any singles group. But our job is not to be a dating service. Nor is it our job to imply by such presumption that singles ministry is a holding pattern for bigger and better things.

ASSUMPTIONS ABOUT LEADERSHIP

The Walls of the Church Do Not Define Ministry

Leadership involves more than simply filling available slots (president, vice-president, directors, etc.) left vacant by the last person who bailed out. We are experiencing a creativity crisis. Ministries are assumed to be "filling-in-the-blank" exercises. We haven't even begun to tap the well of creative ministry options. If nothing were impossible, what would you like to see happen in your church? In your community? We will further discuss these issues in chapter 9.

People Should Have One Job Outside, One Job Inside

We've all heard the statistic that 80 percent of the work is done by 20 percent of the people. That doesn't mean we have to continue the trend. If our purpose is relationship, then part of our job is to see that others don't become overloaded. Therefore, we strongly recommend that people have only one area of responsibility within the church at any one time. (In other words, one job outside—their regular nine-to-five work day—and one job inside the church). The alternative is burnout in six to twelve months.

Leadership Is Not Just Handing Out Assignments

Leadership is about building relationships. It is about building responsibility. It is about encouraging self-responsibility, or self-care. It is about empowering. (See the sidebar for definitions of these terms.)

In Mark's gospel, there's a story about Jesus speaking with compassion to a group of people who were like sheep on the hill. It struck me that His "ministry" was predicated on seeing these people in their particular situation, with their particular needs, wants, and desires. In fact, Jesus never talked to any two people in the same way (except, of course, the Pharisees!). In other words, He talked to people where they were, not where He was or where He (or myths) assumed they were. Jesus did His homework. It allowed Him to touch—and empower—real people and not just force a predetermined agenda or program on the next available unsuspecting audience.

Perhaps Jesus' example will allow us to slow down from our pell-mell hurry to launch the next "program ride" and take some time to read the fine print, which is

---

DEFINITIONS OF TERMS

Empower: Giving others power, responsibility, and ownership for dreams, ideas, tasks, and input. Giving people the ability and power to lead or make choices. Permitting and enabling them to take responsibility.

Personal Boundaries: The ability to say no. Learning your limits. Knowing you can't do everything.

Relational Leadership: Building people, not just starting a program. Creating an environment of nurture where others are empowered. Avoiding hierarchical or autocratic leadership, because the ministry is owned by the people.

Self-Responsibility: Personal development, self-care, and self-nurture to practice personal boundaries.

about people. Real particular individual single adults with dreams, needs, and hopes; single adults to be encouraged, supported, challenged, and empowered.

REFLECT AND REVIEW

Think about the material in this chapter, then answer the following questions. Remember, don't try to do the ministry alone. Whenever possible, discuss these questions with your single adult leadership team.

1. Do you agree that transition is a fact of life? Why, or why not? Discuss the types of transition that impact you and your group, and the sort of impact that transition brings.

2. What are some ways you can offer shorter introductory levels of commitment?

3. List the ways in which the church or single adult groups treat singles as youth. Think about the ways in which your program is hindered by "lumping" single adults together.

4. How have single adults impacted your church? In what ways have single adults contributed? Benefited?

5. Discuss where the following myths may originate. Give some illustrations of how these myths are perpetuated.

    a. Single people have more time than married people.
    b. Single people are less committed.
    c. All single people are hurting.
    d. All single people are looking for a marriage partner.

6. Why is it important for people to believe some of the above myths?

7. Do any of the above myths impact your group? In what ways?

8. Talk about ways in which your group can begin to dispel some of these myths in your group and in your church.

MEMO

TO: Terry

FROM: Rich and Karen

RE: Chapter 2: Leadership: A New Definition

Just saying the phrase "leadership development" isn't enough. People have so many images about leaders and leadership that these images cloud the discussion before we even get going! Maybe you can clarify with:

- Helpful definitions of leadership
- Ideas of what leadership is not
- Observations about becoming an effective leader

With some helpful definitions, we can begin to build a foundation for giving the ministry away.

CHAPTER TWO

Leadership: A New Definition

Terry Hershey

P icture a middle-aged man running breathlessly up a dirt road. He is wearing a Boy Scout uniform. His cheeks are red. The sweat trickles down his brow. His belly heaves with uneven breaths. His skinny white legs protrude oddly from his khaki shorts. Around a corner, he comes to a farmer standing beside the road, leaning lazily against a fence post, chewing on a blade of grass.

"Did you happen to see a bunch of scouts come by here?" he asks, with his hands on his knees, gasping for air.

"Yep," the farmer just stares and chews.

"Well?" demands the exasperated scout leader. "Where'd they go? I've got to find them, I'm their leader!"

WHO'S IN CHARGE?

It's a common scenario. We've all been in single adult ministries where there has been confusion about leadership. Who's in charge here, anyway? What's their job? Is it a calling for the few or the many? What does it mean to "be in charge"?

Does leadership mean taking responsibility?

... or having authority?

... or making tough decisions?

... or doing all the work?

... or blazing an unknown trail for the people who happen to follow?

... or all of the above?

... or none of the above?

If we are the ones in charge, what do we do now?

The confusion is not surprising. Leadership is a loaded term. We see images of tyrants, dictators, "the big cheeses," military commanders, and various categories of "kingdom builders." The common thread among these images is power—leading by force and might, or, more realistically, control. Keeping people and the organization under control is often the intention.

Although we may not want to perpetuate such an image of domination in our own lives (or, in some way, be implicated as one who dominates), we are still influenced by this picture that somehow we need to (or should) be "in control." "Can someone please tell me how I get these people to follow me?" we continually ask with the exasperation of the Boy Scout troop leader. "And once they start to follow, how can I get them to help me and appreciate what I am doing for them?"

At the same time, if we've been given any leadership responsibility, we've experienced the frustration of ungrateful followers, irresponsible committee members, noncommitted volunteers, overcrowded calenders, never-ending tasks, ominous deadlines, unmeasurable goals, changing expectations of others, and lack of appreciation. No wonder we want to find some way to bring it all under control.

Maybe what we need is a book on how to survive!

So we wonder, is it possible to perform our job or task without giving in to the need to dominate those who work with us? Is it possible to delegate and involve others in the task?

Is it possible to motivate other single adults to be involved in decision-making and ownership of the task?

Is it possible to do all this without resenting those with whom we work?

Is it possible not to be absorbed by the job?

Is it possible to be an effective leader without having to be all things to all people?

Is it possible to give a task away and trust that the individuals could do as good a job as we would have if we had done the task ourselves?

Good questions. Before we discuss possible answers, let's look at some faulty assumptions about leadership.

TEAM LEADERSHIP:
A KEY TO MAXIMIZING VOLUNTEERS IN THE CHURCH

The 1990s will bring to the forefront the crisis of lay leadership within the Christian church in this country. People will volunteer less of their time, since time will be the most treasured and least plentiful resource of the laity. Indeed, as boomers reach their forties and fifties, and attain more responsible corporate positions, their free time will decrease due to greater job responsibilities and the pressures of dealing with their adolescent children.

The expected decline in hours voluntarily given to the Church is partly a fault brought on by church leaders themselves. The Church has taken few steps in the past decade to give birth to a new generation of spiritual visionaries—people who devote a considerable portion of their minds to creating a new direction, structure, and movement within the Church that will capture the hearts of the laity at large. The consequences of the failure to cultivate that strata of leaders will be keenly felt by the year 2000. Most churches have utilized volunteers as slave labor, rather than carefully preparing those individuals for future positions of true leadership within the body.

By 2000, churches will recognize that team leadership will be the most effective use of lay leaders and volunteers. The role of the pastor will be to develop workable combinations of individuals who will share, rather than carry, the load of ministry. . . . Once again, this increased emphasis upon management of people will characterize tomorrow's (leader).[1]

MORE ASSUMPTIONS ABOUT LEADERSHIP

As in the story of the Boy Scouts leader, our problem perhaps is our assumptions about leadership. It seems that the North American mentality, is to see leadership in a purely hierarchical sense. The leader is the box at the top of the organizational chart—the person with the VIP status. It is true that all organizations demand leaders. Or visionaries. Or front-runners. Or pilots. Someone must be responsible for guiding and directing the organizational vessel.

With that I have no argument—all tasks require clear communication and a clear line of authority for decision-making. However, there's more to leadership than accomplishing tasks or measuring objectives or counting heads or deciding who resides in what box on the organizational chart. Leadership means more than titles or achieving a stated organizational goal.

Ministry is first and foremost, people. It is not buildings, budgets, reputations, or programs. Translation? Leadership is primarily relational. This assumption is foundational to everything else presented in this book. No longer hierarchical, our picture of leadership is now "circular." In other words, leadership and relationships are connected. We call this philosophy and style "relational" (or "circular") leadership—the charge and responsibility of empowering people, giving them power and responsibility. In the words of one author: "Leaders do not lead to lead; leaders lead to serve. They serve by leading; they lead by serving."[2]

"It sounds good on paper," we may easily object, "but how does all of this translate into our single adult ministries? What does it mean that leadership is relational, or circular? How do we put it into practice?"

Let's begin with what leadership does *not* mean.

Leadership Is Not Crowd Control

It is not crowd control. It is not just another variation on the mass media theme of making people feel good. Where we assume that our job is to be the barometer of people's happiness. Where our minds are consumed by the ever-present public opinion lure: "What will they think? What if there's nothing on the calender for Saturday night? What if nobody comes back? What if the church board doesn't like our new class curriculum?"

Leadership Is Not Entertainment

Relational leadership is not a matter of devising time-consuming activities to occupy single adults or relieve their boredom, or in the words of one urban pastor, "to keep people out of bars and other churches."

I think of a phone call I had with Don, a recently hired single adult minister in a California church. He is young, sincere, well-intentioned, and strongly motivated. Don believes his job is to keep a well-manicured calender of activities—as if church work were like a front lawn, susceptible to the criticism of every passing motorist.

"Why this intensity?" I asked him.

"Because it brings people in," he told me. "It keeps people coming back. And, in all honesty, it keeps the senior pastor off my back."

Because of this view of ministry—continual and relentless entertainment programming—Don does most of the duties himself ("It's easier to do a good job," he confessed) and always keeps an eye out for a better idea to try (which, ironically, was why he called me. He wanted to know what I thought were the top five program ideas for singles).

Leadership Is Not Application of Techniques

Don has not learned the difference yet between maintaining a program and building people. Relational leadership is not just the application of leadership techniques. It is not just program management, where we assume that our primary task is to accumulate the newest and best skills for calendaring and facility use. Where the concern of program management is with reputation and board approval. Whoever has the biggest and busiest (and therefore "the best") program is the winner of the program management contest.

Leadership Is Not People Domination and Manipulation

By the same token, relational leadership is not autocratic, or people domination. Autocratic leaders assume that their job is to change those with whom they work, teach "right" beliefs, or convict those who believe wrongly or differently. They assume that their job is to get people to follow their vision.

These are all inadequate assumptions, because relational leadership is not manipulation. It is not just a matter of having clout. Regardless of our motives, we cannot ultimately change those to whom we are responsible.

Leadership Is Not a Job-Required Obligation

Finally, relational leadership is not a job-required obligation. It is not a scenario for modern martyrdom, where we assume that if there is a task to be done, we will do it, realizing that other people won't actually help. Or, if they do, their commitment will certainly be suspect, and we won't get nearly the recognition we deserve.

So the question still remains . . .

WHAT IS RELATIONAL LEADERSHIP ANYWAY?

Relational leadership is self-responsibility in a place of authority. It is creating an environment for empowering others. Relational leadership is giving responsibility away. Or, to put it more bluntly, it is giving the ministry away. It doesn't matter whether that place of authority is the CEO of a major parachurch agency, the senior pastor of First Downtown Church, the director of young adult ministries, the minister of single adults, or the head of the setting-up-chairs committee for the Christian education year-end banquet. Regardless of the place, our call is self-responsibility and empowering others. That makes leadership relational. (Chapter 4 discusses the issues of self-responsibility, empowering, and self-care in greater detail.)

If I don't understand this indispensable premise, I easily become lost in my own task. Or as Eugene H. Peterson says, the result is to be "preoccupied with shopkeeper's concerns—how to keep the customers happy, how to lure customers away from competitors down the street, how to package the goods so that the customers will lay out more money."[3]

If I don't empower others, I do my best to stay one step ahead of my devouring calendar with its limitless capacity for trivial expectations. I take time management seminars. I buy better Xerox machines and add another secretary. I practice my appropriate public relations skills and buy books like this one. Yet, in the end, I'm back to where I started—a preoccupied shopkeeper.

I become tired ("If only there was one more day in the week."); irritated ("Why is it people are quick to tell me what needs to be done, but not so quick to thank me for it?"); and sometimes successful ("Did I tell you how many people we had in our class last week?"). But I am still a shopkeeper nonetheless.

This is not a book on what people in leadership roles do or should do. It is not just a book on efficiency. Or on better shopkeeping methods. It is intended for single adults and others who are responsible for actions and decisions that contribute to their church or organization. It reminds people that they must make choices based on effectiveness, not efficiency, and people development, not task accomplishment.

Therefore, this book is primarily about responsibility. Self-responsibility. And how self-responsibility is the foundation for relational leadership. (In other words, all the blue-ribbon ideas in the world won't help when our emotional/spiritual/relational well is dry.) With that in mind, how can we creatively learn to give the ministry away? What does it take to empower the people around us? What is the best way to guide others toward self-responsibility and successes in their own tasks? In the end then, this is not a book just about leadership, but about how do we develop leaders from those entrusted to us.

Before answering these questions, I must first make a disclaimer: Giving ministry away is dangerous business. Let's be honest. Ministry is far easier when you do it yourself. It is easier to be autocratic. In fact, leadership as self-responsibility and empowering is subversive teaching. Why? Because the powers-that-be may become angry if you do not entertain single adults, who, in turn, may become angry if you refuse to be their cruise director and entertainment coordinator. With our cultural emphasis on efficiency (measured by competency, productivity, and bottom-line pragmatics), we are susceptible to such pressure. As a result, we begrudgingly respond with our efficient application of our newly learned pragmatic skills and technologies. "Are there more exciting programs I can try?" we ask, throwing our hands into the air.

Giving ministry away, however, means trust—even trusting those who are not nearly as qualified as we are!

It means letting go.

It means not doing the task all alone.

It means self-care.

It means personal boundaries.

Such characteristics go against our cultural grain and our success as a pro-ductivity-oriented world. So let's not kid ourselves by assuming that giving away the ministry will be an easy transition to make. Leadership through self-responsibility and empowering can bring a radical shift in our current organization. Besides, some of us like to do the work all alone. Some are hooked on the martyrdom theme: "Nobody appreciates all the work I do!" We may not know what to do with ourselves if we started saying no to some of our obligations. After all, what will happen to our rep-utation if we start giving some of the ministry projects to "less-qualified" (which may include "less-spiritual" and "less-committed") single adults in our church?

RELATIONAL LEADERSHIP IS NOT . . .	RELATIONAL LEADERSHIP IS . . .
■ Crowd control—or making people happy ■ Entertainment—trying to relieve others' boredom ■ Application of leadership techniques—for reputation's sake or board approval ■ People domination and manipulation—trying to get others to follow our vision; trying to change others ■ A job-required obligation—resulting in a feeling of martyrdom	■ Self-responsibility in a place of authority ■ Creating an environment for empowering others ■ Creating an environment for giving away ownership. ■ Giving the ministry away

CHANGE VERSUS MAKING CHANGES

Relational leadership sounds like a good idea, yet, all too often, when people say they want to change, they really mean "making changes" rather than change. "Making changes" gives us the illusion that we are changing, when in fact we are applying Band-Aids and face lifts. (The same scenario exists when alcoholics quit drinking and become workaholics. They believe they have changed, but they are still "dry drunks," as obsessive as before.)

We don't want to change, we want a fix. In their book *The Addictive Organization*, Anne Wilson Schaef and Diane Fassel define a fix as "any process that the individual or group can get busy about so as not to face their own process, learn from it, and make full-scale changes. The former paradigm based on objectivist sci-ence provided fixes in the form of answers."[4]

In truth, too often that's what we want. Answers. Solutions. Newer and better programs. Making changes is essential to the need to maintain efficiency. Change, however, asks how we can be more effective. Unfortunately, we don't like to be chal-lenged to face the necessary internal changes that must be made. Holding on to our old paradigms is too comforting.

This book introduces a paradigm shift. Making changes calls for efficiency. Change requires effectiveness.

EFFICIENCY	EFFECTIVENESS
■ Program management—merely sponsoring events	■ Lifestyle modeling—ministry is people and relationships
■ Bottom-line pragmatics—concern about accumulating numbers and dollars	■ Influential—effect on people's lives
	■ Valid—everyone has a role
	■ Attractive—warm and user-friendly
■ Competence—only "experts" have responsibility	■ Network—everyone has a dream
	■ Real—honest and open
■ High-poweredness—sophistication for the sake of sophistication	■ Mutual respect—ownership by many
■ Expertise—only "experts" do the planning	■ Teamwork—many involved in seeing the dream come true
■ Consumerability—concern with "Does it sell?"	■ Creating an environment for empowering others
■ Control—ownership by one	■ Giving the ministry away
■ Lone Ranger—ideas by one	

BECOMING AN EFFECTIVE LEADER

What does it mean to be an effective leader? How do we work relationally, not hierarchically? What is the foundation of this new paradigm? Everything that follows, from our look at the theology of leadership to the resources and ideas in the last section, is based on the following five assumptions.

1. *Every Christian is a minister.* The fact that every Christian has a niche, a place, and a role is a biblical truth. In other words, the Body of Christ is owned by the Body of Christ. That statement may sound like a matter of semantics or redundant, but it is nonetheless true. Although we may say we firmly believe it, we seldom practice it. We need constant reminders that the smooth sailing of the Church is not set aside for the elite few who have been "trained" at the professional schools of navigation.

2. *Effective ministries are owned by the people.* Effective ministries are not owned by a select few. Leadership is not just a form of herding, using creative programming to efficiently occupy or move around groups of people. Your single adult ministry can be successful only when shared ownership exists.

3. *Effective ministries empower others.* It is not our job to parade our charisma before an adoring crowd or to impress those around us with our agenda or goals for the good of the group. It is our task (should we decide to accept it) to create environments where people can take ownership and begin to develop responsibility, self-care, and a vibrant faith.

David, a singles pastor, told me about Sharon, a single adult in his church who was the coordinator of the divorce recovery support group. Sharon had been in the singles group for more than a year, having come to the group through her own divorce recovery process. Over the past six months, she had volunteered for various small tasks.

Sharon was surprised when David approached her about becoming coordinator. She was quick to let him know that others were certainly more qualified. But he decided to invest in her. He wanted Sharon to own the responsibility and did not want to treat her just as a volunteer. David watched Sharon blossom over the next two years with a support team of five other single adults. She was more than a volunteer. She was a fellow minister. She became stronger as her confidence and self-esteem grew visibly. She also learned to say no to tasks that were not appropriate for her, while, at the same time, she delegated to other members of her team. Sharon is a picture of an empowered single adult.

4. *Effective ministries are built on a foundation of self-care, or self-responsibility.* Service (or self-sacrifice) does not mean relinquishing boundaries, becoming the victim of public opinion, losing self-respect, or needing to be a junior messiah. Self-responsibility and self-care happen only in fertile, supportive relationships, those times when we are taken from isolation and placed in a circle of friends who encourage, challenge, and energize us. In isolation, we are prone to shopkeeping, competition, and scorekeeping. In an environment of supportive relationships, however, we are reminded that our value is not tied to what we do. We are encouraged in our efforts, and we are challenged to stretch in areas that may be uncomfortable for us.

5. *Effective, successful ministries produce healthy relationships, not just predetermined goals.* I hesitate to use the word successful because of the cultural baggage (of accumulation and productivity) that it brings. Even so, it will not do to disregard the term. Our task is not to start a movement against success, but to reclaim it with a healthy definition. In our definition, success has a relational edge to it. We're convinced no one can succeed by doing a task in isolation. Success is defined by the relationships that develop between those involved in accomplishing the task, making the task itself secondary.

> *No one can succeed by doing a task in isolation. Success is defined by the relationships that develop between those involved in accomplishing the task, making the task itself secondary.*

Granted, to empower others is not easy. We need consistent reminders that our role is to empower others, not to be isolated autocrats, controlling rulers, resentful martyrs, or driving managers. This book is meant to be such a reminder: Ministry and leadership are first and foremost self-responsibility and people development.

Let's walk through the process together.

❖ ❖ ❖

REFLECT AND REVIEW

Think about the material in this chapter, then answer the following questions. Remember, don't try to do the ministry alone. Whenever possible, discuss these questions with your single adult leadership team.

1. Have you allowed others to perform a task in which they did as good a job or better than you could have done alone? Talk about it with your team.

2. What does it mean that leadership is relational, or circular?

3. List some reasons why we give in to the need to dominate those who work with us. Is it possible to delegate and involve others in the task? How?

4. Describe the impact on your ministry when you have allowed other single adults to become involved in decision-making and ownership of the task.

5. What are some ways we can resent those with whom we work? What does resentment do to us?

6. What are some ways we attempt to be all things to all people? What effect does it have on us?

MEMO

TO: Terry

FROM: Rich and Karen

RE: Chapter 3: Obstacles to Effective Leadership

The definitions of leadership in chapter 2 were helpful and got us started, but we realize now that just agreeing on a definition is not sufficient. Let's continue to build a foundation for single adult ministry. Give some insight into:

- The obstacles that are going to get in the way of effective, relational leadership
- How we take ourselves too seriously
- How we assume all problems are "fixable"
- Our confusion about the nature of success
- How we continue to assume single adults are irresponsible
- Our faulty perception of leadership

CHAPTER THREE

Obstacles to Effective Leadership

Terry Hershey

Charlie Brown sits befuddled at the psychiatrist's booth. Lucy is waxing eloquent about life. "Life, Charlie Brown," she asserts, "is like a deck chair."
"Like a what?" he asks in a dazed tone.
"Like a deck chair. Haven't you ever been on a cruise ship? There are hundreds of deck chairs. Some people put their deck chair at the front of the ship so they can see where they're going. Some people put theirs at the rear of the ship so that they can see where they've been." She pauses for effect. "On the cruise ship of life, Charlie Brown, which way is your deck chair facing?"
He responds, "I haven't figured out how to get mine unfolded yet!"[1]

We can learn a lot from Charlie Brown—namely, that effective, relational leadership is more than just knowing the "right answers." In contrast, the process of becoming leaders who empower others begins simply with taking an honest look at ourselves and the obstacles that hinder our effectiveness. It begins with a look at our "folded deck chairs."

As North Americans, when we have a problem, we attempt to resolve it with correct knowledge or the addition of appropriate pragmatic skills. We consume how-to manuals. We faithfully adhere to the troubleshooting checklists obtained at the latest management seminar. The problem still exists, however. Only now it is hidden behind newly developed programming and expertise.

If it is true that effective leadership is self-responsibility, the journey begins with self-assessment. In chapter 2, we stated that our problem was wrong assumptions. The solution, however, is not to simply believe the right things about leadership or acquire enough of the right supplemental programs. Change begins with an honest acknowledgment of the obstacles that exist. In other words, change begins with self-evaluation. What are the roadblocks that prevent us from being effective people developers? Where are we stuck? What wrong assumptions do we have? What attitudes and behaviors are self-defeating, preventing the very thing we desire?

We are reluctant to ask such questions because they are considered negative. That's unfortunate, because all growth begins with an inventory of the obstacles. Change, or growth, occur only when we are willing to take ownership, or responsibility, of where we are today—with the folded deck chairs in our lives. The Bible calls this "confession," meaning more than just reciting sins. It means taking ownership and responsibility. It means the process of change, which begins with self-assessment and continues with action based on that assessment.

If we do not conduct this self-assessment, the obstacles remain subconscious, infecting and affecting the way we do ministry. We become like the "dry drunk," who "changed" from being an alcoholic to a workaholic. But the change is merely decorative, with the real problem continuing to persist, only now in a new form. The dry drunk opts for a fix, never stopping to take the responsibility that comes with self-assessment.

Let's take an inventory. What are the obstacles or impediments to effective, relational leadership? What are our folded deck chairs?

WE TAKE OURSELVES TOO SERIOUSLY

This obstacle results from our image of leadership as control. When in control, we feel responsible for others instead of responsible to others. We approach our task or responsibility with the obligation that we are required to "make something happen." We have moved from being "responsible" to being liable and even compulsive. Through some twist, our identity has become intertwined with our task. Consequently, our reputation is at stake with anything and everything we do. A Catch-22 results— we need even more control. It's a no-win cycle.

We cannot escape the reality that we live in an addictive culture with its obsessive emphasis on "feeling good," being happy, and achieving success by being productive. Not surprisingly, then, many organizations, including the church (and many singles groups), have been coopted by this cultural byline.

Donna, the director of the single adult ministry at a mid-sized church in central Oregon, had a familiar concern. "How can I get more single people committed to the programs I've started? They're all excited about the ideas I have, but they never fully follow through. They never seem to care enough. So, I end up doing everything," she told me, with some exasperation, at a luncheon for single adult leaders.

AN ADDICT

An "addict" can be any individual (or organization, or group) obsessed with a substance or behavior (alcohol, drugs, food, work, success, image, reputation, religion, etc.) that the individual has internalized as essential to his or her identity. Because of a tenuous and insecure core or identity, the individual (or organization) clings precariously to this substance or behavior that promises relief (or fulfillment, happiness, freedom, or success). The result? We become dependent on whatever behavior or program is required to make us "feel okay."

Is Donna's story normal? Probably. Healthy? Not a chance.

Darryl ministers with single adults at a suburban church in the Midwest. The singles group, which meets every Wednesday and Saturday night and Sunday morning, is one of the largest in the area (a fact that Darryl will tell you frequently). It is clear to everyone that Darryl runs the show. He keeps meticulous statistics. He prides himself in the array and flurry of offered activities. He uses a handful of volunteers for every program. ("They're the only ones I can trust," Darryl told me, failing to add that his volunteers burn out after six months.) He works seventy hours a week (which means that he sees his wife—if she comes to the event—more often at church than at home). Yet, he has this nagging sense that somehow it's all not enough.

Is Darryl's story exaggerated? Not by much. Common? Unfortunately.

Rooted in Addiction

It would be presumptuous and unnecessary for me to call Donna or Darryl "addicts." But it will be helpful for us to see that the unhealthy no-win cycle that has Donna and Darryl stuck has its roots in addiction.

Change is threatening. As a result, discussion of addiction and church ministry may be uncomfortable (Did someone say "heretical"?). The discussion of the loss of control frightens any addictive system. To fight any loss of control, the system becomes rigid, ingrown, black and white, right or wrong. In other words, busy singles leaders become busier, controlling leaders become more controlling. Why? Because addiction equates with a sense of drivenness—whether it is an individual with his or her alcohol, an organization with its sacred cow, a leader with his or her need for success (or vision for the world), or a group with its insistent workaholic patterns. Such a preoccupation dictates the life of the singles group.

Like Darryl, we can easily live a one-dimensional existence. If we can find one good thing about our obsession—"after all, people are being helped"—then we imply that it is all good, as is the case with the church and workaholism. We know we have a problem when we require workaholism and consequently reward workaholic behavior. Called the "designer drug for the church" by Anne Wilson-Schaef, workaholism finds welcoming arms because of the ongoing images of the "good Christian" (or good singles leader or volunteer) who works hard and the "selfless" person who ministers to others by never attending to his or her own needs. Without realizing it, we are attached to a system that drives us and which we fuel with more and better—and busier—programming.

Why is this so important? While all may appear "normal" from the outside, the unhealthy drama is played out in a relentless cycle, eventually taking its toll.

Healthy Singles Groups: A Contrast

Like healthy families, healthy organizations (or singles groups) give and take, share responsibility, respect individual opinion, express real feelings, and offer a sense of personal safety. Healthy families, organizations, and singles groups allow and encourage personal development.

CHARACTERISTICS OF HEALTHY FAMILIES/ORGANIZATIONS/ SINGLES GROUPS	DISRUPTIONS CAUSED BY PARENTAL/ORGANIZATIONAL/ OR SINGLES GROUP DYSFUNCTION
■ Safety (physical and emotional) ■ Open communication (conflict allowed and resolved) ■ Self-care ■ Individualized roles (or no rigid roles) ■ Free to change ■ Free to laugh	■ Emotional unavailability or loss of control of parent (or leader) ■ Secrets kept to maintain peace ■ Facade of normality or "spirituality" maintained ■ Feelings hidden ■ Conflict (and anger) denied and ignored ■ Family's (or organization's) needs dictate roles ■ Roles become rigid, especially during times of stress ■ Resists change ■ Always serious

The addiction cycle places all of those characteristics in jeopardy, and development is arrested. Because safety is predicated on performance, and because any give and take (as well as individual opinion) is relinquished in favor of pursuing the addictive goal, and because responsibility (and therefore power) is owned by the few, real emotions are repressed. Honesty and real opinions are abandoned in favor of "not rocking the boat." Craziness in the hierarchy is not challenged, to protect the leaders. And too often, it's done behind the misquoted biblical injunction to "touch not God's anointed."

Keeping the Cycle Going
Darryl found change difficult because his hardworking volunteers helped keep the cycle going. They helped maintain the illusion that their "drivenness" was necessary. (Current literature would label such a person as "codependent.") Such "helpfulness" is also based on insecurity, a way to derive meaning from helping others. In this context, however, helping is not a positive trait, but is more realistically defined as rescuing or relieving others.

GROUP HEALTH CHECKUP

1. In what ways is our group a place where conflict is viewed as threatening and brushed aside?
2. In what ways is our group a place where people feel like they need to please the "powers that be," or a place where they need to conform?
3. In what ways is our group a place where people are afraid to admit that they are not feeling spiritual?
4. In what ways is our group a place where single adults feel safe?
5. In what ways is our group a place where people are free to say no?
6. Does our group laugh a lot? Why, or why not?
7. In what ways do the members of our group feel like they have any ownership of the ministry?

Codependent people feel responsible *for* others. We possess an internalized belief that somehow our behavior can control someone else's feelings and behaviors. We fill a protective role (for control) that is adopted from experience in a family, or organization, with little or no safety, give and take, responsibility, or expression of real feelings. As a result, instead of being real, we wear a mask of controlling through helping, fixing, or rescuing. The "Core of Insecurity/Addictive Behavior Cycle" chart illustrates this cycle—which is the same for "addicts" and "co-addicts" (codependent persons) alike.

CORE OF INSECURITY/ADDICTIVE BEHAVIOR CYCLE

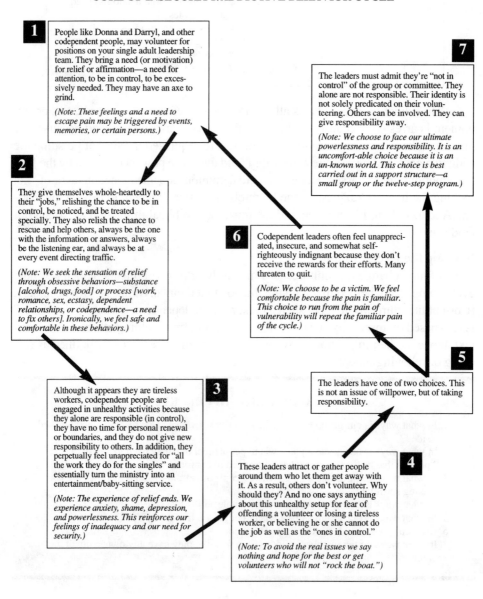

1 People like Donna and Darryl, and other codependent people, may volunteer for positions on your single adult leadership team. They bring a need (or motivation) for relief or affirmation—a need for attention, to be in control, to be excessively needed. They may have an axe to grind.

(Note: These feelings and a need to escape pain may be triggered by events, memories, or certain persons.)

2 They give themselves whole-heartedly to their "jobs," relishing the chance to be in control, be noticed, and be treated specially. They also relish the chance to rescue and help others, always be the one with the information or answers, always be the listening ear, and always be at every event directing traffic.

(Note: We seek the sensation of relief through obsessive behaviors—substance [alcohol, drugs, food] or process [work, romance, sex, ecstasy, dependent relationships, or codependence—a need to fix others]. Ironically, we feel safe and comfortable in these behaviors.)

3 Although it appears they are tireless workers, codependent people are engaged in unhealthy activities because they alone are responsible (in control), they have no time for personal renewal or boundaries, and they do not give new responsibility to others. In addition, they perpetually feel unappreciated for "all the work they do for the singles" and essentially turn the ministry into an entertainment/baby-sitting service.

(Note: The experience of relief ends. We experience anxiety, shame, depression, and powerlessness. This reinforces our feelings of inadequacy and our need for security.)

4 These leaders attract or gather people around them who let them get away with it. As a result, others don't volunteer. Why should they? And no one says anything about this unhealthy setup for fear of offending a volunteer or losing a tireless worker, or believing he or she cannot do the job as well as the "ones in control."

(Note: To avoid the real issues we say nothing and hope for the best or get volunteers who will not "rock the boat.")

5 The leaders have one of two choices. This is not an issue of willpower, but of taking responsibility.

6 Codependent leaders often feel unappreciated, insecure, and somewhat self-righteously indignant because they don't receive the rewards for their efforts. Many threaten to quit.

(Note: We choose to be a victim. We feel comfortable because the pain is familiar. This choice to run from the pain of vulnerability will repeat the familiar pain of the cycle.)

7 The leaders must admit they're "not in control" of the group or committee. They alone are not responsible. Their identity is not solely predicated on their volunteering. Others can be involved. They can give responsibility away.

(Note: We choose to face our ultimate powerlessness and responsibility. It is an uncomfort-able choice because it is an un-known world. This choice is best carried out in a support structure—a small group or the twelve-step program.)

The church is full of Donnas and Darryls. (This is true of all helping professions.) When given responsibilities, Donnas and Darryls will gather more codependent people around them. In this process, we act on our need to rescue and protect those around us. Like the subjects of the emperor in the tale of the emperor with new clothes, we protect the individual or organization from the truth. We are not conscious that we're living a lie, only that we believe we are sparing others from getting their feelings hurt.

When we feel responsible *for*, we assume our job is to make sure others feel okay. We want to provide answers, so we rescue. Why? Because we are afraid of failure. We want others to think well of us, and we feel like we need to perform and impress those around us. We want to ensure no one around us is unhappy or upset. As a result, no division exists between our personal life and job (or volunteer task) life. The two meld together, with our personal life consumed by the need to find our identity in and through what we do.

What happens when we feel responsible *for*? How does that differ from being responsible *to*? The following chart helps.

RESPONSIBLE FOR	RESPONSIBLE TO
■ I fix	■ I share
■ Protect	■ Encourage
■ Rescue	■ Show empathy
■ Control	■ Confront
■ Carry others' feelings	■ Allow others' feelings
■ Don't listen (or selectively)	■ Allow doubt
■ Squelch disagreement (or avoid)	■ Allow questions
■ Manage emotions	■ Am willing to fight
■ Repress	■ Confess
■ Do it alone	■ Involve others

The result? Thinking that we must be responsible for others takes its toll on our emotional and spiritual life.

RESPONSIBLE FOR	RESPONSIBLE TO
I feel more . . .	I feel more . . .
■ Tired	■ Relaxed
■ Anxious	■ At ease
■ Impatient	■ Unconstrained
■ Liable	■ Aware
■ Culpable	■ High self-worth
■ Nervous about reputation	■ Free from obligation
■ Afraid of public opinion	■ Free to be honest

Ironically, in such a scenario, others must live up to our expectations of them, which our experience tells us they will never do. Or, more realistically, they do. For example, we assume people are noncommittal, and they never let us down. So, we continue to assume that it is our role to change (or fix) others. Since the only way to change noncommittal people is through guilt, we become manipulators. But being good codependent people, we manipulate in "helpful" ways.

Putting Out Fires

Addiction cycles thrive on a crisis orientation to ministry. Some have called this the ministry mode of "fire-fighting."

I had just gotten off the phone with Tim, a single adult minister for a prominent Midwestern church. I felt exhausted from listening to his story. "It's so crazy," Tim had told me, his tone tired and angry. "It just never stops. First, I do a divorce recovery workshop, and two days before it begins, three group leaders quit, so I end up combining two groups and lead them myself. In addition, my counseling load has increased. It seems that this month is the month for emergencies. I can't turn them away now, can I? To top it all off, the committee planning the retreat flakes out, and I get stuck making the remaining arrangements and working out the agenda. It's like you can't count on anyone. So now I'm out five nights a week at some singles function making sure everything is going okay."

Fire-fighting: A place where one feels obligated, stuck, and swamped.

I received a letter from a director of Christian education and single adult ministry after I had told an audience that my home phone was off-limits to many in the congregation. "Us peons out here have our phones listed everywhere. We are asked to be all things to all people. Yes, we can limit it sometimes. We can cross off times on the calender and say we are booked for private time. But I have someone who walks in my house at night without knocking and says, 'I knew you would be sleeping, so I came over.'"

If our identity is contingent on what we do and how we look when we do it, it feels traumatic when we are not needed or appreciated. As a result, we create or maintain a crisis that requires our attendance or presence. This reinforces the underlying insecurity and fear of real change—the fear of giving up control. While many complain about the pace of their ministries and the ongoing fires that require their attention, they secretly perpetuate the familiar game plan and derive some satisfaction from this illusion of importance and power.

This material on the addictive cycle is not meant to engender guilt or insinuate that we must all try harder. In fact, it is meant to bring a sigh of relief. "Whew, you mean I don't have to play God in everyone's life! I don't have to rescue and control! You mean it's okay to admit that I don't have all my deck chairs unfolded yet!"

It is vitally important that we begin with the principle that God loves and accepts us where we are, for who we are, and not because of our accumulated score in the game of rescuing, fixing, controlling, and helping. The good news of the gospel is that because God is big enough, we can simply be ministers (or more accurately, reflectors of His grace). We don't need to be the hero. We don't need to be the one with all the answers. We don't need to be the junior messiah. We don't need to be self-sufficient. We can learn to give the ministry away. We can learn to say NO. We can learn to live with doubts and questions. We can learn, in the words of Merle Shain, to be "tough enough to be soft."

It's not as easy as it sounds, however. We must stop long enough to hear the gospel message that cuts through our attempts to earn love (and therefore deflect it) via shopkeeping, scorekeeping, and bravely wearing our mask of "Mr. or Ms. Helpful." The gospel simply says, in Jesus Christ "you are loved." Period. As a result, we have no need to use our leadership or responsibilities as a platform to prove anything, manipulate anyone, or manufacture acceptance via performance.

So what's the lesson of this first obstacle? Effective, relational leadership begins with the permission to be loved as we are—folded deck chairs and all. Only as we are loved, will we have the permission to slowly be ourselves.

WE ASSUME ALL PROBLEMS ARE "FIXABLE"

When we're told we have a leadership problem, what's our response? We want a cure—a logical consequence of the first obstacle. We want to bring all of this under control. It will simply not do, we say to ourselves, to go on wrestling with the under-lying issues, such as the need for control, lack of personal boundaries, absence of self-care, or a cycle of addiction and coaddiction. With a little elbow grease, willpower, prayer, and faith, we can get our act together!

Destination Mentality

This assumes that every problem has a solution and the goal in life is to arrive there. The argument goes as follows: As soon as our problems are resolved, we can get on with our lives, ministries, programs, or relationships. Until our problems are resolved, our life feels short-circuited and our energy is required to find a solution. This mentality is similar to a four-year-old child, five minutes out of the driveway on any family trip: "Are we there yet?" We are so intent on the destination, we forget the journey. We become destination-oriented.

As a result, we are susceptible to any new technique or any expert with some new wisdom on "people skills." In so doing, we are still oriented toward "them," not seeing that every issue is first and foremost an identity issue. We are not free to see our relationships, ministries, or tasks—however large or small—as a journey. We approach life with an "if only" mentality, assuming that life will start when our problems are resolved.

As one single adult minister said to me, "Our program is coming along pretty well, but we're not quite there. All we need now is one or two more committed leaders, a better small group system—along with a few more quality facilitators, some more upbeat music for our Sunday mornings, and a more frequent divorce support group." I hesitated to forewarn him that when this list is accomplished, the next list will be even longer. It never ends.

This cycle of thinking produces myopia, discouragement, a need for comparison, and even depression. With a destination mentality, we never seem to be where we should be. We always fall short of the expected goal. We're never good enough. We become overly concerned with the problems that must be resolved before we can become successful. Unfortunately, if we wait for our problems to be solved before

---

DESTINATION STORIES, ILLUSTRATIONS, OR LANGUAGE

. . . imply the word *should* (for example, "grow up," "settle down," "get married")
. . . leave you feeling that you're never far enough along
. . . don't allow you to embrace or enjoy where you are today
. . . leave you feeling guilty because you haven't tried hard enough

JOURNEY STORIES, ILLUSTRATIONS, OR LANGUAGE

. . . recognize that where you are has value
. . . leave you with a feeling of hope
. . . give you a sense of encouragement for taking the next step
. . . allow you to enjoy or embrace where you are today

---

we can have a successful group, class, committee, ministry, or whatever, we miss the point that success is found in the journey itself.

With a destination mentality, we continue to take ourselves too seriously. This infects our perception of ministry, relationships, and even our walk in the Christian faith. When we tell people to "be Christian," we don't mean become Christian (or be on the journey), we mean act like, talk like, and look like a Christian, which is destination language.

In the same way, a destination mentality affects how we perceive church discipline. We see accountability or discipline as someone conforming to predetermined morals or expectations. They have a destination to realize, a scripted role to fulfill. Consequently, discipline becomes a doctrinal issue before being a relational issue. Journey issues of motivation, concerns underlying the behaviors, personal boundaries, personal consequences, and the need for the support of fellow strugglers are never discussed. In the end, nobody wins.

WE MISUNDERSTAND SUCCESS

This is quintessential Americana. Any effort we make at growth or change is primarily for the final payoff—success. So off we go, following the not-so-subtle hints of ever-present Madison Avenue, which promise happiness—and other variations on that theme—with the accumulation of the right combination of goods. Having baptized that scenario, the church pursues its own game of success pursuit, and the search is relentless. Ironically, we're not taught the real meaning of success, only that we're supposed to get some. Consequently, we're never satisfied that we've got enough. And we probably wouldn't recognize success if it stared us in the face.

If we see success as numbers and are thus traumatized by turnover and transition, our reputation rides the roller coaster of approval via the number of chairs and we will easily burnout. If we see success as homogeneity, we may come to be suspicious of people who are not like us. If we see success as rate of return (people who get involved, money collected, number who become Christians, number of baptisms, etc.), more is never enough in our race with the other competitors down the street. If we see success as amount of programming, then we become victims of the merry-go-round of being all things to all people, and we sacrifice quality for quantity.

The fact remains, ministry is not always cost-effective. A one-for-one payoff for the correct application of programming or management techniques is not guaranteed. We miss the point if we make this a "success-bashing" argument. While numbers are an integral part of expansion, they cannot tell the whole story.

Above all else, success is being responsible to, not for, others (see the charts on page 39). Success is creating an environment of nurture. Success is the encouragement of self-care and personal development. It means being a guide and a facilitator. It means slowly learning to trust, and by giving others responsibility, learning to let go. It means listening and not just hearing. Success is the permission to enjoy the journey. Indeed, it is the permission to be human—and fully alive.

WE ASSUME PEOPLE ARE IRRESPONSIBLE

Perhaps our assumption that people are irresponsible is a reflection of our need for control and our own fear of irresponsibility. No one can be counted on, we often tell ourselves. We'll just do it ourselves! We'll do it right! Consequently, we come to mistrust the very people with whom we minister. Our job is to entertain them until they "grow up."

There's a wonderful story that illustrates this obstacle. A church was hosting a large college-age choir for a weekend and needed persons to volunteer to house individual choir members. As is the case when we all need volunteers, the minister stood to make an announcement: "If you're interested in volunteering your home, please call the church office." As usual, only one or two people responded. What next, then?

The congregation's response only confirmed the pastor's suspicions of their irresponsibility. He believed (as we all do) that the only way to motivate irresponsible people is through guilt. So the next Sunday, his announcement sounded like this, "Those who really love Jesus, please volunteer your homes." Of course, only a few more people volunteered. Finally, the pastor had to spend time on the phone rounding up the necessary volunteers.

The next year, the pastor took a different tack. Four weeks before the singing group's arrival, he stood and said, "If you're new here you don't need to listen, but if you've been here more than a month we consider you a part of the woodwork. You are the church. You share in the responsibilities of the life of the church. And you are needed for a project. We have your addresses and phone numbers and we will be assigning one of these students to your home. If there is some reason your home is not available, please call the church office."

What happened? It turned out to be a great experience for those whose homes were "volunteered." Why had they never volunteered before? The reasons are all too common. "I didn't think my house was big enough." "There are others in the church who could do a better job." "No one ever asked me." "I haven't been a member long enough." "Isn't that the hospitality committee's job?" "What do you feed a college student?"

What's the moral of the story? If we assume people are irresponsible, we will wait for them to mature, while using whatever guilt and entertainment necessary in the meantime to motivate them. The principle is this: Never assume people will take responsibility. Always assume you must give it to them.

To help us overcome this obstacle, we must look at the ways in which we take responsibility away from people. For example, we rescue people. We protect them from failure. We don't trust their decisions. We refer to the ministry, class, or committee as "my church" or "my group," inferring that the best anyone can hope for is to volunteer to help me with "my ministry."

WE HAVE A FAULTY PERCEPTION OF LEADERSHIP

We assume leadership is confined to those who are "charismatic," vivacious, extroverted, and "up front." Leaders are the visionaries who can inspire, sway, and motivate. So much for lay leadership! Or for those of us who are paid for what we do, but are not endowed with the gifts of flair, effervescence, charm, influence, and expertise! As a result, we never allow our small contributions to matter. We can become discouraged, feeling as if we are competing against the megachurches or the vivacious cheerleaders who carry out their work down the street from us. In the end, we compromise who we are, trying to be like someone else. Since leadership involves empowering others, neither expertise nor extroverted flair is a requirement.

Being oneself, however, is.

We must begin by facing the obstacles—those attitudes and behaviors that block our effectiveness, perpetuate addictive organizations, and exaggerate the problem. Change can occur only when there is a willingness—à la Charlie Brown—to face the obstacles that derail us.

REFLECT AND REVIEW

Think about the material in this chapter, then answer the following questions. Remember, don't try to do the ministry alone. Whenever possible, discuss these questions with your single adult leadership team.

1. Since change begins with self-evaluation, think about the roadblocks that may prevent us from effective leadership development.

      a. In what ways do we take ourselves too seriously (at home, at work, at church)?

      b. In what ways do we think every problem is "fixable"?

      c. In what ways do we assume most people are irresponsible?

2. Where are we stuck? Which of our attitudes and behaviors are self-defeating, preventing the very thing we desire?

3. How do we define success here at our church/group? Can we relate to any of the following?

    a. Numbers, the more the better.

    b. Homogeneity, people involved who are like myself.

    c. Rate of return (people who get involved, money collected, number who become Christians, number of baptisms, etc.).

    d. Amount of programming, the more the better!

Any of the above views of success can make us victims of the merry-go-round of being "all things to all people." Eventually, we'll burn out.

4. Take the Group Health Checkup on page 37. What motivates you and the single adults in your group? What ways can you and other leaders begin to give responsibility away?

MEMO

TO: Terry

FROM: Rich and Karen

RE: Chapter 4: A Theology of Being Empowered

Your observation about self-assessment was helpful. We hope it makes us all realize that ministry and empowering begin with us; it's not just something we "do to" a group of people. We think it would be beneficial if you talked more about that dynamic.

- How empowering others comes from a place where we are being empowered
- What it looks like to be empowered
- The characteristics of people who have been empowered
- How being empowered enables us to give to others

CHAPTER FOUR

A Theology of Being Empowered

Terry Hershey

A strong foundation helps ensure a long life for a building. Without it, the building is destined to a lifetime of temporary props to keep it standing. Leadership is no different. Effectiveness begins with a solid foundation.

In the previous chapter, we said that change begins with self-assessment. Consequently, growth is not a programming issue but an identity issue. In other words, you can't guarantee growth by adding a new program or format. Our effectiveness, then, is predicated on the permission to see ourselves as loved and accepted, regardless of performance, numbers, accomplishments, or lingering past failures.

This solid foundation is built upon the heart of the gospel, which says grace gives us dignity and worth. The gospel says our identity is not contingent upon merit, skill, charisma, or charm. The gospel also says none of our attempts to earn that grace (or acceptance or approval) through performance, technique, spectacular feats, or clever management nullify the point.

It is a gospel that seems too good to be true.

What are the implications of such grace?

We must note that our theology of empowering is not specifically about a technique for empowering, but about us—the ones who become the empowerers—the ones who become, in the words of Paul, ministers of reconciliation (2 Corinthians 5:17-20).

Our theology of empowering, then, begins with what God says about us as persons (this is the gospel of grace), not a generic lecture from God about leadership. The purpose of theology is to teach us about our relationship with God and, consequently, to liberate us to become more of whom God created us to be.

Theology is not just information and material necessary to study for a test on life. It is not just God's how-to manual or divine Cliff's Notes on better living. At this point we too easily lose our way. If our questions about the theological foundation of leadership can be answered by objective discussion about leadership, we would

MINISTERS OF RECONCILIATION

Therefore, if anyone is in Christ, he is a new creation; the old has gone, the new has come! All this is from God, who reconciled us to himself through Christ and gave us the ministry of reconciliation: that God was reconciling the world to himself in Christ, not counting men's sins against them. And he has committed to us the message of reconciliation. We are therefore Christ's ambassadors, as though God were making his appeal through us. We implore you on Christ's behalf: Be reconciled to God. (2 Corinthians 5:17-20)

miss the point that leadership begins with our identity, not with knowing the right answers to God's test questions.

Elaine was talented, outgoing, and had a willing spirit. Soon after becoming involved in our singles group, she took a position on the social activities planning team. Elaine clearly was well-suited for her job. She was efficient and committed— a terrific asset to our ministry. There was only one problem. To Elaine, it was just a job, a task to be performed. She eventually felt fatigued, irritated, and depleted. As her minister, I was at fault because Elaine was being used, not empowered. Ministry does not take place with talent alone. Was her job a place where she was affirmed, embraced, and encouraged to grow in her job? Was she in community with people who provided support? Was Elaine being empowered?

We have mentioned several times that building leaders—or giving the ministry away—involves empowering people. Empowering the Elaines in our churches and groups. Still, it's more than that. It also involves how we, who are challenged to empower others, find a place where we are, in turn, empowered. In other words, we can only give when and where we receive.

That sounds good, but what does it mean? What does an empowered person look like? What are the characteristics? What are the visible signs?

AN EMPOWERED LEADER KNOWS TO WHOM HE OR SHE BELONGS

A puppy and kitten stared longingly from the full-page color ad. As an emotional pull, it worked, but not as much as the headline at the top of the ad: "It's who owns them that makes them important."

That's not only good advertising, that's good theology. It serves as the basis for the first characteristic of an empowered person—namely, it's who owns us that makes us important.

As Jesus washed His disciples' feet after supper (John 13:1-17), He was able to have compassion on them and risk rejection, because His identity was not dependent upon His ministry—or public opinion, year-end reports, media response, board pressure, or old "tapes": "Jesus knew that the Father had put all things under his power, and that he had come from God and was returning to God; so he got up from the meal . . . and began to wash his disciples' feet" (verses 3-5).

If we are unsure of who owns us or where our identity ultimately rests, we will use our relationships and our jobs to fortify a depleted self. We will conduct ministry with the wrong motivations—the need to be needed and appreciated, to be important, to feel wanted, to impress someone or prove something, to be powerful (or overpower others), to live up to some unfulfilled expectations, or the inability to say no when we're asked to be involved.

When we forget who owns us, we take ourselves too seriously. For this reason, this characteristic is primary to our theology. Learning helpful leadership principles, though important, is not enough. Knowing right answers is not enough. Applying tried-and-true programming is not enough. Why? Because effective, relational leadership is built on a secure identity.

To which one may respond, "And who among us ever has a secure identity?" Arriving at a completed state is not the point. No one will ever totally "get their act together." Knowing who owns us is an ongoing process and struggle. We will need constant reminders that our identity is not ultimately in the tasks we perform, the titles we wear, or the accomplishments we garner.

Why do you think Jesus regularly withdrew to a solitary place? (See the story in Mark 1:32-39.) He did so, at least in part, for the reminder that His identity was intact in the hands of a loving and faithful Father. This confidence gave Him permission to risk, say no, not give in to public pressure, give responsibility away, not be responsible for others, and in effect—to be Himself.

The gospel message says that if we know we're loved, we have no need to prove anything to anyone.

Why is this message so easy to forget? Why is it so tempting to resort to our standard operating procedure of shopkeeping, scorekeeping, performing, and controlling? I'm not sure of the answer, but I know that if we do not make intentional efforts to be reminded, we are easily drawn into the relentless cycle of more is never enough, bigger is better, and "What will they think?"

I have a three-by-five-inch card on my desk for just such a reminder. It contains the following message:

Dear Terry,

I know being in control makes you feel better.
But I can handle it. Thanks anyway.

Love,
God

IDENTITY REMINDERS

Use these reminders (both for ourselves and others) that our identity is not found only in the tasks we perform:

1. Take a play break (see pages 54-55).
2. Send anonymous thank-you/I-appreciate-you cards.
3. Give lay leaders a mini-sabbatical—one or two months off.
4. Go on a play retreat. No church business allowed.
5. Give a gift certificate for a meal at a nice restaurant.
6. Give a gift of cassette tapes of favorite music.
7. Take a break halfway through your business meetings by taking a walk around the block.

AN EMPOWERED LEADER IS SELF-RESPONSIBLE

In the Gospel of Mark, Jesus frequently leaves whatever He is doing to retreat to a solitary place. His reason? To pray. To be renewed. The response is hardly enthusiastic. In one story (Mark 1:35-39), the disciples hunt for Him. "He's left His duties!" "What will people think?" When they found Him they let Him know in no uncertain terms that indeed "everyone" is looking for Him. In other words, "If You want to be a good Messiah, get back down there."

Jesus, of course, being a PR man's nightmare, opts to tell His disciples that they will go preach in a different town instead. Jesus was letting the disciples know that His ability to heal, change, and love was predicated on His liberty to withdraw to be nourished and nurtured. His capacity to give comes from being able to receive.

Jesus would have a difficult time in our world where identity is tied to productivity quotas. It is no wonder that we—who are so inculcated with the Madison Avenue hype of being "in," or being "somebody," or being with somebody who is somebody, or being able to produce a stellar résumé, or achieving notoriety by a tag line in a *People* magazine article—have difficulty in the area of self-care. We are driven by public opinion, and thus we easily sacrifice who we are today for who we think we should be. We too easily believe that being important is better than being real—that is, to be nobody but myself in a world that wants me to be somebody else.

What does it mean that Jesus was self-responsible or practiced self-care? It means:

- Jesus had boundaries. He was able to say no.
- He was not a victim to every whim of the adoring public (or depending on their mood, the antagonistic public).
- He respected His limitations. (He was, after all, human with all its implications of weariness, loneliness, and doubt.)
- He knew He needed a regular reminder that His identity was intact apart from the jobs and tasks He performed.
- He didn't need to take Himself too seriously (and lose perspective).
- He was not dependent upon needing to fix and rescue everyone around Him.

WHAT IS SELF-RESPONSIBILITY OR SELF-CARE?

1. You have boundaries.
2. You aren't a victim to others.
3. You respect your limitations.
4. You regularly remind yourself that your identity is intact apart from your job
   or responsibility or task.
5. You don't take yourself too seriously.
6. You are able to say no.
7. You don't need to fix or rescue others.
8. Self-care equals effective others-care.

Jesus also knew that self-care translated into effective others-care. The result is that His ministry came from His security, not His neediness. He was not a victim or a reactor.

Throughout the gospel record, we find Jesus regularly withdrawing to a solitary place. Why? To pray; to practice self-care; to gain perspective; to be reminded that reality is more than just the line of people waiting to be healed, counseled, fixed, or stroked. It is not surprising (look again at the story in Mark 1:35-39) that Jesus' disciples were amazed to find Him turning a deaf ear to public opinion in favor of self-care and time with His Father.

It is important to note that self-care is not found just in a solitary experience. A lifestyle of self-responsibility, or self-care, is a two-sided coin that includes both withdrawal and community. Withdrawal without community can easily lead to isolation. In community, which is distinguishable from "general public," we find regular encouragement, affirmation, and challenge in areas of our lives that need change. Community is where I am nurtured by others and not required to be the savior, entertainment coordinator, rescuer, or hero. Just me. (Read more about balancing our need for community in chapter 10, and learning to say no and taking time for ourselves in chapter 11.)

Moving from an academic career to the role of priest for a small house for mentally handicapped adults, Henri Nouwen notes in his book *In The Name of Jesus*: "Living in a community with very wounded people, I came to see that I had lived most of my life as a tightrope artist trying to walk on a high, thin cable from one tower to the other, always waiting for the applause when I had not fallen off and broken my leg."[1]

In isolation, our boundaries can be easily erased and our identity once again wed to our ability to perform and impress.

AN EMPOWERED LEADER IS A WOUNDED HEALER

We all feel the need to be strong, impressive, and powerful. Being above any suspicion of weakness is a cultural requirement. Ironically, God's grace is reflected only through those who have experienced brokenness, forgiveness, and renewal.

Henri Nouwen relates a story from the Talmud about Rabbi Yoshua ben Levi, who came upon the prophet Elijah while he was standing at the entrance of Rabbi Simeron ben Yohai's cave. He asked Elijah, "When will the Messiah come?"

Elijah replied, "Go and ask Him yourself."

"Where is He?"

"Sitting at the gates of the city."

"How shall I know Him?"

"He is sitting among the poor covered with wounds. The others unbind all their wounds at the same time and then bind them up again. But He unbinds one at a time and binds it up again, saying to Himself, 'Perhaps I shall be needed: If so I must always be ready so as not to delay for a moment.'"[2]

Our call, says Nouwen, is to be wounded healers. What does that mean? God's power—to heal, reconcile, and care—manifests itself not in our strengths, skills, techniques, or cleverness, but in our weakness, wounds, brokenness, pain, vulnerability, and even our failures. In other words, God's love is reflected through us in ways we would least expect.

Paul, the apostle, is a good example. He makes it clear that God's strength comes through his own weakness and woundedness. (See 2 Corinthians 1:3-7, 12:9.) Mother Teresa is a modern reminder that God's love is reflected in the wounds, sores, and poverty of poor lepers in Calcutta where she works and cares.

Some of us have paid lip service to our need to identify with people by "sharing" our stories of temptation and disappointment. But being a wounded healer (open with brokenness and forgiveness) involves more than an ability to recite some list of sins from a horrendous past or even hint that we thought about such sins. Under the guise of openness, such sharing is both unnecessary and inappropriate. Vulnerability is not a process of dumping my past—as a catharsis—on an attentive audience. Vulnerability is being real or current without taking advantage of another. To be a wounded healer means that I am in a community where I can bring my whole self— with all its fault lines, confusion, and pain—and can experience confession and forgiveness.

For me, that community is a group of men friends who allow me to be Terry— who may be down, hurt, flawed, or ebullient. They help keep me sane. They help give me perspective.

Riding from the airport with Roger, the single adult pastor at an established suburban church on the East Coast, I was aware he needed this time to unload. His life was coming unraveled. His wife was angry at the church and his job. The senior

---

COMMUNITY

A group of persons who provide support, encouragement, and allow for doubt, frustration, and grief. No singular form of community exists. For some people, community may be an organized small group—a regular weekly meeting of "community." For others, connections with the persons who make up this community may be more spontaneous and irregular.

pastor was unrelenting in his pressure to see the singles group "grow." His own emotional life felt dry and tired.

I listened and was sad, not only because of all his frustration and pain, but also because of his answer to my question, "Do you have anyone in this area you can talk with? Anyone you can open your wounds to and experience support and healing?" Roger was silent for some time, and then answered quietly, "No, I don't. That's why I'm glad you're here."

When self-sufficiency is the rule, we expend too much energy hiding our frailties. *I can't let on that I have any weakness, because I must appear together and in control.* We become ardent protectors of our reputation. We become Lone Rangers. Life becomes a survival of the fittest. Ministry becomes a competition. There is easily an us-versus-them mentality.

But as we are becoming wounded healers, ministry no longer equals technique, special tricks, or gargantuan willpower. Ministry can only be a reflection of God's grace in our broken places.

AN EMPOWERED LEADER KNOWS HOW TO PLAY

In his book *Work, Play, and Worship in a Leisure-Oriented Society*, Gordon Dahl writes: "Most middle-class Americans tend to worship their work, to work at their play, and to play at their worship."[3]

This statement rings with truth. When we take ourselves too seriously, we forget that the sign of the Christian is not faith, but joy. We forget that life is a gift to enjoy. We forget how to let the child within us come to life. We forget how to play.

> *"Most middle-class Americans tend to worship their work, to work at their play, and to play at their worship."*

While writing this, I took some time out to sit in my garage for a "play break." I joined my three new kittens, who were already in the midst of an enthusiastic play break. I sat while they raced, pounced, tussled, snuggled, and attacked. As far as I can tell, we had a twenty-minute version of a king of the mountain/hide 'n seek/jungle gym/wrestlemania/relay race. I hardly know who won. Which is precisely what makes it a play break—winning doesn't matter. On my garage floor, I learn from my kittens. I smile; I laugh; and I frolic. I also forget, for just a little while, that a deadline hangs over my head, threatening to make my life only a series of projects and assignments.

When was the last time you had a play break?

To play is sacramental. It is to embrace life. It is to give up keeping score. It is to savor. It is to relish. It is to celebrate today.

Play is also contagious, just like caring is contagious. You can't teach joy, caring, or involvement. You can only catch them. They are infectious. You simply can't infect others by trying harder, or training harder. People change when they are in the presence of people who know how to celebrate. Joy and caring happen with people who no longer need to keep score.

AN EMPOWERED LEADER CREATES A NURTURING ENVIRONMENT

In Romans 14:4, Paul talks about our tendency to set ourselves up as someone else's master: "Who are you to judge someone else's servant?" We become critic, expert, judge, and jury for those around us. It's as if the Holy Spirit is too busy, so we take a crack at the people-changing business. It's understandable. Once again, it stems from taking ourselves too seriously. When we become responsible for others, we see ourselves as their master. They exist to measure up to our expectations; therefore, our job is to shape them up by providing answers, a fix, or a rescue.

If it is true that we are not responsible "for" others and our identity is not dependent upon their choices, their being fixed, or their changing, we are free to create a nurturing environment where their master Christ can develop them. Maybe, just maybe, we can begin to see others with a sense of wonder and expectancy.

What does it mean to create a nurturing environment? Larry came to our church as a new convert to the Christian faith. Characteristic of new converts, he was enthusiastic and willing to help. He was given a responsibility in the single adult ministry for planning social activities. His ideas were quite different than mine, and my first inclination was to change his way of thinking to align with mine, temper his zeal, and tone down his idealistic optimism. But all of that was my agenda. Not God's.

I needed to see that my job was to create a nurturing environment for Larry. As a result, I invited him to be a part of a weekly small group for discussion and prayer, where he could find support and encouragement. On my part, I made sure I encouraged the small successes in his job. Larry never did social activities the way I wanted them done. But there was still a change. The result was not just a change in Larry, who was feeling more empowered, but a change in me.

AN EMPOWERED LEADER SEES BEYOND THE IMMEDIATE TO THE POTENTIAL

Jesus gave people the freedom to grow. He didn't confine people to His predetermined expectations of them. His ministry was not taken from a pre-published script. He saw people as unique, as individuals. He always saw beyond the immediate to the "more" they could become.

There's a great story about a woman who crashes a party where Jesus is being wined and dined by the religious and social muck-a-mucks (Luke 7:36-50). She walks into the room past the flabbergasted servants, kneels where Jesus is reclining, and performs a curious ceremony with tenderness, affection, and passion. Pouring perfume on Jesus' feet, she begins to wipe them with her hair. Needless to say, the religious hosts were stunned. One finds voice enough to question Jesus: "If you were really a prophet, you would know who this woman is," implying, "She hardly deserves your civility! She's only an accumulation of her résumé—a prostitute, a down-and-outer, an outcast, a nonreligious nobody from the other side of the tracks."

Jesus replies (in paraphrase), "I think you miss the point. A prophet is not someone who sees the way things are, but the way they can become, and I tell you this woman will be remembered throughout all of history for her kindness."

This message speaks loudly and clearly about how our worth is predicated solely on who Jesus is and what He has done for us through His life, death, and resurrection. It says we can be an effective, empowered leader precisely because we don't have to take ourselves too seriously. Because grace takes us seriously, we don't have to impress, prove, or overpower.

The forgiveness scene in the movie *The Mission* plays out all the terror and beauty that come with such self-revelation. Robert De Niro portrays a slave trader, capturing Indians for profit, who has been accused of killing his brother. Although the law said it was self-defence, the stark realization of the extent of his selfishness drives De Niro to despair and self-pity. The Jesuit priest Father Gabriel, played by Jeremy Irons, offers De Niro the possibility of hope and redemption. In a damp, isolated cell, De Niro wallows in his self-doubt. "Do you know who I am?" he challenges Irons.

"Yes," is the response, "you are a slave trader and a mercenary, and you killed your brother. And you loved him very much, although you chose a funny way to show it."

Undaunted in his self-hatred, De Niro cries, "But for me, there is no redemption."

The scenes that follow play out the theme of a man in pursuit of a new identity. De Niro accompanies Irons and other members of the Jesuit order on the arduous and dangerous trek into the South American jungles above the falls, where the Jesuits had started a small mission and where De Niro had previously captured and killed members of the Guarani tribe. On the journey, De Niro carries with him a cumbersome and heavy assortment of soldier's armor, held together by a netting and attached to a strong rope that is tied to his neck and back. It is his penance, and he is determined to carry it to completion. The task appears impossible, and some members of the Jesuit band offer to relieve De Niro of his bondage, so great was their empathy with his burden. But De Niro is determined—determined to prove something, maybe to God, to the Indians, or to himself.

At last, the small band of missionaries arrives. As the Jesuit priests are warmly welcomed by a group of the Guarani tribe, De Niro appears on the pathway, some one hundred yards away, slowly making his way stooped over by the weight of the liability of his personal frailties. When the Indians spot him, silence reigns. They know who he is. They know he has killed some of their tribe and sold others into slavery.

Rushing forward, one of the young Indians grabs De Niro by the hair, now matted and wet with mud and perspiration, and raising his head and face for all to see, stands poised with his hunting knife drawn, waiting for some confirmation as to

De Niro's fate. His fate is literally in the young Indian's hands. Time stands still. Finally, the decision is made. Grabbing the rope, the young tribesman uses his knife to quickly sever the load that DeNiro carries.

Over the ledge the netting of armor plummets, landing in the river below. With that, comes the emotion. De Niro begins to sob uncontrollably, and with his tears comes all of the guilt, sorrow, and humiliation. He is free from his need to prove anything to anyone. Not understanding the sobbing, the Indians see De Niro's contorted, tear-streaked face and begin to laugh. Soon all join in the laughter, and as the fine line between pain and joy evaporates, the tears and laughter mingle together in a sweet symbol of reconciliation.

As ministers of reconciliation, we give people the permission to see that they are more than the sum of their parts—their behaviors, their past, their sins.

> *As ministers of reconciliation, we give people the permission to see that they are more than the sum of their parts— their behaviors, their past, their sins.*

When Debbie first joined our single adult group, she was antagonistic and anti-establishment. Simply, she was difficult to love. My response to her came from my codependent cycle. I assumed I had to fix her, change her, and bring her under control. None of those worked, and I was quickly frustrated. I assumed that Debbie was only the persona she projected; that she was, like the woman at the party, only the sum of her parts. I failed to see there was more to Debbie than the anger and pain.

So I changed. I asked myself how I could find ways to trust Debbie, then I asked her if she would be responsible for a monthly concert sponsored by the single adult ministry. She said yes. The result, I must confess, surprised me. Debbie was a terrific leader. And the responsibility allowed her to channel her anger. The responsibility became a place for her healing. I discovered that Debbie saw herself as unlovable—a collection of hurts, rejection, and broken dreams—and needed someone else to give her the permission to see the Debbie beyond the immediate.

AN EMPOWERED LEADER IS PATIENT

We don't want growth, we want security. We don't want an invitation to a journey, we want a destination. We want solutions. We want a nice how-to formula. In response, Jesus gives us permission to continue the journey; to see life and ministry as a journey; to see that ministry is not the absence of our problems. In fact, it is our problems. This permission set me free to see ministry happening even in the middle of my "stumbling, bumbling" attempts.

As I was developing a small group program for our single adults, I was infected with a need to see my work as a destination. I was restless, expecting the ministry to flourish "when" certain changes happened—when the new leaders were trained; when we had a better curriculum; when our problem people were taken care of; when we had more people involved; and when . . . the list was endless. This mentality never allowed me or the people involved to enjoy the groups as they were. The groups had to be perfect before they could be enjoyed, I thought.

We have this ongoing temptation to expect to arrive somewhere. As soon as this or that set of problems is resolved, we say to ourselves convincingly, then life will begin. We quickly discover, however, that such an internal dialogue only perpetuates itself with "if onlys" ad infinitum.

AN EMPOWERED LEADER IS
WILLING TO GIVE MINISTRY AWAY

The upshot of all that has been said in this chapter is this last characteristic. As we begin to believe that our identity is intact in God's faithful hands, we learn that we gain nothing by overpowering those with whom we minister. We gain nothing from being a one-man band. We gain nothing from continually working to the point of exhaustion.

When we don't need to control people, we're free to love them. When we don't need to be God, we're free to be used by Him. When we don't need to win the game, we're free to enjoy being on the team. When we don't need to create an impenetrable reputation, we're free to give the ministry away.

Unfortunately, many people feel some guilt after this material is presented. We read it through our scorekeeping filter and don't feel like we measure up. We wish we didn't come up short in certain areas, so we make more promises and commitments to try to work harder. We feel put out by others who are not pulling their weight to help make this "leadership thing" work. As a result, we feel more obligations—more tyranny of the "shoulds." But the Bible never says that we "should be" ministers of reconciliation. It says simply that we are. Isn't that a scary thought? Our God is crazy enough to reflect His love through a community of broken people. But it is true, and that truth is the foundation of effective, relational leadership.

REFLECT AND REVIEW

Think about the material in this chapter, then answer the following questions. Remember, don't try to do the ministry alone. Whenever possible, discuss these questions with your single adult leadership team.

1. The gospel message says that if we know we're loved, we have no need to prove anything to anyone.

    a. Why is this message so easy to forget?

    b. What does it look like when we resort to our standard operating procedure of shopkeeping, scorekeeping, performing, and controlling?

2. What or who helps remind us that we are owned by God?

3. Review the following characteristics of self-responsibility. What does it mean to . . .

    a. Have boundaries? (Give an example.)

    b. Not be a victim?

    c. Respect your limitations? Say no?

    d. Regularly remind yourself that your identity is intact apart from your job, responsibility, or task?

4. This chapter refers to our need for community.

    a. Where are you being nurtured?

    b. Where is your sounding board?

    c. Where is your source of affirmation? Challenge?

5. In what ways do you attempt to hide your woundedness (your fault lines, confusion, and pain)?

6. In what ways are you reminded of our need for grace? Where and with whom do you experience forgiveness and renewal?

7. When do you play? How do you play? Do you celebrate life? How?

8. How do you treat others as your servants?

9. In what ways can you begin to see people with new eyes? How can you nurture them and affirm their successes? Do you know anyone who could be encouraged about a potential beyond his or her immediate circumstances?

10. Where have you seen growth in yourself and in your singles leadership group in the last three months?

11. In what ways do you allow others to receive praise?

KEY INGREDIENTS FOR BUILDING A CORE TEAM OF LEADERS

HOW THIS SECTION WILL BENEFIT YOUR MINISTRY

The following chronological outline will help you visualize the steps in building a core team of leaders. Most of the material in the outline is covered in this section. Your ministry may fit anywhere in the outline (you may already have selected leaders, for example), but it is important to understand the entire team-building approach because it is an ongoing, never-ending process as leaders rotate in and out of your ministry.

Use this outline as an A to Z guide as you build and nurture an effective singles ministry core leadership team.

A. How to Build Your Ministry on a Solid Foundation (section 1)
  1. Determining your ministry needs (chapters 1-4)
  2. Understanding and addressing obstacles (chapter 3)
  3. Beginning steps to develop a philosophy of ministry (chapter 7)
B. How to Select Leaders (chapters 4-5)
C. How to Develop and Nurture Your Leaders (chapters 5-6)
  1. Building a team (chapters 6 and 7; the Team-Building Assessment, chapter 14)
  2. Addressing team expectations (chapters 6-7)
  3. Fine tuning your philosophy of ministry (chapter 7)
D. How to Maximize the Gifts and Skills of Your Leadership Team (chapter 8)
  Using the Role Preference Test (chapter 14)
E. How to Communicate with Team Members (chapter 7)
  1. Role preference—an ongoing evaluation (chapter 7)
  2. Developing job descriptions (chapter 6)
  3. Handling failure (chapters 6-7)
  4. Resolving conflict (chapter 7)
F. How to Develop a Ministry Strategy (chapters 7, 9)
  1. Conducting a dream/brainstorm session (chapter 9)
  2. Using the Rocket planning method (chapter 9)
  3. Rocket planning review (chapter 9)

MEMO

TO: Terry

FROM: Rich and Karen

RE: Chapter 5: Team Selection

This all sounds good to us. We certainly believe that effective, relational leadership begins with a solid foundation. We believe with equal certainty that effective ministries are places where we give responsibility away. But now what? Where do we go from here? Talk about what this process looks like in practice.

- Steps to implement what we believe
- Steps to building a core team of single adult leaders
- The importance of selecting leaders

CHAPTER FIVE

Team Selection

Terry Hershey

I know the temptation. "Now we're getting to the stuff that really matters," we want to say. "This is the practical material we've been waiting for. This is the how-to section!"

I understand the temptation, which means we must clarify our intention before continuing. It is not our purpose to devise five easy steps that will guarantee programmatic success. It is not our purpose to design a program that will eliminate leadership problems. It is not our purpose to devise a way to eliminate failure as we give away responsibility. Granted, it would be nice to have such a guarantee.

We cannot, however, escape the fact that any success from the use of this section's ideas is based upon the material in the first section. In other words, if we do not understand the principle of "who owns us" (that our identity is not built upon our program's success or failure), the implications of the addiction cycle on organizational life, or the reality that the ministry is owned by the people, then all of the blue-ribbon program ideas in the world will not do any good.

We get so caught up with achieving a goal or reaching the destination that we have forgotten that ministry itself is a journey. Ministry is the training, changes, interruptions, problems, and problem solving. Therefore, we don't need a guaranteed ticket for entry at the destination, but effective tools for the journey.

In the first section, we discovered that those tools are found in a model of ministry that develops people (versus programs) and gives responsibility away. Now let's put those tools to work.

HIERARCHICAL VERSUS RELATIONAL MINISTRY

Let's start with semantics. Throughout the first section, we used the phrase relational, or circular, leadership. We want that term to be more than just a catch phrase. The best way to further understand relational ministry is to compare it to hierarchical ministry.

Hierarchical Ministry

In the hierarchical model of ministry, power is limited and must be divided. Only a certain amount of power exists. Consequently, it must be allocated. We do this in a recognizable way with our organizational chart. The person at the top of the chart is given the greatest percentage of power, with the remainder divided among the "lower" boxes.

To fully understand, we must differentiate between power and responsibility. Not all persons in an organization have the same authority or areas of authority. In other words, their areas of responsibility differ. One may have a larger, and therefore quantitatively different, load of responsibility and authority. One may be responsible to another, thus coming under the other's authority. In the same way, one may have several others report to him or her.

EXAMPLE OF HIERARCHICAL MINISTRY STRUCTURE

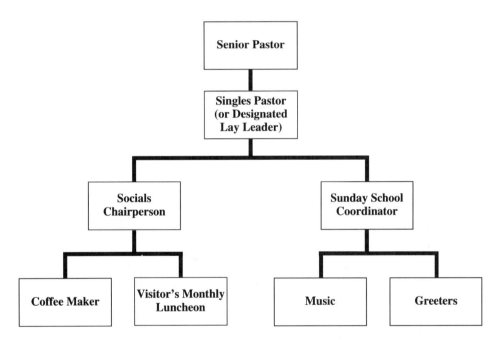

To assume, however, that these differences imply a difference in power (or the capacity for power) is a qualitative distinction. *Power implies ownership and a capacity to effect change.* If this property is limited to the few "at the top," we subsequently discourage creativity and the best we can hope for is a set of faithful volunteers to help us do "our" ministry. In other words, the people who work for us would be, at best, servants, not co-workers.

Relational Ministry

In the relational model of ministry, power is limitless. Every person has potential ownership and, therefore, power—the capacity to effect change. Each has the power to make decisions, have choices, give input, solve problems, plan the future, and take responsibilities. The hierarchical model, by contrast, considers power to be zero-based and thus it must be redistributed. Consequently, a continual struggle exists over who gets to keep the power. This struggle eventually occupies much of the organizational life.

The following chart continues to outline the differences.

HIERARCHICAL	RELATIONAL
■ Power divided—diminishing capacity to effect change	■ Power created—every responsible person is given power
■ Power allocated—only so much to go around	■ Power limitless—enough for everyone, even "low" person on the totem pole
■ Division of turfs—a spirit of competition	■ Building a team—everyone can win
■ Ownership for the few	■ Ownership for the many
■ Creativity stifled	■ Creativity encouraged
■ Planning done by one (or a few)	■ Planning by a team

In the book *Megatrends 2000*, the authors tell us that effective organizations have shifted "from management in order to control an enterprise to leadership in order to bring out the best in people and to respond quickly to change." Effective leaders "inspire commitment and empower people by sharing authority. [They] win commitment by setting an example of excellence."[1]

We don't want to create an artificial delineation just to make a point, nor do we wish to engage in a hypothetical discussion for the fun of it. Our assumptions here truly determine our direction in ministry. It makes a difference—a big difference.

Granted, it is a fantasy to think that power is (or can be) distributed equally to all participants. But that's not the alternative. We're not painting an all-or-nothing scenario, with hope for a utopia. In the real world, crises arise, a fact that necessitates the use of the hierarchical system.

Even Jesus in the temple, overturning tables and expelling moneychangers, resorted to the hierarchical system. In His mind, selling in the temple was a crisis that warranted hierarchical power. In other words, Jesus said by His actions, "All the power is in My hands now. I make the decisions. I call the shots."

In a contemporary less sensational example, Chris was leading a group of single adults on a short-term mission trip in South America when their rental van broke down. The situation required immediate and direct attention. Chris didn't appoint a committee meeting or a team planning session to decide to rent a new van. The crisis necessitated hierarchical power—complete decision-making power in the hands of one person. Chris made the decision.

Is it possible that many churches perpetuate a mode of existence where they move from one crisis to another—maybe even creating them—as a means to keep power and control in the hands of the one or the few?

In the real world, some jobs (whether we like it or not) carry more "power" than others (and this power may be recognized formally on an organizational chart, or it may be recognized informally by members of the organization). We must ask: Does the system allow for power to be created at all levels of the organization? Are creativity and ownership encouraged and affirmed? Are people at all levels being empowered, or is there only so much power to go around, with the lucky few with the correct organizational lottery tickets being the winners?

What are the essential elements to implement relational, rather than hierarchical, leadership in your single adult ministries? First, you need to build a team. Building a team involves three steps: selecting your leaders, spending time with a few, and continuing development as you give them ownership.

BUILDING A LEADERSHIP CORE TEAM

Anxious to return home to practice newly learned empowering principles presented at a training conference, a pastor asked me the best way to convince his congregation that empowering was a good way to do business. (As we said earlier, this may be a subversive teaching, especially if the people have been trained to think that it is one person's job to do the ministry. This thinking is usually the rule and not the exception. But there's the rub—empowering begins with a team.)

I told him, as I am telling you now: Gather three or four people (eight to twelve maximum) from your single adult ministry or church who are willing to walk through this material with you. Don't assume you can build a ministry alone. Giving away ownership begins at the developmental stage, in which we begin to build our "leadership core team." Team building is a three-step process.

Select Your Leaders

We do not believe in leadership by volunteerism. Let me explain. I've worked in many churches where I begged for volunteers, and once people responded, I spent the remainder of my time trying to get certain ones to "unvolunteer."

This is not to say that people should not or cannot volunteer their time or services, but just because people volunteer doesn't mean they should be given the specific tasks for which they volunteered. It may be inappropriate in cases to offer a task just because a person is willing (or guilt-ridden, enthusiastic, or new to the church).

> *I agree with Peter Drucker: "There are no more 'volunteers.' There is only unpaid staff."*

Just as "the squeaky wheel gets the grease," many people also volunteer because they have an axe to grind or another hidden agenda to accomplish. In some cases, they may be too emotionally needy.

Since we're on the subject, I must confess I have difficulty with the word "volunteer." It seems to connote that I am the one doing the ministry, and the best anyone else can hope for is to volunteer to help me with "my ministry." Too often, no implication of any ownership is given. As an alternative, some churches effectively use the words *co-worker, lay minister,* or *team member—even unpaid staff.*

I agree with Peter Drucker: "There are no more 'volunteers.' There is only unpaid staff." In his book *The New Realities*, he tells the story of a 13,000-member church with a paid staff of 160. To effectively manage the variety of activities, they ask new members after a few months to become "unpaid staff." They are thoroughly trained and given a specific assignment with performance goals.[2]

Semantics aside, the issue remains the same: We shouldn't wait for people to take responsibility, we should give it to them. That's selective leadership, the beginning of the process of giving responsibility away—tapping people on the shoulder and asking them to be a part of a team. Jesus used this approach with His disciples. He didn't set up a table after one of His talks to take applications for the Twelve. He asked them individually to join Him. When the disciples came to Him to point out the obvious, that several thousand people had been listening all day and were hungry, He didn't say, "I'll take care of it" or "Are there any volunteers?" He said, "You feed them." (Rich talks more about the "Jesus Model" of ministry in chapter 6.)

The principle applies whether you're a pastor, singles minister, lay leader, or social committee chairperson. Who are you tapping on the shoulder? Who's helping you? Who are you inviting to be a part of the ministry?

You may be saying, "Wait a minute, here. It sounds good. We're in favor of giving responsibility away—handing the ball off. But you've never been to my church, have you?" I understand the objection. We look around and don't see any exceptional candidates for the selection process. Those who are exceptional are already up to their ears in volunteer work around the church anyway. What if Jesus had adopted the same attitude? Can you hear Him, "You know, Father, I've been here on earth awhile. You asked Me to find some disciples. But You haven't been to Galilee lately, have You? There aren't exactly discipleship-quality folks here. I mean, the best I could find are a fisherman who swears a lot, a tax man who steals from the people and the government, and two brothers who take their mother everywhere!"

Jesus knew He was not to wait for charismatic, exuberant, "together" people to appear and volunteer for duty. He knew He was to develop leadership, to spend time with a few people and empower them. And the process began with selecting people who were, at the time, gems in the rough.

I suspect many people in our single adult ministries are, at best, gems in the rough. We may need to return to our ministries with new glasses. For me, it meant identifying those individuals who had a learning and giving heart. Skills can be taught, but people with a desire to grow and learn are a resource too precious to pass by.

Spend Time with a Few

This is the logical consequence to the first step. At this point, we must make a choice in our ministry. We must choose between program management (hierarchical ministry) and lifestyle modeling (relational ministry). These are not mutually exclusive categories, but they are choices that determine values and priorities in our ministries.

Program management emphasizes efficiency. It is primarily task-oriented. Lifestyle modeling emphasizes effectiveness. It is primarily people-oriented. Lifestyle modeling begins with a commitment to spend time with a few. I must recognize that team development is my primary job description, not the accomplishment of program goals, the administration of projects, or the execution of programs. My primary job is to create an environment where a team of people can be empowered to accomplish their dreams and goals.

We must learn to be the people of God before we can do the work of God. In a purely program management style, power is divided and held by those in charge. Volunteers are recruited to carry out the work efficiently. Business meetings are held to iron out problems blocking efficiency. Don't get me wrong. A good deal of work does get accomplished under this scenario. But I wonder, is there more to ministry than implementing programs?

Here's why I ask. Under the program management style, I soon discovered that my primary reason for meeting with people was task oriented. There was no relationship other than the job. I think there are two reasons for that.

First, since power is allocated and held by the few, those with power tend to mistrust all others. Why else would we spend time during a committee meeting rehashing the type of salad to be served at a banquet, unless we didn't trust the person or the capability of the person whose job it was to make that decision in the first place?

Second, we can easily relate to someone if the connection is primarily task-oriented. Real relationships—which include conflict, affirmation, stretching, risking, learning, and trusting—are never easy or efficient.

The choice of a lifestyle modeling ministry also affects our calendar. In my case, the purpose of our meetings was no longer business, but mutual support. So what did we do? The leadership core team met for brown-bag dinner every Tuesday night in my office. Why Tuesday night? Because that was program night at the church, and I didn't want to add more night meetings to people's calendars. Our agenda? No business allowed. Instead, we focused on three items:

1. We asked, "How's your week been?"
2. We took turns sharing some lesson that we had learned
   from the gospel or some area of personal growth and challenge.
3. We prayed for each other and the ministry.

I have to be honest; our first few meetings ended in about fifteen minutes. Why? We were not used to being together as people, only as business associates. We were continually tempted to discuss business. We wanted to get the prayer time over with so we could get on with the "real" ministry—namely, the business that continually cried for our attention.

You may say that this type of meeting is easy for someone with a light and open calendar. In fact, it is not easy (initially) for anyone. It requires choices. Effective ministry is not just what you say yes to, but what you say no to. I made a commitment to meet weekly with our leadership core team and monthly with each team member. To accomplish this, I had to schedule fewer business meetings. I had to attend fewer committee meetings. I had fewer hours on my calendar for individual counseling. I had to make choices.

This style of ministry will definitely get a reaction. The grapevine was quickly buzzing with the rumor that "Terry just isn't available anymore." At first, I was defensive. Then I recognized the myth that I could or should be available to meet everyone's needs. This myth was built on the premise that no one else in the church was capable of ministry. And if we are indispensable, then we're assuming people are irresponsible.

In addition, many people considered this "time with a few" to be snobbish, the formation of a clique. Perhaps, but it makes me wonder why we tell single adults to get into relationships, and then when a group forms, we tell them to get out of their clique. Relationships do not a clique make. How do we ensure that the leadership core team does not become exclusive? We make sure new persons are added as others rotate off the team on a regular basis. (This will be covered in greater detail in chapter 7.)

In part, the rumors were right. I was no longer available to everyone. I was more available to a few, however, so that they, in turn, could be more available to another few and so forth. In the end, everyone's needs were met more effectively because we were not all spread so thin.

Continue Development as You Give Leaders Ownership

How are gems in the rough turned into competent leaders on a core team? It certainly isn't luck or serendipity. The answer is a continued commitment to development—a commitment to ongoing training. In my own ministry, this training took one of two forms.

1. *A semi-annual leaders retreat.* I scheduled a retreat for anyone who had been on the leadership core team, had served on one of the committees, or had been invited to serve and wanted to see what this ministry was all about. This leaders retreat was a highlight for me because it involved not just those with "titles," but anyone who had any part in making our ministry programming work. The retreat said loudly and clearly, if you are involved, you are considered leadership. It gave us an opportunity to affirm our purpose and to affirm one another. At the end of the retreat, each person was able to stand up and answer these four questions:

> *It makes me wonder why we tell single adults to get into relationships, and then when a group forms, we tell them to get out of their clique. Relationships do not a clique make.*

- What am I responsible for? (Where do I fit?)
- Who am I responsible to? (Who do I work with?)
- Who is helping me so that I am not doing the job alone?
- Where am I being nurtured?

(Keep reading. These questions are addressed later in this section. Resources for leadership retreats and seminars are included in chapters 12 and 13.)

2. *A leadership development group.* This second form of leadership training met for four weeks between the two retreats. We met whenever there were enough people—between three and ten—to form a group. (Note: We met on Tuesday night, our regular singles activity night, so we did not add another night to people's calendars.) In a strictly volunteer model, I discovered that I knew nothing about some of the people working with me and for me. They were doing the job simply because they volunteered. Our leadership development group attempted to correct that weakness through the group's three purposes.

   a. The group gave us an opportunity to tell our stories to one another—our personal history, our God story, our church story. It let us see where others had come from and what they valued.
   b. The group gave me an opportunity to talk about the single adult ministry, the purpose statement, and our particular philosophy of ministry. It was an opportunity for briefing, for making sure we were all, as one friend says, "playing the song off the same sheet of music."

(Purpose statements are discussed in chapter 9, philosophy of ministry is discussed in chapter 7.)

c. The group gave us an opportunity to explore spiritual gifts and look at service opportunities (not just in the singles ministry, but other areas of the church as well).

Through team building, we do not seek elimination of problems or failure, but the initiation of the first steps to become the people of God before we do the work of God. These are the first steps toward relational leadership.

Let's review. You want to build an effective model of relational leadership in your church. To do so, you must build a leadership core team, beginning with these three steps.

- Select your leaders.
- Spend time with a few.
- Continue development as you give leaders ownership.

If we want to practice relational leadership, building a core team is a non-negotiable.

REFLECT AND REVIEW

Think about the material in this chapter, then answer the following questions. Remember, don't try to do the ministry alone. Whenever possible, discuss these questions with your single adult leadership team.

1. Look at the characteristics of hierarchical and relational ministries found in the chart on page 66. According to the chart, in what ways is your ministry hierarchical? In what ways is it relational?

2. In your current ministry, how do you select leaders? Can you name who you're "tapping on the shoulder"? Who's helping you? Who are you "betting on"?

3. Review your calendar. How do you spend time with your single adult leaders?

4. Is it true that if we are available for everyone, we're available for no one? Explain.

5. What ways do you develop leaders? In your current ministry, in what ways are leaders given ownership? In what ways do you do most of the work?

MEMO

TO: Rich

FROM: Terry and Karen

RE: Chapter 6: Time with the Team

This second section tells about key ingredients for relational ministry. In chapter 5, Terry gave a thumbnail sketch of the steps to building a team. We'd like to hear your input on how you used these steps in your experiences with single adult ministry.

- How did you select leaders?
- What were some practical ways you spent time with them?
- How did you give leaders ownership?
- How do job descriptions help your leaders succeed in their tasks?
- How do we make sure we aren't setting people up for failure?

CHAPTER SIX

Time with the Team

Rich Hurst

Giving the ministry away is a good idea; giving it away wholesale to a group of people is a bad idea—this constitutes "dumping" the ministry. You can't dump a ministry on a group of single adults. You can, however, intentionally give the ministry to individuals by spending time with them, communicating with them, and developing leaders. Each time you give a piece of the ministry to an individual, you give that person an opportunity to achieve a kind of stardom.

"Come on," you're thinking, "I mean, being in charge of Sunday morning greeters hardly constitutes stardom!" The apostle Paul might not agree. In Philippians 2:14-16, he wrote to the church at Philippi:

> Do everything without complaining or arguing, so that you may become blameless and pure, children of God without fault in a crooked and depraved generation, in which you shine like stars in the universe as you hold out the word of life—in order that I may boast on the day of Christ that I did not run or labor for nothing.

Paul affirms the importance of his investment in the individuals at the church of Philippi. He acknowledges that when he stands before God, he wants to present the individuals he invested in—his stars—not the programs he started and maintained. He wants to boast of the people he empowered. In the same way, your investment in individuals says to them, "When I stand before God, I want to be able to hold you up as evidence that I did not labor for nothing."

In the previous chapter, Terry talked about three steps in building a leadership core team. In this chapter, I'll elaborate on how I applied those steps in my single adult ministry.

CHOOSING LEADERS

When Jesus began his ministry, He did not start a mass recruitment program, asking for volunteers. Instead, He looked around and said to specific individuals, "Come with me." In the same way, choosing single adult leaders must involve more than asking for volunteers to write their names and phone numbers on a sign-up sheet.

A few years ago, we needed a second co-chair for a single adult retreat we were planning. The two co-chairs, along with the team they selected, were responsible for every aspect of the retreat. It was a big job with a lot of far-reaching responsibilities, so we were anxious to select the right person. A co-worker and I asked several people, all of whom had turned us down. Finally, I sat in my office and prayed: "God, who do You want to be the other person?"

A name immediately came to mind: Melissa. She was one of our top leaders, but after completing her leadership term in singles, she chose to be more active in other church ministries. I hadn't spent much time with Melissa recently, but knew she had remained active in the church ministry. At first I disregarded her name as a passing thought, but I couldn't get her name out of my mind. Finally, I said to my co-worker, "I know this is crazy, but how about Melissa?" She also knew that Melissa was active in other areas, but we took a chance and called her. To our delight, Melissa said yes. As we talked to her, she was clearly the perfect person for the job.

Prayer is a great starting place for leadership selection. Many times, God will bring a specific person to mind. Most often, though, the choice is much less obvious. In those cases, guidelines help. I have a few guidelines I follow.

Watch for People Who Are Committed to Service or Willing to Help

In Acts 6, the Christian leaders of the day chose new leaders because they were "full of Spirit and wisdom." These people's lives had communicated their availability to help accomplish whatever was asked of them. The leaders of the day knew who they were and apparently had seen their work.

Sometimes we're so hungry for helpers that we ask people to be responsible for too much too soon. Be patient. Look for people who have shown they can follow through on the little tasks and can handle increasing responsibility until a project is done. Be aware of stereotypes of single adults (see chapter 1). Look for people in whom you want to invest. Watch for the type of faith visibly demonstrated through caring or leadership qualities.

Give people a chance to show their willingness to invest in others in ministry. Find those who are wanting to help others, not just trying to be "show boats." I was once involved with a leader who was in front of the group nearly every week. By his attitude I could tell that a primary reason he was doing the job was to get attention, not to encourage others. Make sure people are willing to be involved in encouraging others in ministry, not just self-gratification.

Involve Unemployed or Underemployed People in the Ministry

Those who are between jobs generally have three pressing needs. We tend to think only of their need for income. We often don't consider two other important concerns: the needs for affirmation and to plug into a place. Involving the unemployed or under-employed in single adult leadership can provide them with the missing sense of worthiness and a meaningful, significant place to focus their creative drive. It can also provide you with a wellspring of energy, creativity, enthusiasm, and talented leadership.

As the pastor, director, or single adult leader, you do not recruit people to fulfill your dreams. Rather, you invest in individuals to whom God has given dreams of their own.

Do not use or misuse your under-employed or unemployed people, however. If someone is underemployed, use this time to encourage and challenge him or her to try bigger things. If people are unemployed, they may be tempted to use this ministry opportunity as a replacement for their job search. As a result, set time limits and encourage them in their job search.

Rely on the Opinions of Lay Leadership
Sometimes group or congregation members can see other members in a way that professional ministers or staff people often overlook. Lay leaders have the benefit of being a part of the group and can sometimes get to know other members better and faster than the pastor, director, or key leader. Trust the instincts of those leaders you have previously identified. Consider their input.

GETTING TO KNOW LEADERS

Once you've selected the right people, your next responsibility is to spend time with them. Spending time with people means finding out who they are. Here are some "discussion-starter" ideas to get to know them.

Start with their God story. Ask your single adult leaders how their faith journey has led them to this point in their lives. Don't make this a perfunctory group exercise for new leaders. Spend time with each person individually, asking them to share their story with you personally.

Ask about their family life. Spend time with your leaders to get to know and understand them. Learning how people relate in their families gives you clues to how they'll relate in leadership core teams.

Ask about their dreams for ministry. As the pastor, director, or single adult leader, you do not recruit people to fulfill your dreams. Rather, you invest in individuals to whom God has given dreams of their own. As a leader, tell your dreams to people, and then ask them about their dreams:

- What would you like to do if there were no money, time, family, or educational restrictions?
- In what ways would you like to change the world, given a complete absence of limitations?
- What one thing would you like to change about your work environment?

- Who is one of your heroes? Why?
- What is something your hero did/does to help change the world?
- What is one thing our city could do to improve how it meets people's needs?
- What is one thing our church could do to improve how it meets people's needs?

Your leaders may never have been asked to share their dreams. Once they do, ask them to be accountable to you to see that one of their dreams is accomplished. For example, one single adult leader dreamed of taking graduate classes. I asked her to take the first step and call a nearby university to inquire about courses, then tell me about it. Another leader dreamed of feeding the homeless. I asked her to try it, then tell me how it went. She decided to fill a picnic basket with breakfast food— scrambled eggs, toast, fruit, and juice. She went to a park and asked homeless people there to join her for breakfast. She still does this on a regular basis. Sometimes she feeds as many as twenty people.

By asking people to be accountable to you, they feel you care for them. They feel that someone is interested in them and their dreams. When people feel cared for, their ministry will soar.

SPENDING TIME WITH YOUR LEADERS

When you spend time with your leaders, you get to know them better, and they learn more about you. Here are several ideas or ways to spend time with the people you've selected.

Meet them on their turf. Go to where your single adult leaders work. Have lunch with them. Meet for dinner after work. If you are paid staff, don't expect your leaders to come to your office. If you are a lay leader, don't expect them to come to your house. Meet them when and where it's convenient for them.

Use your telephone. If you have time limitations, use your phone to get to know people. Don't make long bothersome calls, but make short calls. "Hi! How are you? I was thinking about you and wanted to let you know." As time goes on, ask deeper questions. Ask people what they enjoy doing for fun. Ask questions about their work, families, and friends. Later, as you become closer, ask them about their relationship with God. Who is God to them, and what do they think God is like?

One leader had a small boat that he kept docked on a lake near downtown Seattle. We spent hours talking and bobbing in the waves, surrounded by the tall masts of passing sailboats. Our maritime discussions were the foundation of a relationship that could not have been built inside the walls of a church office.

Schedule a lunch date. I make a point to have lunch with my top leaders at least once a month. In a complex ministry with many leadership teams, this is sometimes hard to maintain because of the time it consumes. You may need to give up something to be able to spend time with leaders in this manner. For example, don't attend every program or activity. (Chapter 11 tells you more about the importance of being able to say no—not being available for everyone, but spending quality time with a few.) The return on the hours spent in this type of relationship is higher than merely investing time in programs. Programs may or may not change lives, but spending time with people will.

Send notes. Send short notes to your leaders on a regular basis. Let them know you are thinking about them and that you care. In the note, give them the responsibility to call you in the near future.

Involve them in other activities. Several years ago, I had just joined the staff of a church and needed help moving into a new house. On my first Sunday, one of the staff announced to the church that I could use help moving. Only one man showed. Darryl had recently moved to town and wanted to make some new friends. We had a great afternoon together, wrestling the furniture into place as we talked.

Not long after, he became involved in the church's singles ministry. After I was able to observe and get to know him better, I offered him a leadership position. Although Darryl's first leadership experience was less than successful, I stuck with him and continued investing in him. (Later I came to believe that it was me who had failed him because we had not fully discussed the job or our expectations of one another.) I met with him weekly, sometimes spending the majority of our time talking about ministry issues, but often just talking about real-life issues each of us was facing. During our time together, I tried to make clear to him that his value was not related to his performance.

After a period of time, he said something I'll never forget. "It changed my life that you didn't give up on me; that you continued to give me your time week after week. Thank you. You won't be sorry." Sometime later, I got the highest compliment a person could possibly receive: Because of his leadership experience and the seminary training he had received years earlier, Darryl was asked to assume my position when I left that church.

You only have so much of yourself to go around. A healthy leader understands that premise. One person can be responsible for building only so many relationships. Most single adult ministries have between three and six top leaders (a good rule of thumb is fewer than ten). Invest in them. You'll see amazing results.

TRUSTING YOUR LEADERS—GIVING THEM OWNERSHIP

In single adult ministry, we must remember that single adults aren't teenagers. Most are professionals in the marketplace. We need to trust them, to give them ownership. This point was driven home by the following experience.

At a meeting with the leadership core team for Cornerstone, the young singles ministry at University Presbyterian Church, I found myself in a debate with the team about the Sunday morning class. They had asked me to clarify who was responsible for the program.

"You are," I said, "but I choose the speakers."

That's when the debate started. The speaker consumes 75 percent of the class time, they argued. How could I say they were responsible for the program when they had no authority to select its major component? They felt I was holding out on them. I tried to explain that I felt responsible for the type of program we presented. A lot rode on the quality and content of the speaker's message. As the staff person overseeing this ministry, I felt I needed the final word about speakers.

They told me that they felt I didn't trust them. They felt the responsibility they had been given was not accompanied by the corresponding authority. I realized they were right, a hard thing for me to discover. I thought I trusted them, but communicated a different message by continuing to choose the speaker.

Finally, Matt, one of the leaders, said, "Let us try it! Let us select speakers for a while." I told him I was worried about them failing.

He responded, "Let us fail then!"

He was right. The time had come for me to live out the principle of giving away ownership.

At the beginning of this chapter I said that giving the ministry away "wholesale" to a group is a bad idea. I couldn't just say, "Okay. Here. You want it? You can have it." I could work with individuals—together as a team. I could (1) *give input*, (2) *trust them*, and (3) *give the ministry away*. So, Matt and the rest of the team developed a list of potential speakers and asked me for suggestions. My role as a participant on the team was to approve the list of speakers. Afterward, they enlisted the speakers for the Sunday morning classes.

Giving away ownership can sometimes be the toughest of the three steps mentioned above. Although you maintain contact with the leaders, give input where needed, and continue their development, you must trust them and let go. You quickly put the other two steps to the test. You hope that you have chosen the right people and your investment of time is paying off. But the real test comes when you actually hand them the keys to the ministry. You find out how much you trust your chosen leaders. You also discover whether you're willing to give them responsibility and authority.

There are times, however, when you do not give people responsibility.

1. If they have proven they will misuse that trust.
2. When you're not sure they understand the overall needs of the people they are to serve.
3. If the direction they're headed is destructive to the overall ministry.

For example, you have just assumed a new position and did not choose your current leaders. It would be unwise to walk in and immediately give away all respon-

---

WAYS TO SPEND TIME WITH YOUR LEADERS

1. Meet leaders on their turf.
2. Use your telephone.
3. Go out to lunch once a month.
4. Send them notes.
5. Involve them in other activities.

sibility. Take time to assess the current level of commitment and maturity. Giving people wholesale authority and responsibility can be destructive if you find they do not have a clear vision of their task. You may discover leaders who are there because no one else would do it. Some people are in leadership positions because of their own needs as opposed to a need to serve. This can be destructive to the ministry. Take your time. Go slowly. When you move too fast you devalue people and run the risk of losing them.

THE JESUS MODEL

Jesus demonstrated each of these three steps in His own ministry. The gospels tell that He handpicked His own disciples; they didn't volunteer. He spent time with them, then gave them responsibility and authority. Let's look at an example of Jesus giving His disciples ownership of the ministry.

Picture this scene in Matthew 14:14-20: Thousands of people have gathered to be touched by the hand of this mysterious healer. It is now evening. The disciples come to Jesus and say, "Let's get rid of these people and get some dinner!" The disciples are hungry and tired, and no doubt a little cranky. But Jesus feels compassion for the crowd and doesn't want to leave. So He says, "They do not need to go away. You give them something to eat!"

The disciples react with surprise, quickly informing Jesus that they have little to give. Their response has a bit of an edge to it: "We have here only five loaves of bread and two fish."

But Jesus says, "Bring them here to Me." He asks His guests to sit down. Jesus then gives thanks and sends out His "stars" to feed the thousands of hungry people with five loaves of bread and two fish.

Easy? Hardly. Can you imagine walking into a crowd of several hundred hungry people, not knowing if you really have enough food to go around?

Jesus knew that investing in individuals—spending time with a few—is risky business. It's risky to receive empowerment because it implies ownership and responsibility. It's also risky to give the ministry away. Jesus had given the disciples the tools they needed to succeed, but the real possibility of failure also existed. Jesus allowed them to walk into the crowd on their own. He didn't do it for them.

Jesus modeled effective, relational leadership. He could have simply fed the crowd Himself, but He chose to give the ministry away. He had chosen this band individually; He had spent long hours sharing His life with them; and now He was giving the ministry to them.

WHEN YOUR LEADERS SEEM TO FAIL

Sometimes your handpicked leaders seem to fail. Remember how Darryl got off to a rocky start in his first leadership role? I tried to diagnose the possible cause. I carefully selected him. I met regularly with him. I gave him ownership of a part of the singles ministry. Yet Darryl appeared to be failing. Upon further analysis, I discovered I was the one who failed him. Remember these important factors:

1. I did not clearly define what I expected him to do. I had merely given
   him a task. I assumed Darryl knew how it should be done. But he
   didn't, and he was unsure of what I wanted.
2. I discovered the task was not appropriate for him. The job I had given
   him required a different set of gifts and talents than he possessed.
3. I did not help Darryl find anyone to do the ministry with him. He was
   on his own.
4. I never asked him to be accountable to me for anything. I just expected
   him to "get the job done." Then I was disappointed when it didn't
   happen.

How do we make sure we're not setting people up for failure? This situation
pointed out to me five important questions we all need to ask ourselves before giving
someone a task.

HAVE I CLEARLY DEFINED THE JOB?

Have the people clearly articulated their own dream? In other words, did we agree?
Did we verbalize expectations?

As people commit to a job or ministry, take time to work through what is
expected of them. What will it take to accomplish the task? One of the most effective ways to hinder leaders is to attempt ministry by assumption, to assume they know
what we want them to do.

Another way to handicap leaders is to assume we understand their dream. I
once listened to a tired, frustrated leader tell me about how the pastor had given her
the green light to pursue her dream for ministry. He had not taken the time, however,
to find out what that dream entailed. Once she successfully began the ministry, con-
troversy arose within the church. The pastor asked, "What are you doing?" "I'm doing
what we talked about," she replied. Unfortunately, they hadn't really talked about the
details of her dream. In the end, she felt abandoned and frustrated. The message is
clear: Take time to clearly define the dream or specific area of responsibility.

Melissa is an example of clearly defining a job. Camille served as the other
co-chair for the retreat planning. I met with both of them to discuss our philosophy
of planning with a team—with each team member having specific responsibilities.
They could ask people from the three different Sunday morning single adult classes
to be on the team. I gave them a workbook that Sheri, one of the singles, had com-
piled. The workbook was a guide to planning retreats, and contained flyers and ideas
from past retreats. It also contained job descriptions for team members. I asked them
to sit down with my co-worker, Sandy, to go over the budget and other details. Sandy
and I would approve the budget and any literature. (We had learned through a bad
experience that if you don't check printed materials, you can leave out needed information. One time we left out the dates of the retreat.)

Outside of these details, they were free to plan the retreat any way they wanted.
I asked them to think about what they wanted to do, and we would meet again in a

couple of weeks. I challenged them to dream big and not to allow their former retreat experiences to hinder what they'd like to do.

Melissa, Camille, Sandy, and I met two weeks later so the two co-leaders could describe their creative dream for the retreat. It had a western theme, complete with a chuckwagon barbecue. They also presented a mockup of the publicity brochure. It was perfect—one of the best-looking brochures I've ever seen. I listened to how they decided to involve their team members and help people at the retreat get to know one another. They had understood their job and had now placed the stamp of their dream on it. (Chapter 14 contains specific job duties for retreat team members. It also includes sample budget worksheets and report forms.)

Job Descriptions

Job descriptions help ensure leaders know what is expected from them. To develop a job description, ask the following questions.

1. What is the position title (for example, team member, team facilitator, divorce recovery coordinator, retreat coordinator, etc.)?
2. What will this person be doing, generally? In other words, what is the purpose of this position?
3. What are the specific responsibilities?
4. Who does the team member report to and from whom does he or she receive information (for example, how much money the person has to work with, what facilities are available for a seminar, etc.)?
5. With whom does the team member work closely?
6. What gifts or skills are required?
7. What are the expectations of the team member (for example, lifestyle, church involvement)?
8. What is the term of this position?
9. What are some time-measurable goals during this term?
10. When and how will we evaluate this job description, based on the accomplishment of the goals?

A sample job description for a leadership core team facilitator appears on the next page. In this job description, I completed all sections except where I had the facilitator fill in three measurable goals for the term. (By having leaders set their own goals you give them ownership and responsibility for their ministry.) Prior to the facilitator beginning his term, we discussed the job duties, made sure the goals were measurable, and answered any questions. We set the date for an evaluation halfway into the term. During the evaluation, we reviewed how that person was doing in his job, if he was accomplishing his goals, and if I was available for him when he needed my input. A blank job description appears on page 202 in chapter 14. You can adapt it to fit your needs, or use it as it is in your ministry.

IS THE TASK APPROPRIATE FOR THE LEADER?

Not every task is appropriate for every person's gifts and skills. By placing people in the wrong ministry, we can set them up for failure. Sometimes a job or ministry is too big for a person to handle.

At a single adult seminar, a man raised his hand and asked, "What do you do when someone doesn't follow through?" He recounted an incident in which the church was hosting a holiday potluck for singles. The tables were set, and the silverware was polished and laid out perfectly. Pumpkin pies were being kept warm in the oven. The group was waiting only for the man who was to bring the turkey. Finally, he arrived . . . with nothing! The organizers were devastated.

JOB DESCRIPTION

Position Title: *Team facilitator*

General Description and Purpose for Position: *This person leads the team meetings and ensures that every team member feels supported and understands his or her assignments.*

Position Responsibilities:
- *Lead the team meetings.*
- *Meet regularly with department staff and turn in monthly reports.*
- *Coordinate team in the selection of speakers for Sunday morning classes.*
- *Establish policy; make decisions regarding Tuesday single adult meeting format.*
- *Make announcements at singles meetings.*
- *Be at all team meetings.*

Reports to: *Church staff*

Provides Information for/Receives Information from: *Team members*

Works Closely with: *Co-facilitator*

Gifts/Skills Required: *Organization; administration; leadership; positive outlook; ability to resolve conflict.*

Expectations/Standards: *It is expected that you be a self-starter. It is also expected that you be living a constant Christian lifestyle. It is important that you be a team player, as you will be working closely with the church staff and your team members.*

Three Measurable Goals for Term:
1. *Increase our attendance on Tuesday night class from forty to eighty.*

2. *Develop quality leaders within our group by offering a leadership retreat.*

3. *Publicize our group within the church and community with the use of flyers, bulletins, and news releases.*

Term of Position: *June 1, 1991 to June 1, 1992*

Date of Evaluation: *December 1, 1991*

Assigned Person's Signature: *Matt Codman*

Date signed: *April 5, 1991*

The man who asked the question wanted to know what he should have done to prevent this minor catastrophe. We suggested that perhaps the expectations had exceeded this man's resources. In other words, was a turkey the appropriate responsibility for this man? Had he previously brought turkey? Did he know how to cook a turkey? As it turned out, the man didn't know how to cook a turkey. He was horrified with the task. His responsibility didn't fit his talents.

We suggested that that person be asked to bring a precooked ham to the next holiday potluck! In short, make sure the task fits the person's ability to complete it.

DOES THE LEADER HAVE A TEAMMATE TO HELP WITH THE JOB?

Since ministry is not tasks but relationships, why would we give anyone a job to do alone? Did Jesus?

In the gospels, we read that Jesus sent out the disciples in teams. Why? Because He knew the value of support. As Jesus traveled the countryside, He went with others. He talked about being a part of the kingdom—a kingdom of relationships, not tasks. This kingdom not only involves a relationship with God the Father, Son, and Holy Spirit, but also with each other.

In Luke 10:1-24, Jesus sends out the seventy disciples two by two. Imagine the finish to this adventure: They all come back excited. They tell Jesus all they've accomplished. You can feel the excitement. The room is full of the buzz of voices as the teams tell their stories. They say, "Lord, even the demons submit to us in Your name." He replies, "I saw Satan fall like lightning from heaven." Imagine Jesus joyfully saying, "I know! I saw Satan himself fall before you. Great job! I have given you authority to trample on snakes and scorpions and to overcome all the power of the Enemy; nothing will harm you. However, do not rejoice that the spirits submit to you, but rejoice that your names are written in heaven." Jesus is saying, "Yes, you have done a great task, but what's most important is that you are related to Me—your names are written in heaven on the welcome list." Jesus' ministry was about relationships.

Working with a teammate helps build relationships. At the beginning of the retreat that Melissa and Camille co-chaired, I took the speaker out to breakfast.

"Are you excited about the retreat?" he asked.

I told him I was looking forward to it.

He continued, "How are the numbers?"

"Oh, they're okay," I said, "but what I'm really excited about is that the two people in charge of the retreat have established a great friendship. Before they began working together on this project they hardly knew each other. Now they're becoming great friends."

The point of ministry is not task, but relationship. It's people learning to support one another, to encourage one another. Then why would we ever give someone a task to do alone? In fact, if someone is doing a job alone, we should seriously ask, "Why is that task necessary?"

WHO IS THE LEADER ACCOUNTABLE TO, AND FOR WHAT?

Accountability acts as a support structure for the leader. With accountability in place, people understand who they are to report to and for what. Accountability does not mean playing God in your leaders' lives, but rather allowing leaders to analyze how they're doing and what they're expected to do well.

People who attempt to give the ministry away sometimes have a tendency to overdo it. Their technique might be more appropriately called "abandoning the ministry." These people will carefully choose a leader, then dump the whole ministry in his or her lap and walk away, only to show up later to criticize the failure. A good accountability structure provides a clear idea of the responsibilities of all parties involved. The following questions should help you and your team establish accountability. (Chapter 7 describes more ideas for team communication.)

1. Have we agreed upon a job description?
2. Have we agreed upon times we'll check in with each other to report progress and concerns?
3. Have we agreed upon finances and a plan for the activity? (Chapter 14 gives you sample sheets to work with budgets and plans.)
4. Are we communicating support for each other? If so, how?

As I was driving on the freeway behind a truck, I saw the following message on its rear doors: "Our goal is safety and courtesy! How are we doing? Call 1-800-555-5555." That's a fine example of accountability. The job is well-defined. The driver knows it; the supervisor knows it; and you know it.

Accountability structures show leaders they are measuring up to the established standard. Next time you see a truck driver doing something right, call the 800-number and let the boss know! That brings us to the next item.

HAVE I AFFIRMED THE LEADER?

Affirmation is one of the greatest tools for a person who empowers. People respond to recognition and encouragement. People like to receive credit for what they have done. Follow these affirmation suggestions on the next page.

Dear Pam,

Thanks so much for organizing and coordinating the seminar "How to Slow Down in a Hurry-Up World." You worked well with your team—everyone seemed to enjoy all aspects of the event. You communicated clearly with your team members and the church staff throughout the entire process. I greatly appreciate your upbeat personality and your warmth and friendliness. You made the team members feel important and you made all participants feel welcome.

God's blessings to you. You're great!

Rich

1. Thank people publicly. Tell people about the leaders. Brag about them.
2. On all publicity, calendars, and literature, print as many leaders' names as possible. Include who's in charge and their responsibilities.
3. Send certificates or letters of commendation to those who have helped or succeeded on a leadership core team or project. Acknowledge people who've received degrees or awards. Write the letters so people will want to keep them. Don't just write a note that says, "Thanks for the help." Detail how you feel the person has helped and what it has meant to you. (See the sample letter and certificate on pages 85 and 87. A certificate you may want to use in your ministry appears in chapter 14, page 201.)
4. In leadership meetings give people credit for the work they've done. Word gets around about who takes credit for activities.
5. If possible, give small gifts or flowers. Take the leadership core team out for dinner when the project is completed.

Remember that the person who practices this relational model of leadership commits to stand alongside the chosen leaders, even in times of failure. I once read that failure is always an event, never a person. That's good theology. When we view ministry with that adage in mind, it helps us give it away.

Effective, relational leadership is not measured by our performances, but the relationships we build. In Mark 1: 9-11, God's voice is heard immediately after Jesus' baptism: "You are my Son, whom I love; with you I am well pleased." God says He is happy with Jesus before He has done anything. Jesus has not started His public ministry, yet God says, "I like you!" If we as pastors, directors, and leaders can keep this in mind—that we're investing in people, not the success or failure of programs—we'll go a long way in developing healthy, competent, and committed leaders.

LET'S REVIEW

1. Carefully choose your leaders. Do so after prayer and observing them.
2. Spend time with your leaders.
3. Give away ownership. Let go of the power. Trust your leaders.
4. Avoid failure. Ask yourself five questions:

   ■ Is the job well-defined?
   ■ Is the task appropriate?
   ■ Is there a helper—a teammate?
   ■ Is an accountability structure in place?
   ■ Do leaders feel affirmed?

5. Leadership is measured by the quality of the relationships developed.

SAMPLE CERTIFICATE

CERTIFICATE OF APPRECIATION

To: _____ *Sandy Gwinn* _____

For: _____ *Single Parent Ministry* _____

We appreciate your help with:

Planning Our Single Parent Ministry

Signed: **Rich Hurst**

Date: *June 1, 1991*

You are a winner!

FIRST

❖ ❖ ❖

REFLECT AND REVIEW

Think about the material in this chapter, then answer the following questions. Remember, don't try to do the ministry alone. Whenever possible, discuss these questions with your single adult leadership team.

1. Who are potential leaders in your single adult ministry? Write down their names. Spend a week praying for them.

2. Think of a few top single adult leaders in your current ministry. How are you spending time with them now? Choose one way to spend time with them this upcoming month.

3. Do you find it easy to let go of power, to trust others? Why, or why not? How does this affect your ministry?

4. Think of a time when a leader seemed to fail (or think of a task you took on that seemed to fail). Check the boxes that apply to the situation:

❑ The job description was clearly defined.

❑ The task was appropriate for the leader.

❑ The leader had a teammate with whom to work.

❑ The leader knew who he or she was accountable to and for what.

❑ The leader was affirmed.

5. What steps could have been taken to make the failure a success? Don't remain focused on the failure. Learn from it, practice forgiveness, and move on.

MEMO

TO: Rich

FROM: Terry and Karen

RE: Chapter 7: Team Communication

Your ideas for team building are great, but without clear communication, it all falls apart. We think you have some helpful things to say about this key ingredient for building a core team—keeping the lines of communication open.

- What are elements of effective, healthy teams?
- How do teams develop a philosophy of ministry? Why is this important?
- What steps can teams take to identify problems and resolve conflict?
- What are some helpful forms and procedures to facilitate communication and build effective teams?

CHAPTER SEVEN

Team Communication

Rich Hurst

Effective, clear communication is a key ingredient for any single adult ministry—especially when you want to empower leaders and give them ownership. With clear communication, leaders:

- know their job responsibilities,
- know who they're accountable to and for what,
- feel like they're working on a team, not isolated and working "out on a limb."

With healthy communication, you don't have unexpected, "crisis" turnover. Your ministry experiences smooth transitions, because leaders know the length of their terms and when evaluation takes place. With healthy communication, tasks are accomplished as a team and relationships are built. Without communication, tasks are accomplished alone. Life, as well as ministry, was never meant to be lived out in isolation.

I recently asked the single adults in a leadership core team if they felt communication and teamwork were important to the success of their ministry. Each agreed they were primary factors. However, when I questioned them further about how they ensured that everyone communicated with each other and worked together as a team, it became evident they were working as a group of Lone Rangers.

They were not spending much time together. They would come together once a week and call it their leadership core meeting. No coordination of events, much less brainstorming on how they could work together on projects, took place. Each team member decided individually what plan was best for his or her area, and did it. No sense of community, or caring how the other person was doing, was evident. The group members felt unsupported and burned out.

When examining our team's communication, we must critically ask: To what extent do we choose to communicate with each other and build teams of people, instead of solely focusing on better programs? We somehow need to find a balance between relationships within the leadership core team and the work to be done by the team. As we communicate and build the team personally and relationally, we more effectively get the work done.

Single adults feel affirmed in this situation because they understand their roles and responsibilities as they work together to minister. Even when we are committed to building teams and relationships, we still may fail. When we communicate and pursue unity within our teams, however, we will have the strength to learn from success as well as failure—together.

WHAT ARE TEAMS?

Teams are groups of people who trust one another to help them reach a common goal. In healthy teams, people who work in isolation are the exception, not the rule. In healthy families, we operate as team members, creating an environment for trusting, caring relationships. Sports are team activities, for the most part. Even in boxing where one person is pitted against another in the ring, the boxer has a team of supporters and trainers in the corner. Each person on the boxer's team has an important role.

In ministry, clear communication and teamwork are important no matter what the church size. I have seen this chapter's principles applied with equal success in churches of less than 200 to churches of several thousand. "Sure," you say, "I'm trying to minister to singles and I'm a part-time, non-paid leader. I don't have the time or energy to communicate clearly and build a team. It's much easier and faster to do it myself."

These concepts apply whether your singles ministry employs several paid staff or is directed by one or two unpaid lay people. If you're an overworked, unpaid lay leader, the key to success in ministry is doing less and doing it with others. Therefore, it's worth your time and effort in the long run, because with a team of people you get more done.

The Bible offers several examples of leaders who clearly communicated to build teams. Read Nehemiah 3:1-32 in which Nehemiah gives everybody a job— everybody worked and was responsible. Read Exodus 18:13-26 in which Moses learned to delegate. Read Luke 10:1-23 in which Jesus gave the ministry away to seventy people. These leaders built a group of people who worked together toward a common goal. Each team member was important. Each one had a role.

When you build a healthy, working team, people get to know one another. They learn how to deal with conflict. In healthy teams, people feel they can share their dreams and fears. They won't feel used. Ministry without healthy teams always leads to people feeling isolated, lonely, and discouraged. I have listened many times to people in their sixties talking about their loneliness in ministry. They never took the time to build groups of people who not only got things done, but encouraged one another in their ministry dreams.

TYPES OF TEAMS

Each year, professional basketball, baseball, and football hold their respective all-star games. If any of these all-star teams were to play any league team, the all-stars would lose, because the league team knows how to play together—as a team. The all-star teams are made up of outstanding individual performers.

Our churches operate in much the same way. We develop individuals one-on-one, then thrust individuals together in leadership core teams, boards, and committees. We throw these individuals together—most of the time without any training—and hope they'll be able to work as a team. We leave little room for the team to develop a common goal or work at true fellowship and encouragement. Relationships are not the first priority, rather a particular task becomes their primary objective. We think we are building teams when we are actually developing programs with groups of individuals.

> **When we make the choice to work toward people-oriented ministries, we build teams in which everybody has a role. When we focus on building successful programs, only the few superstars have roles, while the rest watch.**

This would be disastrous on a basketball team—a group of players trying to win using their own skills and abilities. Unfortunately, many single adult ministries find themselves in this condition—players operating on their own trying to create a successful ministry.

As we try to build teams, we must answer this difficult question: Is our first priority to build people or programs? When we make the choice to work toward people-oriented ministries, we build teams in which everybody has a role. When we focus on building successful programs, only the few superstars have roles, while the rest watch.

Continuing with our analogy of the sports teams, we see four types of teams.

1. *Boxing team.* As described at the beginning of this chapter, one person is pitted against another in the ring. The boxer has a team of supporters and trainers in the corner. Each person on the boxer's team has an important role.

2. *Collegiate team.* Basketball produces what we call a collegiate team. This is a small team with flexible roles. Players can play both offense and defense. Although some flexibility exists, the team must work together as a close-knit group.

3. *Positional team.* A football team has a larger dynamic because more players are involved. The roles are more defined. Few players play both offense and defense. Others play a more limited role on "special teams." In professional football, three sub-teams—offense, defense, and special teams—make up one larger team.

4. *Strategic team.* Baseball is a different sport—it involves strategy. Each of the nine players on the field at the same time have a specific role. The only time players take another player's role is when they cannot do it themselves (for example, the pitcher covering first base). The players work together only when one person cannot handle the task alone.

As leaders, we need to decide the type of teams we want to build, or what type of team we already have. That team is dictated by our ministry size and circumstance. Since the types of teams differ, the ways we build them will vary as well.

One of the primary ways teams vary is in size. Some teams are as small as two or three members, others are as large as twenty people or more. I work in two different team environments. I am on a church staff, which is a strategic team of forty people. We are all on the same team and have the same visionary leader, our senior pastor, but we actually operate on smaller teams, or departments, which work somewhat independently of each other.

Within that larger team, I cannot develop close relationships with each of the forty team members, but it's still important for me to communicate with them. Clear communication means being prepared with detailed reports for our weekly two-hour meeting. Clear communication also means sending memos or making phone calls to other departments that may be affected by my single adult department's programs and activities.

My smaller departmental team of eight single adults meets two hours each week. We must communicate with each other—asking for help with our needs and listening to our teammates. Clear communication means having a common goal and participating at the highest level possible at all times—being enthusiastic, attending all meetings, begin considerate of each other. In this smaller team, we have an opportunity for greater fellowship and encouragement, because we are in closer contact with each other.

ELEMENTS OF EFFECTIVE, HEALTHY TEAMS

When you are building a leadership core team, what characteristics do you aim for? How do you know you have an effective team of leaders? Healthy teams are characterized by four different elements. Members enjoy fellowship and encourage one another. The members plan a strategy for their ministry and operate with a philosophy of ministry. Let's look more closely at each of these elements.

Fellowship
Effective team members enjoy one another—they experience true fellowship. Bruce Larson, in his book *Setting Men Free*, says these four things about fellowship:

1. Fellowship requires commitment to one another—being willing to spend time with one another, not judging one another, supporting one another, and being there when someone needs you.
2. True fellowship consists of honesty to the point of vulnerability—being

willing to share who you are as a person, sharing some of your struggles as well as your successes.

3. A group must have relevance to the world—relationships must make a difference in your life on Monday morning, not just on Sundays.

4. True fellowship involves accountability to one another—people can count on you to get your job done, to be a teammate.[1]

Ask yourself and your leadership core team these questions: Are you committed to each other? Are you honest to the point of vulnerability with each other? Do you reach out to others? Do you know your purpose? Are you accountable to one another? Work through these questions as you read this chapter. The answers to these questions are important when building healthy, effective teams.

Encouragement

Another characteristic of effective teams is encouragement—taking the time to believe in each other and letting each other know that. It is celebrating the great times and comforting one another during the difficult times.

Building a team of people means we encourage people to be their best. Alan Loy McGinnis offers several ways to do so.

1. Expect the best from the people you lead.
2. Capitalize on people's strengths rather than getting obsessed with their weaknesses.
3. Maintain high standards and keep large dreams clearly in view.
4. Use success stories to inspire excellence.
5. Build into the relationship an allowance for storms.
6. Create an atmosphere where enthusiasm can build.
7. Take steps to maintain a high level of personal motivation.[2]

Unfortunately, encouragement is a rare commodity. As Christians, we face struggles: to choose to celebrate others' success, when we are taught to win at all costs; to choose to comfort one another in failure, when in our church culture we shoot our wounded; to choose to stop and listen to another's problem, when we want to give the person some quick advice and move on to our next agenda item; to give away the opportunity for credit, when we want to be known ourselves.

By encouraging each other, we build relationships and establish a healthy environment as we minister to single adults.

A Strategy

Healthy, effective teams plan their ministry. They develop a good strategy for working with single adults and giving the ministry away.

1. Start on a solid foundation. (See chapters 1-4.)
2. Select quality leadership. (See chapters 5-6.)
3. Spend time with a few. (See chapters 5-6.)

4. Continue to develop leaders as you give the ministry away. Give leaders ownership. (See chapters 5-8.)
5. Keep your ministry focused and intentional. The Rocket planning process described in chapter 9 helps leadership core teams further develop their strategy for their specific ministry.

A Philosophy of Ministry

A philosophy of ministry helps team members communicate off the "same sheet of music." It answers the question, "Why are we doing things like we are?" Teams operate best when team members know why they operate as they do. Developing a philosophy of ministry begins by asking questions.

1. Who do we believe God is? What role does He have in this ministry?
2. What role does Scripture play in the ministry?
3. What role do people play in our ministry? How do we see them as "players"? What are they responsible for?
4. How do people do ministry? Do they do programmatic ministry? Do they spend time with people? Do they do "big events" ministry?

A committee at our church developed the following philosophy of ministry:

The starting point of our ministry is God. The guide for our ministry is the Bible. The focus of our ministry is people, not programs. The environment of our ministry is teamwork, not individualism.

This is one philosophy. Add to it and change it, but use it as an example for you and your team to develop one of your own. A worksheet for your team to use in creating a philosophy of ministry for your single adult ministry appears in chapter 14, page 209.

Although essential, a philosophy of ministry is useless unless you communicate the information and review it on a regular basis.

1. Write your philosophy of ministry and post it in places where people will see it (for example, bulletin boards, newsletters, flyers, church bulletins, etc.).
2. In all new member sessions explain why you have a philosophy of ministry and what it means.
3. When you train single adult leaders, review the philosophy of ministry. Make sure your leaders agree and understand its importance. This can be done at leadership retreats or seminars. (See chapters 12-13.)
4. Review your philosophy every couple of months to keep it fresh in your team members' minds.
5. Practice decision-making during a leadership core team meeting. Use the case studies included in chapter 14. The case studies describe a

potential problem situation. Your team members must decide how to deal with the problem—basing their decisions on your philosophy of ministry.

BUILDING TEAM COMMUNICATION

Depending on your current situation, you may be on your own in single adult ministry, but wanting to build a new team. Or else, you may have an existing team and want to build relationships, establishing clear lines of communication with the members.

When we develop a new team, we have a great opportunity to begin "fresh," to start off on the "right foot." The primary tasks facing new teams are similar to those facing existing teams: We must establish relationships; decide on a common goal and purpose; and determine how we will resolve conflicts, how we will communicate, who the leader will be, what role each team member will fill, and how we can support each other.

> *In all new member sessions explain why you have a philosophy of ministry and what it means.*

A new team does not have to deal with "old tapes" of inherited history, as does an existing team. The new team can begin by asking the question: "How do we want to operate so that we can work together as a healthy team, with the best results for all single adults in our church?"

When we want to build healthy communication into our team of leaders, we must take three steps.

■ First, take time to evaluate the group's needs.
■ Second, determine what, if any, problems exist.
■ Finally, ask, "What are our options to meet needs and solve problems?"

The Team-Building Assessment—a tool to help you and your team members evaluate needs and determine problems—is included in chapter 14 on page 220. Chapter 14 also includes quick quizzes to help you with each of the following three steps.

EVALUATING THE TEAM'S NEEDS

Take the time to find out each team member's agenda and what he or she might be feeling. Some of your team members may not feel empowered. They may feel that their ministry goals are not being realized. They may feel frustrated that the single adult ministry is not growing as they'd hoped it would. Start by asking a few questions of the team.

1. What is our philosophy of ministry? (Read page 95.) The philosophy reminds members why they operate as they do.

2. What is our goal? (This question can be easily answered after the team has worked through the Rocket material in chapter 9.)
3. Are people supporting our efforts? Are singles showing up at our activities?
4. Do team members feel supported, affirmed, and encouraged in their efforts?
5. Are people complaining about our ministry?
6. Is there a lack of interest in what we are doing?
7. Are decisions made that cause confusion?
8. Are people having unresolved conflicts with each other?
9. Are team members taking risks? Are they being imaginative?
10. Is our single adult ministry moving ahead, maintaining, or disintegrating?
11. Are team members serving in roles they truly enjoy? (Read about role preferences in chapter 8. Take the Role Preference Test in chapter 14, page 224.)

After you determine needs by asking the above questions, move to the next step and determine existing problems.

DETERMINING PROBLEMS

Identifying problems usually means looking at the issues that surface in the form of unhappy people, or evaluating why the ministry is not getting the results for which the team had hoped.

When team members are unhappy or do not support the ministry, a problem usually exists between individuals or perhaps people misunderstand the goals. We will examine two potential problems.

A Problem Between the Leader and the Team

While I was working with a group of single adults, they began a lengthy, negative discussion about their pastoral leadership. They believed the leadership was totally ineffective—one of the most commonly identified problems in the church today. This ineffectiveness is usually more evident to the team than the leader. The accompanying symptom of this problem is team members who become either passive or uncooperative. Both are deadly to a team. Leaders may fail for several possible reasons:

Lack of communication. The leader doesn't communicate his or her expectations of the job and doesn't listen to the dreams of the other team members. (This was one of the ways I failed Chet—see chapter 6. I didn't clearly communicate my expectations of the job. He was basically on his own and had to guess what needed to be done.)

Ego. The ambitious, political leader wants to win no matter what it costs the rest of the team. The leader may also be more concerned about looking good than the quality of team relationships or encouragement of team members.

Insensitivity to people. The leader's disregard for team members' feelings or needs destroys the team's motivation.

Inability to delegate. By lack of delegation, the leader gives the team members the message that they are not trusted, or needed, to do the work.

Criticism of others to make self feel or look good. We have all experienced someone like this. This type of criticism doesn't motivate anyone; it simply destroys all respect and trust for the leader.

Betrayal. When a leader betrays a teammate by going behind his or her back or betraying a confidence, any existing trust dissolves. We must let people know that not only do we have confidence in them, but that they can have complete confidence in us as well.

No vision for the future. Leaders are visionaries. If a leader cannot see past today, then that leader will have difficulty leading the team toward any significant goals.

Arrogance. In this case, the leader possesses a cool personality. We build our teams by letting our teammates know we care about them, not that we care only for ourselves.

Lack of training of others. As leaders, we must build up the body by training and equipping others for ministry.

People seen as commodities. If we see people primarily as a way to get something, they will see through our motives and will have little reason to remain on the team. As leaders, we don't use people because of their talents or areas of expertise. We work alongside and support them as fellow ministers.

Laziness. Leaders who want others to do the work and then take the credit themselves are bound to fail.

Hurting leader who doesn't ask for help. We don't air all our dirty laundry and problems with our teammates, but we do share our needs and concerns. No one said leaders cannot have needs. As leaders, we model for our teammates, which includes being honest enough to seek the help of others.

Problems Between Team Members

Another problem occurs when people on ministry teams cannot get along. Any time people gather, the potential for conflict exists—whether in families, organizations, or singles groups. Conflict is normal and healthy, but when it persists without resolution, problems arise. Don't ignore it. People who are on the same team must constantly work on conflict resolution. The next step offers you and your team ways to resolve conflict.

RESOLVING CONFLICT

Read through the following ideas. Review them with your team. These guide lines help meet needs and resolve conflict so that your team can function in a healthy manner.

Hear feelings, not words. Attempt to be empathetic. During conflict, people often say things that hurt others. When this happens, stop and ask yourself, "What is this person really feeling?"

Be congruent. Be in touch with your feelings and, therefore, responsible for them. If you are angry with a person or upset with a situation, ask yourself, "What am I really feeling? Why am I so angry about this? What's going on that this is so important to me?"

Avoid you *messages. You* messages cause others to be defensive. Use I messages, instead. For example, don't say "You make me so mad when you always criticize my ideas." Instead say, "I feel hurt when I offer an idea and it's criticized and not considered."

Don't use never *or* always. Avoid generalizations.

Be ready to forgive and ask for forgiveness. Real empathy brings genuine apologies and repentance that will soften hearts and free us from the slavery of bitterness, hostility, and vindictiveness.

Be responsible for personal change. Do not take the responsibility to change another. Read Matthew 7:3: "Why do you look at the speck of sawdust in your brother's eye and pay no attention to the plank in your own eye?"

Stay with one issue at a time. Don't be tempted to bring up past grievances that may or may not be connected with the current issue.

Call time when the discussion becomes destructive. The person who calls time is responsible for arranging a new time (preferably within twenty-four hours) to discuss the matter further, once the feelings have been tempered.

Stay with the here and now. Avoid bringing up the past or referring to the future.

A HEALTH CHECKUP FOR YOUR TEAM

The ideal team is one where groups of people trust one another to help them reach a common goal. Answer these questions to check the health of your team.

1. Is your job well-defined? Do you and your team members understand what you are supposed to do? Do you operate under rules, goals, objectives, and understandings? (If not, develop job descriptions as described in chapter 6, pages 81-82.)

2. Have you and your team developed agreed-upon common goals? (If not, work through the Rocket process described in chapter 9.)

3. Are your assigned tasks appropriate for you and your teammates? Do you enjoy your role? (Read about role preferences in chapter 8. Take the Role Preference Test in chapter 14, page 224.)

4. Does each team member have a helper? (Make sure each person isn't doing his or her job alone. Read about this in chapter 6, page 84.)

5. Do you and your team members know to whom you're accountable? To whom do you report? (Make sure this is a part of your job descriptions. See chapter 6, page 85.)

6. Do you and your team members feel valued and encouraged? (See page 94.)

7. Does fighting exist between circles and cliques? (This was the problem Paul addresses in his letter to the Philippians.)

8. Do you and your team members know how to deal with interpersonal problems? Do you know where to get help? (See pages 98-100.)

9. Are some team members intimidated by the leader and consequently passive? (If so, discuss these feelings and work toward resolving them. See pages 97-98.)

10. Is the team leader threatened by the success of his or her team members? (Examine the health of your leadership style by taking the Determining Problems quiz on page 211 in chapter 14.)

Avoid "below-the-belt" remarks. Do not make remarks such as, "I can see why you have problems at home." These remarks are insignificant to the issue; they are only designed to hurt. They also abuse a confidence. Attack the problem, not the person.

Address the conflict yourself, when possible. Approach the one, and only the one, with whom you have the conflict. If that person is unable or unwilling to hear, meet with a referee (preferably a mutually agreed-upon person). Finally, approach with a group. Jesus offers this approach in Matthew 18:15-17. (A word of caution: Approach as a group only as a last resort. This is often used as a power move, not as a healing tool. People in the small group must be committed to confidentiality, the restoration of the person, and the moving forward in restored relationship.)

Avoid blaming, placating, and distracting. Instead, attempt to be adult. Attempt to resolve the situation. Hear feelings. Be rational, logical, and intelligent.

Above all, be loving. Show love that is accepting, supportive, and caring.

Learn to clarify. Since most problems arise out of misunderstandings, this is one of the most helpful steps to remember in resolving conflicts. Once we clear up misunderstandings within the team, moving forward becomes easier.

Read the health checkup on page 99. See how well you and your team members trust and help each other reach a common goal.

HELPING TEAM MEMBERS DO THEIR BEST

Team members do best when they know what's expected of them. Besides giving detailed job descriptions, other procedures can help team members successfully tackle their responsibilities. One such procedure is called the "Team Members Covenant." We have included this covenant in chapter 14, page 214, for you to give to your team members.

PRINCIPLES OF TEAM MEMBERSHIP

These principles are meant to enhance a team of single adults and help everyone understand the expectations. Whether you are building a new team or upgrading an existing team, these eight ideas will help team members work together. (Chapter 14 includes a copy of these principles for use in your ministry.)

Always be willing to do more than your share. When we each commit to do more than our own share, we help ourselves, as well as everyone else, get the work done. If team members only do what is in the confines of their job description, problems arise. Cooperation is the key. When team members each decide to contribute more than required, the team's morale grows. (Remember, however, don't push yourself and others to overload and burnout. You have a team with whom to work—all of you shoulder the load.)

Do not say uncomplimentary things about other team members behind their backs. Talking behind the back of your team members undermines trust and respect. Although common with team members who are unhappy with leadership, talking behind others' backs is destructive and relationally lethal.

Accept reality. All members do not have the same duties. Not everyone on a team can do the same things. Each person is gifted in different ways. This is why we have job descriptions to clarify who does what. Leaders always have more responsibility, and sometimes they are called on to make decisions that affect their team's duties. Respect this and accept the reality that if everyone had the same duties, the ministry would be unproductive.

Participate in team activities even when inconvenienced. When we agree to be a team member, we agree to be connected and accountable to our teammates. This is not always convenient. Make every effort to be a team player. Attend meetings, get-togethers, special occasions, and celebrations with the team. Participation facilitates self-disclosure and mutual respect, both of which are important to team development.

Confront your conflicts. Every team will experience conflicts—a normal and healthy part of team development. Conflicts that go unaddressed become destructive. A commitment to resolve conflicts strengthens team relationships.

Don't be late or absent for trivial reasons. Show respect for others by demonstrating they are as important or more important than we are. Being late says that we think we are more important. For this reason, arrive on time and do not miss meetings unless there is a valid reason. The team should predetermine the validity of various excuses.

Be concerned with your personal growth. Team development and personal growth cannot be separated. When we grow, our team benefits as well. Make it a priority to expand your knowledge and abilities through personal growth. Take classes, attend seminars, and read. Whichever method you choose, your own growth will stimulate the team's growth and success.

Contribute to other team members' personal growth. Contribute to the personal growth of others through sharing resources and information, but only when it is appropriate. Do not be an advice-giver or fixer. In the appropriate context, however, helping team members will contribute to a stronger team.

Through periodic review of these principles, remind team members of potential aspects that may damage your team's health (for example, consistently being late for meetings). Reviewing the principles reminds members what they need to do to maintain a healthy team.

COMMUNICATION BETWEEN TEAMS AND CHURCH STAFF

In chapter 6, we mentioned that giving the ministry away to single adults doesn't mean abandoning the ministry, it means leaders must work together. Clear communication is the link between teams and church staff. To help facilitate this communication, we've included examples of several forms: the Team Report (page 102), the Event Finances Checklist (page 103) and Worksheet (page 104), and the Activity Request Form (page 106). University Presbyterian Church prepared the following information about staff/team communication and responsibilities. Adapt it to fit your situation.

What Do Individuals on Staff Do?

Since team leaders, team members, and church staff work together as a team, team members must stay in touch and work together. To do so, staff members have certain responsibilities:

1. To encourage you in your ministry. The staff is not here to do your ministry. Through encouragement, we will help you accomplish your goals and make sure you have the resources you need.
2. To communicate with you about what is happening in the overall ministry. Good communication is important so you can see the bigger picture; when we see the bigger picture, we can work better as a team.
3. To help you work through your difficulties and frustrations in your ministry. Staff does not necessarily have the answers, but sometimes it helps to know we care and will listen. We're here to serve you when it gets tough.
4. To be a part of seeing your dreams come true. Share your ideas and dreams for the ministry.
5. To approve your plans.
6. To provide proper channels to secure finances for your event.

How Can You Help the Staff Do Their Ministry?

The church staff is like the coaching staff of a sports team. They rally the team and motivate it toward a common goal. They are chosen to help you be successful and win, and they do best when you help them win as well. The way you can best help the staff is to be a team player; ministry has no place for Lone Rangers. You can also help by completing these communication tools:

Team Reports. Throughout my ministry career, I've asked leadership core team

---

TEAM REPORT

Name: *Susan Pearce*
Area: *Singles Retreat Coordinator*
Date: *June 10*

1. I need decisions from you for the following items:
   Can we have a barbecue on Saturday night?

2. I am having a problem with the following:
   I'm still waiting to hear back from you on the flyer approval.

3. I am planning to:
   Have David organize the food committee. If you have a problem with that, let me know.

4. I am making progress in the following areas:
   Saturday afternoon activities and small group facilitator selection.

5. I would rate my personal happiness factor at (1=suicidal, 100=best I've ever been): *80*

   I say this because:
   I'm happy with the progress the team has made with the retreat planning; however, I'm a bit nervous about completing what still needs to be done.

6. Please pray for me in the following areas:
   For my relationship with my boyfriend due to my time constraints.
   That I'd be able to encourage my team members, not criticize them.

facilitators to complete a monthly report to give me or to the church staff person to whom they're accountable for decisions and support.

The sample on the previous page shows a report that was completed by a singles retreat coordinator. She handed it to me because I was the staff person in charge of the singles department—she was accountable to me. This report allowed her to remind me of decisions I needed to make for her. She could tell me any problems she was having with her team, the event planning, or any other concern she wanted to share. She detailed her plans and progress, rated her happiness factor and gave a reason for her feelings. She also listed prayer requests.

Leadership core team leaders can ask each team member to complete one of these forms for their specific area of responsibility. For example, you may have a team of three leaders for your overall single adult ministry. One leader is responsible for the singles Sunday class, another for the upcoming singles retreat, while a third is responsible for once-a-month fellowship events. Each team member could fill out

---

EVENT FINANCES CHECKLIST

Good stewardship means wisely using the abundant resources that God has given us. In planning and running a singles event at University Presbyterian Church, you are responsible for the financial viability of the event. Events should be planned to generate at least 15 percent more income than expenses. This "profit" goes to fund outreach ministry projects through the singles department, a vital part of our work as Christians.

For each singles event (retreat, workshop, social event, etc.) the designated event coordinator is responsible for finances. The event coordinator is expected to follow these steps:

- ❑ Fill out the budget section of an Event Finances Worksheet. You may need to call rental facilities to obtain cost estimates.
- ❑ Submit the form to Rich (or your assigned staff person) for approval. He will discuss your plans and keep a copy on file.
- ❑ Telephone any rental facilities and confirm your reservations. If a deposit is required, ask for a copy of the rental contract and an invoice. Bring the invoice to Rich for payment.
- ❑ As the event approaches, you may need to purchase supplies. You may request a cash advance from Rich for your budgeted items (such as decorations or groceries) that cannot be invoiced and paid by check from the church. You are personally responsible for this money and must have receipts for anything you spend. Any money not covered by receipts must be returned to Rich.
- ❑ Items that are invoiced must be budgeted and an invoice copy brought to Rich—no surprises please.
- ❑ As you sell tickets or accept donations, you must turn in the money to Rich within three days. Do not spend this money. Keep a running count of tickets sold and dollar amount.
- ❑ Partial scholarships for people who can't afford the event may be available. Talk to Rich before you say anything to anyone.
- ❑ On the day of the event, you will have people paying at the door. Be prepared and turn in the money then to Rich or his designated representative.
- ❑ Meet with Rich after the event to review your financial results. This will help you and help us plan future events.
- ❑ Have fun!

Staying in touch:	Rich Hurst	Church Office
	Phone: 555-5000	Phone: 555-1500

the report on a monthly basis and give it to the team leader (as well as the church staff person). The report communicates progress and needs, and helps leaders feel they are working as a group, not by themselves. A copy of the report is included in chapter 14, page 216, for use in your ministry.

Event Finances Checklist and Worksheet. Each church has its own process for handling finances. The checklist on the previous page shows how finances were coordinated for the singles department at University Presbyterian Church. Use it as a guide for creating your own checklist to give leaders so they know your church's specific process for handling funds.

The Event Finances Worksheet below shows how team members can keep track of the money received and spent for an activity. It includes space for leaders to

EVENT FINANCES WORKSHEET

Event Name: *New Years Party* Location: *Meany Tower* Date: *Dec. 31, 1991*

Coordinator: *Jeff Hussey* Phone # (Day): *789-6817* (Evening): *Same*

Event Price: *$25* Event Capacity: *300* Possible Income: *$7,500*

INCOME:	PAST	PROJECTED	ACTUAL
Number of Paid Participants	209	300	273
Other			
Total Income (number paid x price)	$5,225	$7,500	$6,825
EXPENSES			
Facility	1,000	1,000	1,000
Transportation/Music	600	500	500
Speaker Honorarium	200	0	0
Adult Leaders Honorarium			
Printing/Publicity	1,000	500	652
Food/Refreshments	0	750	891
Other *(Smoke Machine/Decorations)*	225	300	712
TOTAL NET COST	$3,025	$3,050	$3,755
NET COST PER PARTICIPANT	14.47	10.17	13.75
# Scholarship (incl. staff)	160	100	200
$ Scholarship (# x cost per)			
TOTAL COST	$3,185	$3,150	$3,955
TOTAL PROFIT	$2,040	$4,350	$2,870

write the funds spent in past events of a similar nature, funds they're planning to spend at this upcoming event, and the actual amount spent on the event or activity. A blank copy of the worksheet appears on page 217 in chapter 14.

Activity Request Form. The Activity Request Form is yet another effective communication tool. Team members complete this form and give it to church staff so they have a clear description of a possible singles activity. Team members fill out the activity's purpose, write their names, phone numbers, and areas of responsibility. The form also includes space to write a promotion plan and a possible event schedule. A completed example form appears on pages 106. A blank copy of the form is included in chapter 14, page 218.

RECRUITING TEAM MEMBERS

Shaping a group of single adults into an effective, healthy, communicating team of leaders is a continuous process because team selection is a continuous process. Terms end. Past leaders leave as new leaders come on board. The team-building retreats described in chapter 12 provide excellent opportunities to ensure past leaders communicate with new leaders as they "pass the baton" of their duties. (See chapter 12 for more details.)

Throughout the entire process, communication is essential to successfully give the ministry away. How do we continue the cycle? How do we recruit new team members when the terms end?

When the singles group at University Presbyterian Church began, it operated for several months with informal leadership—whoever wanted to help did so. The first "official" team was selected by vote of the informal leadership team and the church staff. The official team was formed in order to have a smaller body of leaders who could discern needs, set goals, lead the singles ministry, and enable others to do the same.

The following qualities of potential leaders were deemed important: Christian maturity; an ability to relate to people; motivation; time availability; consistency in lifestyle and commitment; experience and/or training in leadership; and vision for the singles ministry.

Lay leaders and church staff combined to recruit new leaders for the following reason:

> While the team suggests a list of candidates, we believe that the church staff should have the opportunity to take anyone off the list for any reason, without question by the team. We want to have this church staff involvement for two reasons: First, a pastor or staff member may know confidential information regarding a person's appropriateness to serve on the team to which the team may not have access (for example, regular church attendance versus sporadic attendance, personal lifestyle, or major theological differences that would cause division). Second, it is perceived as an honor for a person to be recruited by the pastor or staff member and this begins a relationship of communication between the prospective team member and staff.

ACTIVITY REQUEST FORM

Event Coordinator: *Jeff Hussey & Jerry O'Leary*   Phone (Home): *789-6817\524-7300*
                                                              (Work): *789-6817\621-1333*

Address: *725 Spring*

City and Zip: *Seattle, WA 98105*

Event Name: *New Years Eve Party*

Event Date: *Dec. 31, 1991*   Event Place: *Meany Tower Hotel*

Statement of Purpose: *Have Fun*

Team Members	Phone (Day)	(Evening)	Teammate/Phone
Contact Person: *Becky Arnette*	*235-6782*	*789-5111*	*Suzanne Sikma\624-9192*
Promotion: *Greg Crum*	*782-6400*	*989-4131*	*Earl Slokum\789-1392*
Registration: *Brad Brucker*	*923-1289*	*633-5620*	*Hugh Wilson\234-0142*
Setup: *Kris Saldin*	*774-3121*	*321-1942*	*MaryAnn Pirsol\524-7311*
Supplies: *Karen Caldwell*	*923-4121*	*774-1862*	*Helen Turner\832-1961*
Cleanup: *Ann Natzke*	*235-1300*	*235-2159*	*Merilee Barr\232-1341*
Decorations: *Suzanne Bergon*	*789-1323*	*221-4721*	*Tim Jernberg\231-1500*

Other (specify):

Promotion Plan (Include specific steps you will use to publicize this event. Include dates
for proposed bulletin inserts, mailings, posters, etc.):
   1. Bulletin Announcements (8 weeks ahead)   *5. Ticket Sales at Weekly Meetings*
   2. Flyer\Mail to List (4 weeks ahead)   *(Weekly for 4 weeks)*
   3. Newspaper (4 weeks ahead)   *6. Signs\Posters (2 weeks ahead)*
   4. Radio (PSA) (2 weeks ahead)   *7. Skits During Classes (3 weeks ahead)*

Event Schedule:
   6:00 - Friendship Hour
   7:00 - Dinner
   8:30 - Games and Dance
   12:00 - Celebration Prayer and Communion

Does this event have a budget? ❑ Yes ❑ No
(If yes, budget must accompany this request.)

Approved by: *Rich Hurst*   Date approved: *October 11, 1991*

When replacing team members, the church used the following steps:

1. Current team members create a list of candidates by making suggestions during a team meeting. No discussion occurs about the candidates at this time.

2. The list of candidates is passed among the team. If anyone knows a valid reason why a candidate should not be considered, the candidate's name is removed without discussion. (Note: a "valid reason" is information which would render the person inappropriate according to the above criteria. A personality conflict, unless extreme, is not a "valid reason." We trust leaders to make mature decisions in this

process. We allow no discussion because our purpose is to form a list of candidates, not do a "character assassination" on people.)

3. The team facilitator submits the list to the church staff.

4. The church staff has the opportunity to remove a name from the list without discussion. The list then goes back to the team.

5. The team takes the returned list and votes by written ballot on the top choices.

6. The team submits the list of top candidates for the necessary slots and two alternates to the church staff member, who, in turn, calls the candidates, asks them to be on the team, and communicates to them about the job responsibilities and length of term. The church staff member then confirms with the team who the new members will be.

This process worked well for this church's singles ministry. Use it as a guideline to develop your own selection process for new team members.

WITH A HEALTHY TEAM MEMBERS ARE MORE LIKELY TO . . .	WITHOUT A HEALTHY TEAM MEMBERS ARE MORE LIKELY TO . . .
■ get to know each other. ■ learn healthy ways to deal with conflict. ■ share dreams and fears. ■ feel affirmed and sure of their role.	■ feel isolated and lonely. ■ feel discouraged and used. ■ hold in ideas and keep feelings to themselves. ■ feel uncertain and unsure of their roles.

REMINDERS ABOUT BUILDING TEAMS

Building teams is a learned process. Building a team does not happen by accident, but because someone chooses to do it. Changing from the Lone Ranger model of ministry to the team model involves a choice.

Change is hard work that takes time. When you decide to take the team approach to ministry, everyone affected—senior pastor, committee, etc.—must agree on the approach and the steps to get there.

No magic answers exist. While teams sometimes do not work, they beat the alternatives. Don't let setbacks and failures stop you.

The people who are in power must support change. Change in any organization cannot take place without the support of those in positions of power. If pastoral staff members do not support you, meet to discuss what they'd like to see happen in single adult ministry. As you share your dreams and expectations, try to form a consensus. After that, if the staff still doesn't support the ministry, ask yourself, "Is this the place for me?" Conflict of this sort is not healthy for you nor the people with whom you're trying to work.

Give yourself credit when you create change. When a group of people works together as a team, reward each other. Celebrate your success as a team.

Ownership enhances commitment. People support what they have participated in creating. This principle cannot be overstated.

Do not hesitate to ask for help. Fellow leaders, peers, and good consultants are ready and willing to help you develop team ministry.

TEAM-BUILDING ASSESSMENT

We've referred to the Team-Building Assessment throughout this chapter. It's an important tool to help you and your leadership core team evaluate how you are doing as a team. It helps determine needs and potential problems. It assesses goals, ideas, personal growth, and ministry roles. If your leaders serve one-year terms, wait to give the assessment until your leadership team has served together for at least six months. Following the initial assessment, conduct it again at three-month intervals. See how your leaders stay on target with team communication. Schedule a special meeting or retreat to discuss the results. Discover and discuss the areas in which your team can improve, and the areas in which your team is strong. Celebrate!

REFLECT AND REVIEW

Think about the material in this chapter, then answer the following questions. Remember, don't try to do the ministry alone. Whenever possible, discuss these questions with your single adult leadership team.

1. Do you already have a healthy, effective, communicating team? Check the characteristics that apply to your group of leaders:

❏ We are committed to each other.

❏ We are honest to the point of vulnerability with each other.

❏ We reach out to others.

❏ We know our purpose.

❏ We are accountable to one another.

❏ We encourage each other.

❏ We have an established strategy, plan, or goals for our singles ministry.

2. Build an effective team by doing these three steps:

a. Evaluate your needs. What is your goal? Have you worked through the Rocket material in chapter 9? Are people supporting your efforts? Do people feel supported in their efforts? Are people complaining about the ministry? Are decisions made that cause confusion? Are people engaged in unresolved conflicts with each other? Are people taking risks? Are they being imaginative? Are you moving ahead, maintaining, or melting down?

b. Identify problems—the issues that usually surface in the form of unhappy people or unachieved goals and objectives.

c. Think of ways to resolve these problems. Reread pages 98-100 for ideas.

3. Develop a philosophy of ministry if you don't already have one. Use the worksheet found on page 209. Invite your leadership core team or any interested individuals to help.

4. Pages 100-101 list eight principles that enhance a team. Which of the principles do your leaders follow?

5. If your leadership team has served together for at least six months, schedule a time to take the Team-Building Assessment found in chapter 14, page 220. Discover how you are doing as a team.

MEMO

TO: Karen

FROM: Rich and Terry

RE: Chapter 8: Team Roles

We're on track with the needed ingredients for a
relational ministry. We're building a team of single
adult leaders. What we want to avoid is setting
people up for failure by shoving them into the
wrong role. Many people think that ministry has to
be all work, no fun. How can we help each other
find places to fit in, to minister to one another, and
enjoy it in the process? Any suggestions?

- Tell how single adults can determine tasks
  they most enjoy.
- What are some team ministry roles?
- How do these roles fit into a ministry that is
  given away?

CHAPTER EIGHT

Team Roles

Karen Butler

A few years ago, our single adult ministry core team created individual job descriptions for each team member. David, one of the men in the group, had "unofficially" planned our singles social activities for more than a year. People called David if they wanted to know what was going on during a given week or weekend. He always knew what events were planned or, if he didn't, he would find out for you.

David was a natural party organizer. However, when it came time for his job description, he said, "I don't want to plan social activities for the group. I don't think it's an appropriate ministry role for me because I enjoy it so much." After some discussion, we convinced David that because organizing social activities was so fun and enjoyable, he'd be the person for this ministry role. This role fit David's preferences more closely than anyone else in the group.

UNDERSTANDING ROLE PREFERENCES

When we understand our role preferences—the tasks we most enjoy doing, where we "fit" in the ministry—we are most effective at empowering others. Single adults in the church see that we enjoy what we're doing. They sense the contagious excitement. The ministry doesn't look like work, but fun. Do you know your preferred role? Do those on your singles leadership team know theirs? Find out by reading this chapter and taking the Role Preference Test in chapter 14, page 224.

This chapter describes four ministry role preferences: creators, developers, caretakers, and participants. People may show any combination of these role preferences at any one time, and these preferences change as people change. This chapter shows how to make your single adult ministry more effective by making sure people are doing what they like to do.

Whether we are first-time leaders or veterans looking for new direction, each of us has reached a point where we've asked ourselves, "What more can I do? Where do I fit?" We can determine our fit in ministry, or ministry role preferences, by asking ourselves these questions:

- What things do I do well?
- What activities and contributions give me a sense of worth?
- What seem to me and others to be my gifts?
- In what activities do I feel I am most myself?
- Whom do I most admire?
- What is fun for me?
- What—in my wildest imagination—would I like to do in ministry?

As we stop with our team members to ask ourselves these questions, we facilitate our growth as ministers. We discover that we really enjoy what seems to be a natural fit for us. Some of us may think this is contrary to the nature of ministry and service because we think service must be exclusively solemn and difficult. Yet serving God can bring joy and touch a real need at the same time. Mother Teresa puts it more eloquently: Ministry is "where my joy touches a human need." Ministry does not need to be unnatural or awkward; it may actually bring great joy. God knows our hearts, desires, dreams, preferences, and goals. He created them. He wants to best use us for building His Kingdom.

Doing What You Enjoy
The choices we make both consciously and unconsciously demonstrate our ministry role preferences. Some people enjoy planning activities. Others enjoy serving behind-the-scenes—setting up chairs for worship, making sure everyone has a songbook, etc. Others enjoy teaching and leading groups. Still others choose to organize Bible study groups or minister to new people in the church setting. We may choose to plan in one program and simply participate in another. Choices do not dictate our personality type or permanent ministry role, but they are important to determine our preferred ministry role—right now.

Our senior pastor challenged our single adult leaders by saying, "Never do anything in ministry that is not joyful for you." We take that seriously. If we do not enjoy our ministry, perhaps we are in the wrong place. Ministry will never be all fun and no work, but we can (and should) enjoy our work. God has given us the gift of desires, which we can use to help focus our ministry role in an area where we can be effectively used by Him and enjoy the experience at the same time.

Church Size Not Important
Choosing your ministry role preference seems easy to picture in a large church, where so many jobs literally ensure "something for everyone." A smaller church doesn't seem to offer as many choices. Can we still do what we prefer instead of what needs to be done in a small church? I believe we can. Although a smaller variety of tasks and activities exist, there will be tasks that fit into each of the preferences described in this chapter. These role preferences are general, not narrow and specific.

For example, imagine you attend a smaller church with fewer than 200 members. Your singles group consists of fifteen people in their thirties to fifties. The leadership core team consists of three singles representing the various age groups. One enjoys planning social activities and is currently working on a retreat. Another is concerned with the spiritual growth of the group and spends much of his time planning and teaching Bible studies. The group needs someone to be in charge of enlisting people to provide refreshments for the weekly singles get-together. You ask the third person on the core team if he'd take this responsibility. Understanding his ministry role preference, he says, "No. I'd hate to do that."

So what do you do? Do you forget the whole thing? Do you take on the task yourself? Do you keep searching for someone who would enjoy the task? The obvious answer is to find someone who may enjoy organizing refreshments. You may ask, "Who would ever want to do that kind of work?" Many would. For some, this is a great way to serve behind-the-scenes. If a member of your core team isn't interested in organizing refreshments, look to others in the congregation who would enjoy this role.

Negotiable Versus Nonnegotiable Tasks

You may, however, spend a lot of time searching for a person to fill a specific role and never find anyone. You must then determine whether the task is negotiable (a task that can be passed over at this time without harmful effects) or nonnegotiable (a task that must be accomplished). For example, organizing refreshments is a negotiable task. If you can't find a person to organize refreshments, don't offer refreshments. It probably won't become a pressing issue unless someone else notices it, sees a need for it, and helps find a way to fill the need. Activities planning and small group coordination are other examples of negotiable tasks.

Nonnegotiable tasks include cleanup, setup, nursery care for single parent activities, etc. When tasks must be done but nobody wants to do them, equally divide the

---

A ROLE PREFERENCE OVERVIEW

Creator
- Starts new ministries or programs.
- Has innovative ideas for existing programs.

Developer
- Knows how to make dreams happen.
- Applies practical thought to creative ideas.

Caretaker
- Provides encouragement to people and programs.
- Senses needs and sees that they are met.

Participant
- Participates with a limited ministry role.
- Observes ministry programs and roles therein.

tasks among the team members. This way, the tasks will still be accomplished as needed while you continue your search for others to fill the slots.

Leadership according to our ministry role preference is enjoyable and fulfilling. Unfortunately, many single adult ministries don't operate according to ministry role preferences. I was already involved in a singles ministry before I learned about role preferences. The ministry once needed someone on the leadership core team to organize small groups. I didn't want to and luckily had another job, so the task went to someone else. He tried it for a few weeks, came back to the group, and said, "I don't have time. This is an overwhelming task."

Somehow—I still wonder how—the task got "dumped" on me. Being an organizer, I thought I could handle it in no time and move on to something else. The job was a nightmare. People called me all hours of the day and night. (That's one reason I bought an answering machine.) No one was ever happy. I don't like making phone calls, so the job was difficult for me. I dreaded putting people into groups. I sat on my living room floor with scraps of paper spread out all around me, trying to match people with some consistency. I did the best I could, but eventually had to find someone else to take on this task.

Leslie actually volunteered to organize small groups. She gathered names of people wanting to be in a small group on a weekly basis, matched them with each other, called them, and later followed up to see how the groups were going. The best part was that she loved doing it—she did it for more than two years. I clearly did not prefer the job, but someone who was great at it did.

MINISTRY ROLE PREFERENCES

When we're excited and enthused about ministry, our excitement spreads. When we're bored or think "it's a dirty job, but somebody's got to do it," we communicate that our tasks are drudgery. To give the ministry away, to empower others, we must be excited about our role. We do this best by doing what we most enjoy.

Since God has made us unique, we each have different preferences. The Meyers/Briggs Type Indicator, as well as several other tests, help us discover our preferences (see more about these resources in the Bibliography). However, we have developed our own test, the Role Preference Test, to help people understand the following four ministry roles:

1. A *creator* is someone who sees a need, such as a ministry to divorced people, and decides to try a divorce recovery workshop he's heard about from other churches.
2. The *developer* takes that idea, researches other divorce recovery programs, and modifies or adapts the program to fit his or her singles ministry.
3. The *caretaker* is a small group facilitator or leadership core team member who supports those in attendance, encourages the leadership, and is enthusiastic about the program.
4. The *participant* is any of the persons attending the workshop.

At any given time, our ministry role preference may change. We may be a developer, but then need a break, so we become a participant for a while. We may start out a participant, develop great visions, and become a creator. People's ministry role preferences are subject to change due to personal growth and other circumstances.

Ministry role preferences aren't mutually exclusive. We may prefer more than one role at the same time. Sometimes I am a creator/developer, and sometimes I care more about developing and caretaking. At times, I step back and simply participate. These preferred roles are not mutually exclusive nor are they necessarily permanent. Let's take a closer look at each role preference.

CREATOR

Creators are dreamers and visionaries with new ideas cascading from their hearts and minds at any given time. Creators continually surround themselves with new ministries and become the center of new activities. Creators usually do not work within a system. They either create a system or do without. Creators may work in tandem with a developer to establish specific steps of action to make the dream come about, then trust the developer or caretaker to make it happen. Creators are most satisfied when left alone to create, to come up with new ideas. Likewise, a creator may be unsatisfied with having to work with someone else's dream.

In singles ministry, creators say, "We minister to people in their twenties and thirties, but offer nothing for those in their forties. Let's get the people in their forties together and start something." In a smaller church, creators say, "We need a program for singles," then start getting people mobilized.

In Mark 2:1-5, four men in Capernaum who were frustrated by their circumstances used a creative solution. They wanted Jesus to heal their paralyzed friend, but they were met by an obstacle—a great crowd surrounding Jesus. Rather than taking the conventional approach of pushing themselves through the crowd, they became creative. They dug through the roof and lowered their friend into the room where Jesus was preaching. So great was their faith that Jesus forgave their friend's sins.

Characteristics of Preferred Creators

1. Creators get more excited about ideas and dreams than the practical application of those dreams. Although creators say, "Let's start a large singles ministry," they may not have thought through that their small church has only four singles, so to "start a large singles ministry" will mean starting small at first and then networking with other area churches.

2. Creators are more theoretical than practical. This characteristic ties in with the previous one. Creators may devise wonderful ideas, but the ideas may not be practical for a given situation.

3. Creators are original. Frequently creators' ideas are not just a repeat of what another ministry is doing, but are fresh and new, something never tried before

(for example, a new way to do music for the group, a unique approach to reaching unchurched singles, or a new format for the newsletter).

4. Creators take pride in their own ideas. This characteristic can be a plus or a minus. It is great for creators to take pride in their original ideas, but in ministry it is not wise to hang on to your ideas as "mine." Giving the ministry away means letting go of your ideas, even when you are proud of them.

5. Creators don't worry about roadblocks to ideas. Creators look at roadblocks and say, "So what?" I have frequently benefited from a creator who will say, "What if money weren't an issue, what then?" This has helped me to dream, where I wasn't able to before, because all I could see were the roadblocks. However, in ministry you need both roles, someone practical to see the roadblocks and someone creative to see around them.

6. Creators prefer to work alone rather than with a committee. Along with taking pride in their own ideas, creators don't need a committee. As a result, they frequently see committee members as getting in the way, not aiding in the process. If you are a creator, acknowledge this about yourself and try to work with others. Avoid being a Lone Ranger.

7. Creators encourage others to dream. They ask, "What's something that's never been done?" or "What is a new approach to this situation?" Creators find a new twist to an activity, program, or newsletter. Creators instill energy and enthusiasm for the dream session discussed in chapter 6. They encourage others to think, "What in your wildest dream would you like to do in a single adult ministry?"

Healthy Versus Unhealthy Creators

How do creators fit into a ministry that has been given away? Creators may try to fit their role into a given ministry in either a healthy or unhealthy manner. Healthy creators are the ones who give the ministry away. They dream a dream and then let it go for others to develop and implement. Unhealthy creators are unwilling to let their dream go for fear that it will be mistreated or improperly implemented.

Creators must recognize that they cannot effectively carry out the dream alone and still share ownership in ministry. They must share ownership and build teams of ministers who encourage and empower one another. In a team, healthy creators can work with others to develop the dream all the way through its application. While creators may become frustrated when sitting down with a planning team to implement the ideas, their communication and input is a key ingredient throughout the entire process. The originator best communicates a vision.

I worked on a singles team with a creator. His ideas were tremendous. We frequently tried new and different activities. We tried ideas that most of us thought would never work, but often did. However, he was impatient with planning, working as a team, and looking at the big picture. He wanted to plan a retreat and "just do it" when we didn't even know if anyone wanted to attend a retreat. The rest of us worried, prayed, and called everyone we could to see their interest level.

Effective single adult ministries need healthy creators to work alongside those with other ministry preferences.

DEVELOPER

Developers prefer to channel dreams by establishing goals and making them happen. They ask, "Where do we go from here? What shape will this ministry or program take in terms of fellowship, instruction, or worship? What are our goals to achieve this program?" Developers are both practical and theoretical, and will likely understand a creator's dreams. Developers carry those dreams one step further to see that they can be properly implemented.

Timothy's role as a developer is evident in the New Testament. Paul had developed strong relationships during his stay at Ephesus, but was called to move on through Macedonia, preaching the gospel. Paul knew he might not return for some time, so he asked Timothy to care for the church at Ephesus. Paul instructed Timothy to speak against the false teachings, supervise the growing Ephesian church, and develop its leaders. Paul knew he could leave the Ephesian church in Timothy's hands to continue to develop the leaders and affirm the true gospel.

Several years ago, a few people had the same dream in our church: to gather a group of young adults for fellowship. We met as a team of six people—the pastor included—to simply explore, not specifically plan, this dream. For an eight-week period, we shared, studied the Bible, prayed, and discussed what shape we wanted the dream to take. One problem arose, however; we each had a different picture of the dream and different goals for this new ministry idea. Therefore, our dream began with prayerful small steps of faith.

First, we voiced our individual thoughts about the dream. Some wanted a small, intimate group such as we already had, while others wanted to extend the fellowship to include the other young adults in the church who were not involved in any fellowship group. We also wanted to offer worship and instruction.

Next, we further developed the dream. We experimented with an 8:00 a.m. summer Sunday school class. After sending letters to all young adult church members and friends, we waited for that first morning to see what would happen. We had the custodians set up eighteen chairs, thinking that with the six of us we might be able to reach about twelve more. On that summer Sunday morning at 8:00, eighty young adults gathered in the room—eighty young adults who said, "Yes, this is our need too. We want fellowship, instruction, and worship with one another. We want relationships that will help us in our growing relationships with God and the world."

The team's roles drastically changed. We could no longer all be creators. We needed to diversify and develop more leaders—creators, developers, caretakers, and participants.

Today, several years later, we still have a strong fellowship of young adults in the church. The leadership has changed, as have all of the roles, but team members are still being empowered to seek their preferred roles in the church and outside the church as well.

Characteristics of Preferred Developers

1. Developers are practical. Developers are not simply content with an idea, but need to see a way to make it happen.

2. Developers take the dream one step further and say, "That's a fantastic dream. Now what? What steps do we take to organize the program?"

3. Developers discover resources to facilitate dreams. Developers are sensitive to creative ideas that meet needs. They find appropriate people and use them to implement the creative dreams.

4. Developers are problem-solvers. They thrive on the challenge of finding solutions to problems.

5. Developers draw on experience. This can be a benefit or a detriment, depending on how it is used. Developers learn from experience; they know what has and hasn't worked in the past. Since they know, they may be hesitant to try something again, failing to realize that what works for one singles group may not work for another, and vice versa. For example, a camp out may work great for the twenties and thirties group, but fail for the fifties group.

6. Developers are organized. Developers make lists of what needs to be done and how to do it. Developers working on a one-day seminar will make a list months before of all that needs to be done: getting the speaker, publicity, registration, refreshments, room setup, and so forth.

7. Developers ask, "How can we make this happen?" This again stems from their practical side. A developer in a group who wants to plan a ski trip will find the location, rates, transportation, perhaps even swing a deal for the group. Developers help leadership core teams develop targets and goals (see chapter 6) as they plan their Rocket (see chapter 9). They ask "How can we make this dream happen?" They help put the dream into action.

> *Developers are organized. Developers make lists of what needs to be done and how to do it. . . . Developers ask, "How can we make this happen?"*

Healthy Versus Unhealthy Developers

Healthy developers have a good idea of the "big picture" in the ministry. They understand why we are doing what we are doing and what is needed to implement programs and activities. Healthy developers ask practical questions necessary to make a dream happen:

- What are we trying to do?
- How can we make it happen?
- Where do we go from here?

Unhealthy developers may bring a halt to conversation and dreaming by saying, "That'll never work." Unhealthy developers may disregard the creator's input into the dream and possibly ignore the team to get the job done in the most efficient manner.

Unhealthy developers may take the dream and say, "The only way to get this job done right is to do it myself." This defeats the purpose of giving the ministry away so that a group of individuals may each be empowered in ministry.

CARETAKER

Caretakers are vital to effective, relational ministries. They take the game plan outlined in the Rocket process and make sure the single adult ministry stays on target by meeting needs through accomplishing the set goals. Caretakers ask, "What needs to be done? What needs are being met? Are we accomplishing our goals?" Caretakers may be team leaders who gather members to work in all areas needed to meet goals. Caretakers are also sensitive to the ministry's needs. They are nurturing. They see the needs and meet those needs, either directly or by delegation.

The Samaritan in Luke 10:25-35 was a caretaker. He stopped along the road to help a man who had been beaten and robbed on the road from Jerusalem to Jericho. "He went to him and bandaged his wounds, pouring on oil and wine. Then he put the man on his own donkey, took him to an inn and took care of him" (10:34). The next day, the Samaritan paid for the injured man's care before he continued on his journey. This caretaker saw the hurting man and was willing to do what was obviously needed to provide for the man.

My friend Nancy is a caretaker, both in ministry roles and in her friendships. She is a caretaker whether ministering to the sick in a health care program or finding provision for physical needs of a mission with whom we are working. She comes alongside other leaders to support and care for them. She has been known to leave gifts or even emergency money on my doorstep in times of need. For other friends, she provides babysitting one afternoon a week so the parents can enjoy some time out. Nancy is a true caretaker. She sees a need and finds resources to meet that need.

A caretaker involved in the development of single adult leadership seeks people out, gets to know them, and encourages them in ministry opportunities. The caretaker is sensitive to people and wants to see them succeed. This person is crucial in team building, both initially and in the ongoing support and affirmation of leaders.

Characteristics of Preferred Caretakers
1. Caretakers feel strongly that programs or plans must be carried out "right." They are willing to help make it happen. They are often willing to spend extra time to make sure the work is done appropriately—preparing a mailing, setting up for an activity, planning a coffee hour, etc.

2. Caretakers see their own contribution to the general working of a ministry as important. Caretakers know their contribution is important, no matter how big or small.

3. Caretakers are detail persons. They take registrations for an event or put people together for small groups.

4. Caretakers like people and are sensitive to their needs. Caretakers enjoy helping others. They don't simply plug people into groups. They make sure people are in the right group to fit their needs.

5. Caretakers know what needs to be done and either do it or delegate the work. They usually are the ones who notice that the speaker needs a glass of water or that more chairs must be set up. They will either do the job themselves or have someone else do it. In fact, they may anticipate those needs ahead of time and take care of them themselves.

6. Caretakers don't care about being up front or the leader. They are willing to take (or may even prefer) a behind-the-scenes place on the team. They have a healthy ego, and don't see any task as beneath them.

7. Caretakers ask, "What needs to be done?" In a singles ministry, this person may ask, "Who looks like they need a friend?" or "Who doesn't have a Bible?"

Caretakers' places in ministry today are endless. They may arrange to set up the room for a meeting. They may make sure mailings get out, people are called, and songbooks get to the retreat. They may spend all their time with people: drawing them out, encouraging them, affirming them in their ministry. All of us, whether we are creators, developers, or participants, need caretakers to help us succeed in ministry, and we can all be caretakers to one extent or another.

Healthy Versus Unhealthy Caretakers

Healthy caretakers see that jobs get done and draw out people to do the ministry. They see that people are involved, the program "works," and that whatever else needs to be done gets done.

Unhealthy caretakers play the victim or the martyr. They do all the work themselves and then whine that they have so much to do. Some unhealthy caretakers may be termed "codependent," always taking care of others' needs to the exclusion of their own. Unhealthy caretakers can use their position to give others the "dirty work" while keeping the glorifying jobs for themselves.

PARTICIPANT

Many participants take their places in our singles ministries. Richard Halverson, in his book *How I Changed My Thinking About the Church*, gives us this perspective on participants:

> I asked . . . "How many do we need to really do the work of the organization of this church?" . . . Suppose that each [member] could hold only one job, how many would it take to do the work of that large congregation? At the time, the membership was about 7,000. To my amazement I found that it would require only 365 to do the work that was required to maintain the program of the First Presbyterian Church of Hollywood. . . . This meant that most of the members of the church could never have a job in the institution.[1]

In other words, the supply of participants is greater than the demand of tasks or responsibilities. It's okay to be in this majority, but we should try when and where we can to encourage participants to accept leadership roles.

We often see the participant as a passive role in ministry, but the participant is a valid role for a new person or one who needs refreshment. This may not be a long-term role, but an opportunity to reflect on personal roles and where to fit into the ministry. Leaders can cultivate other leaders from within the participants, encouraging and empowering them to ministry in a given area. Tragically, some people participate for years before they are encouraged to discover other ministry roles, or they leave altogether.

People may be participants for a number of reasons. Here are a few reasons:

1. They are new to the ministry and haven't had a chance to find out where they fit.
2. They are seeking renewal and relief from overdoing it in another ministry role.
3. They may be in pain, not having the energy to give elsewhere. They may be going through grief, a divorce or separation, or struggles with their children or parents.
4. Participants may be unsure of their abilities.

In Exodus 3-4, Moses is shown as a participant when God called him into leadership. In fact, if Moses had it his way, he would have continued to be a participant. As he met God on Mount Sinai, God told him to go to Pharaoh and bring His people out of Egypt. Moses responded, "Who am I that I should take on this task?" God pursued, telling Moses to tell the people that He had sent him. Moses feared the people would not believe him. God showed Moses His power, entreating him to go to the people. Moses again responded, "O Lord, I have never been eloquent, neither in the past nor since you have spoken to your servant. I am slow of speech and tongue" (4:10). God reminded Moses that He made him and would teach him what to say. Again, Moses asked God to send someone else.

We see Moses, the participant, as a person who was unsure of his abilities. He lacked confidence both in what God had given him and in his ability to do God's work. Just imagine how the Israelites' history would have been altered radically if Moses had insisted on remaining a participant.

Another biblical participant is found in John 5:2-9. The paralytic at the pool at Bethesda had laid there for thirty-eight years, claiming he was unable to get to the pool. Jesus' response to this man was, "Do you want to get well?" (verse 6). When the man responded that he had no one to help him, Jesus commanded him to get up, pick up his mat, and walk. The man did just that.

Like the paralytic, we sometimes prefer to stay the participant, even if we are unhappy doing so, rather than make the choice for health. The healthy thing for this man was to get up and walk, healed by Jesus. Many times, the healthy action for participants is to take a risk and let God act. We need to make healthy choices for our ministry roles.

The transition from participant to another role is a choice. Moses chose to follow God's call to lead the Israelites out of Egypt. The paralytic chose to pick up his mat and walk. For those of us who are participants, regardless of our reason, a time will come for us to choose to move to a more active role. While we are spectators, we can enjoy the time of refreshment and challenge, contemplating the choices ahead of us and dreaming about how God might use us in another role in His timing.

As leaders, we can encourage participants to make that choice. We can encourage participants to dream and then support their movement into another role. We can give ownership to them, perhaps in small doses so as not to overwhelm them. We can help them move from the passive participation role to a more active leadership role. However, we must not make participants feel guilty or less important for filling their current role.

Characteristics of Preferred Participants

1. Participants may not understand where they fit in the ministry. This includes new Christians and ones from experiences where ministry wasn't given away. They may not understand that they, too, can minister.

2. Participants may be new members or newcomers to your ministry. They may even be newly separated or divorced people in your singles ministry, or a newly married couple to your couples ministry.

3. Participants see many choices before them. Unlike developers and caretakers, some participants may be like a "kid in a candy shop," not sure which great role to pick—too many choices may exist.

4. Participants may be tired and just want to enjoy the ministry outside of a leadership role for a while. Many leaders need this time to regroup or just enjoy the ministry.

5. Participants may have been hurt and need encouragement. They may have been a leader in a failed activity. They may hesitate to try anything again. They may have felt hurt in the process of trying to work with unhealthy team dynamics.

6. Participants ask, "Where can I fit in?" This is the most positive characteristic of the participant because the possibilities are endless and there is room for growth.

Healthy Versus Unhealthy Participants

Healthy participants are acute observers in the ministry, studying the people and program, understanding what opportunities are available when they are ready to make that choice. Healthy participants also allow others to encourage them and invest in their lives. This doesn't mean participants are "sitting ducks" for every leader who wants to pressure them into a job. Healthy participants don't show up late and duck out the door as soon as the program is finished; instead, they invest, inquire, and learn about themselves and those around them.

Unhealthy participants close themselves to people and opportunities. They let hurt or fatigue make them bitter. They criticize the current leaders and do not offer any help. They will sometimes decide that because there is no apparent place for them (because no one has asked them to do something), they are not wanted or adequate for ministry. Unhealthy participants are likely to remain participants for a long time—

becoming a drain on the ministry—or become dropouts. Regardless of our ministry role, we can be sensitive to others' needs and give encouragement to those around us, whether they are participants or ministers in other roles.

OUR CHANGING ROLES

As I mentioned earlier, our ministry role preferences may change or become combined over the years as new experiences and opportunities arise. Sometimes I am a creator, sometimes a developer, sometimes both. Sometimes I just need to be a participant. Any of these preferences played out in excess are unhealthy. People cannot always be participants without feeling lack of direction or satisfaction. By the same token, people cannot always be caretakers without feeling overburdened at some time.

> *Effective ministry is not conducted Lone Ranger style. Effective ministry is relational. It's working as a team. Effective ministry is not programs; it's people and relationships.*

Discovering our ministry role preference is not just for our own health, but is an opportunity to understand our team members. In each of the four ministry role preferences shown here—creator, developer, caretaker, and participant—relationships exist with people who prefer different roles. A struggle can develop when we prefer our own role so strongly that we view the incorporation of others' ministry roles into our own as tiresome or a waste of time. We know we can accomplish our own task within the scope of our individual role, so why work in a team?

That brings us back to the original point of this book. We want to give ministry away. We want to empower others. Effective ministry is not conducted Lone Ranger style. Effective ministry is relational. It's working as a team. Effective ministry is not programs; it's people and relationships.

As we learn our ministry role preferences and as we work together in community—as a team—we enjoy one further benefit: We have help in times of change. When we change our roles, either intentionally or by circumstances, difficulties often arise. During the times when I need to be a participant and step back from a leadership position to reflect on which way to go next, I become insecure about my worth. During these times, I need a community around me to support me and to help direct me toward the next plan God has for me. Once again, none of us can do it all alone.

If you find that you and your team members are not functioning well within your roles, read about communication and how to build a healthy team of leaders (see chapter 7). Read about working together and encouraging each other as a valuable member. We need each other to help shape and guide our response to our ministry role preferences.

OBSTACLES TO MINISTRY ROLES

Some obstacles may hinder us from finding and utilizing our ministry role prefer-ences. We can learn from potential obstacles and honestly confront them.

Confusion

We can occasionally become confused about our roles. We may think: "Everything is already being done by someone else," "I don't even know what I like to do much less what I can do," "If it was really a good idea, someone would already be doing it," "I'm sure there is not enough money to do it," or "They'd never go for it."

At this point, we must remember our preferences—tasks we tend toward over and over again, tasks we enjoy. When we prayerfully reflect on past enjoyable tasks, we see where our preferences lie. We still may wonder where to plug those preferred areas into a ministry role, but our fellow ministers are there to help us find our place.

Here are some ways to clear the fog of confusion about our roles, whether we are team leaders, team members, or participants wanting to plug into a ministry:

1. Carefully read this chapter and consider each ministry role preference.
2. Take the Role Preference Test in chapter 14, page 224.
3. Prayerfully reflect on activities you have enjoyed in the past.
4. Talk to people who know you and have been around you. What do they see? What opportunities do you and others see around you? Where is there a need that you'd like to meet?
5. Try meeting one of those needs. Consider the ministry an experiment. That way, if after trying it you don't think it is for you, you haven't failed but just gathered more information. If you enjoy it, you have learned something new about yourself and found a role at the same time.

Burnout

When we are tired or discouraged and don't want to play anymore, determining our ministry preference role can be difficult. Perhaps the stress of our last ministry role has taken its toll and we want to be left alone. If we are working within a healthy team environment, this likely won't happen. When we find ourselves burned out, for whatever reason, we can use that time to redetermine our ministry role preferences and evaluate why we are burned out. Burnout doesn't necessarily mean we are in the wrong role. It may simply mean that we need a break.

FOUR MAJOR OBSTACLES TO MINISTRY ROLES

- Confusion
- Burnout
- Lack of encouragement
- Competition

For a long time I was a creator/developer in a particular single adult ministry, but then my term ended. That was okay, because I was tired and looked forward to a change. I asked myself, "Now what? Where do I go from here?" At various times since then I have had differing ministry roles, from participant to creator/developer again. Along the way, I have disciplined myself to continually redetermine my role preference to ensure that I am where God has called me to be and where I enjoy serving Him. Those close to me have been crucial in that determination and implementation process.

Here are some ways to deal with burnout:

1. Ask, "Why do I feel so burned out? Am I just tired, or am I angry or hurt?"

2. If you are just tired, perhaps you simply need to stop and take the time to be renewed. If you are angry, try to restore any deteriorated relationships, or possibly your own spirit.

3. Talk to those around you. See how they view the situation. Then compare their views with your own viewpoint. Perhaps you have been unintentionally hurt or are angry out of pride.

4. If your burnout is a result of overextending yourself, learn to rest. Use that time to figure out how to honor your relationship with God by serving Him without overextending yourself. It is possible to reach a balance, but it takes discipline to stop for time with God to become refreshed and renewed.

5. Read the discussion in chapter 11 on your need for Sabbath—a time to renew yourself. An effective minister is able to say no to overcommitments and yes to time alone.

Lack of Encouragement

Another obstacle to discovering and implementing our ministry role preferences is a lack of encouragement. This is a continual challenge for leaders. A pastor once said that a lack of encouragement is like standing on a hose. When we stand on a hose, we cut off the water supply, which was the reason we turned on the hose in the first place. The hose backs up and possibly bursts under the pressure. Without encouragement, we, too, can crumble under the pressure. We eventually defeat the purposes for which we are in ministry in the first place.

We can encourage others in a number of ways, not just verbally:

Give ownership away. When we keep ownership to ourselves, we discourage those around us. We in effect tell them, "You are not needed," "I can do it better myself," or "Your contribution is not worthwhile."

Empower others. When we do not empower those in ministry around us, we discourage them. We may think we are doing them a favor by running the program for them, but we are limiting their growth and opportunity in ministry.

Encouragement is vitally important to the determination and enjoyment of all of our ministry role preferences. As we intentionally encourage those around us, we enable them to be healthy ministers in our community. Read chapter 7 to learn more specific ways to encourage leaders.

Competition

Competition tears at the fabric of all ministry role preferences, essentially stopping the process. Competition may stem from a misconception that one role is more important than another. If I am motivated to have a "better" role in ministry than another, or if I want to be up front more than others and want the most respect in the room, I cannot honestly determine my ministry role preference.

Comparison cannot be a factor in this process, because it has less to do with what we really prefer and more to do with how we want to look to others. Likewise, ego undermines this process. A desire to be "king of the mountain," or the great controller, must be dealt with separately from the discovery of our ministry role preferences.

Overcome feelings of competition by these ideas:

1. Remember why we minister in the first place—to serve God, wherever He guides, directs, and wants us. Remember that God has created our dreams, desires, and preferences.
2. Don't focus on ourselves. When we do, we can expect to find ministry roles that feed our insecurities, which will remain, making us miserable when we need to move on after our ministry role is completed.
3. Don't compare yourself to others. Give thanks for both your strengths and others' strengths. A healthy relational ministry requires a variety of leaders working together, all with unique gifts and talents.
4. Focus on God and discover ministry role preferences that we enjoy while we effectively minister where He has called us. This brings fulfillment that keeps us along the healthy path of interaction with our Christian community.

ROLE PREFERENCE TEST

Chapter 14 offers a tool to help people discover their preferences in ministry roles—the Role Preference Test (page 224). You can give this test to anyone at anytime. Administer it to leaders on your core team as you try to hammer out job descriptions. Give it to single adults at a retreat or workshop titled, "Ministry Roles: Where Do I Fit?" Help single adults who are new to your ministry discover areas in which they

---

BIBLICAL EXAMPLES OF ROLE PREFERENCE

Read about these biblical examples of the four ministry roles:

- Creator—four friends who creatively solved a problem (Mark 2:1-5).
- Developer—Timothy who developed leaders in the Ephesian church (1 and 2 Timothy).
- Caretaker—the Samaritan who helped a man in need (Luke 10:25-35).
- Participant—Moses who was a participant called into a powerful ministry leadership role (Exodus 3-4).

can minister. Administer the test at least once a year, or any time you determine roles in your ministry.

When we all work together to discover our ministry role preferences and live them out, we function as a healthy community of ministers, doing God's work for His people and the world. As a community, we are called to help each other define those activities we enjoy and can do for God's service. As leaders, we are called to empower and encourage others around us to become involved in roles they enjoy. To do this, we must give away the ministry to those around us, while continuing to offer encouragement and training.

REFLECT AND REVIEW

Think about the material in this chapter, then answer the following questions. Remember, don't try to do the ministry alone. Whenever possible, discuss these questions with your single adult leadership team.

1. Reread the characteristics of the creator, developer, caretaker, and participant. Which role do you see yourself in right now? Why? Which role would those around you see you in now? Why? Are the roles different or the same?

2. This chapter talks about the following obstacles to ministry roles. Think about them in relation to your singles ministry.

   a. What are ways you can clear your confusion about ministry roles?

   b. What are ways you can avoid burnout and help other leaders avoid burnout?

   c. How can you encourage others in your single adult ministry?

   d. How can you avoid competition?

3. Schedule a time for you, your team leaders, and any other interested single adults to take the Role Preference Test found in chapter 14. Discover people's preferences. Are they doing what they enjoy? If not, how can you change this?

MEMO

TO: Rich

FROM: Terry and Karen

RE: Chapter 9: Taking Aim

A final important ingredient for relational ministry
is the need for a target, or, more specifically, the
steps to determine the target at which to aim. What
method have you used to make your singles ministry planned and focused?

- Describe a planning process for us to use.
- What steps do we need to "take aim"?
- How can we make sure that we are not
  aiming at everything?

CHAPTER NINE

Taking Aim

Rich Hurst

A fter working in a church for a few years, I wanted a refresher course in ministry, so I decided to take a firsthand look at other single adult ministries on the West Coast. I jumped in my car and headed south, where I spent a few weeks visiting churches from Seattle to San Diego, looking at single adult programs, and talking with several single adult pastors. Of all of my conversations, one stood out from all the rest. The pastor asked me a question that changed the way I do ministry.

"Why are you doing ministry?" he asked. I was too embarrassed to admit I had never really given the question much thought. Having been a hurting young man who found grace and encouragement in a single adult ministry, I had become an active lay leader. From there, one leadership opportunity led to another, and soon I was the singles pastor on a church staff. Everything had seemed so natural, so "preordained," that I had never felt the need to ask myself "Why?"

But here was the question, hanging in the air in front of my face: "Why are you doing ministry?"

I stared blankly at my interrogator.

He continued. "What is your purpose? Why are you a leader?" Now I had the answer! I said what I knew he was after.

"To tell people about God!" I felt like a college kid on a television quiz show. I hoped my answer would end his line of questioning. I had never met this man, yet here I was being asked fundamental questions about my ministry. I wanted to run for the door.

He looked at me again and began to speak. Apparently my answer had not satisfied him. "Yeah, I know you want to tell people about God, but how do you intend to do it?"

I left his office that day and headed north with a new concept of ministry—intentional ministry, a concept for ministry that causes me to continually ask myself, "What is my purpose for ministry and how do I intend to achieve it?"

This chapter is going to explain a process we call the "Rocket." Other organizations use names such as *planning grid* or *planning arrow*. We have chosen to use the name Rocket because we want to suggest to single adult leaders that they are trying to hit a target with their ministry.

This process can be used by leadership core teams as well as individuals. However, we believe the best results happen when groups of people take the time to decide what they intend to do in their ministry. This process will help teams intentionally plan. Let's look at more details about the Rocket planning process.

SHOTGUN MINISTRY VERSUS INTENTIONAL MINISTRY

"If you aim at nothing, you will hit it. If you aim at everything, you hit nothing!" We have a choice in ministry. We can take a shotgun approach, which is to aim at everything and often hit nothing, or we can take the laser-beam approach, zeroing in on purpose. In our fast-paced world, the shotgun approach is not as effective as the targeted, intentional ministry approach.

Each of the people I met on my trek south taught me some important lessons.

Out of a church of 300, only twenty-five singles regularly attended. We operated a shotgun ministry. We tried to do everything all at once and ended up hitting nothing.

- Unintentional (or shotgun) ministry can lead to overly busy leaders, as urgent matters take up disproportionate amounts of time.
- People in an unfocused ministry will often shift their attention away from Christ, the Head of the Church, to a member, often the highly visible pastor.
- Intentional ministry allows us to recognize other people's needs and carefully aim our ministry, rather than spraying a shotgun blast of programs and hoping some people find them meaningful.

When I started in single adult ministry, I read every available book and singles newsletter. I decided I needed to begin with a large group meeting, singing, and some kind of presentation. I noticed a lot of singles ministries were doing divorce recovery so I thought, "Let's start one of those." I had come from a church that believed strongly in small groups so I thought, "Let's have those too." Next, I noticed we didn't have any outreach to unchurched single adults so I thought, "We need a program for that, too."

Before long, everyone was burned out. Out of a church of 300, only twenty-five singles regularly attended. We operated a shotgun ministry. We tried to do everything all at once and ended up hitting nothing. We didn't have the resources and didn't take the time to train people properly.

By necessity, we moved to the laser-beam approach. We learned the hard way, by burning out. We were forced to become intentional and focused. So, we stopped and asked a simple question: "What could we do well with our resources?" We decided we could not do everything well since we didn't have enough people and resources, but we could continue to have our Tuesday night meeting, with singing and a speaker presentation. We could also offer divorce recovery since there was no other service like it in our town—not only could we do it well, but it would also act as our outreach in our community. By focusing on a few areas and doing them well, we avoided burnout. This exemplifies intentional ministry.

THE ROCKET

People-building ministries must be focused. The Rocket is a tool to help your ministry become focused and intentional. The Rocket—like other tools used by consultants and trainers to help ministries and other organizations—is designed to help focus your aim for maximum results. The process is more important than the Rocket diagram itself. (See the Rocket on next page.) If the image deters you, gather as much as you can from the principles and develop your own image and process.

The Rocket is comprised of several elements to help you plan and execute your ministry goals.

THE LAUNCH PAD

The first step in establishing an intentional ministry is to build a solid launch pad of prayer and research. A successful spaceship launch depends upon the combined efforts of many individuals. In the same vein, we must gather a team of like-minded people around us as we begin this process.

Nehemiah provides a good example to those attempting to follow a biblical model for intentional ministry. In Nehemiah 1, the author describes how Nehemiah wept when he heard about the condition of the walls of Jerusalem. He was moved by a need.

In your single adult ministry, ask yourself what makes you weep like Nehemiah when he saw the state of the walls in Jerusalem. What makes you angry? What do you want strongly to change?

The best ministry comes from the heart, whether you feel moved by a person or project. We can conceive intentional ministries through many means, but all are born of deeply felt needs. Gather people who feel as you do. Pray about these needs. Research them.

Several years ago, my wife and I went on vacation to Mexico. Upon our return, we were burdened by a strong feeling for that country. We wanted deeper interaction, more than visiting its beaches and then leaving. We talked about the needs that we had seen, and decided to pray about what we could do. In later talking with a friend, we discovered others had similar feelings.

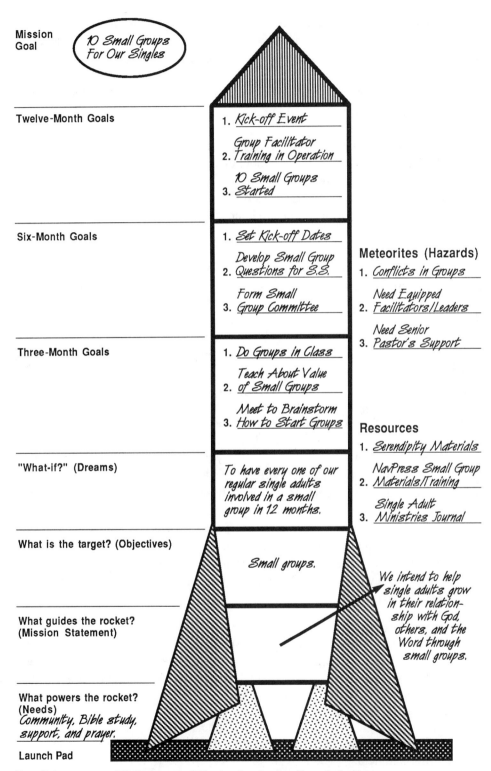

Mission Goal
10 Small Groups For Our Singles

Twelve-Month Goals
1. *Kick-off Event*
2. *Group Facilitator Training in Operation*
3. *10 Small Groups Started*

Six-Month Goals
1. *Set Kick-off Dates*
2. *Develop Small Group Questions for S.S.*
3. *Form Small Group Committee*

Three-Month Goals
1. *Do Groups in Class*
2. *Teach About Value of Small Groups*
3. *Meet to Brainstorm How to Start Groups*

"What-if?" (Dreams)
To have every one of our regular single adults involved in a small group in 12 months.

What is the target? (Objectives)
Small groups.

What guides the rocket? (Mission Statement)
We intend to help single adults grow in their relationship with God, others, and the Word through small groups.

What powers the rocket? (Needs)
Community, Bible study, support, and prayer.

Launch Pad

Meteorites (Hazards)
1. *Conflicts in Groups*
2. *Need Equipped Facilitators/Leaders*
3. *Need Senior Pastor's Support*

Resources
1. *Serendipity Materials*
2. *NavPress Small Group Materials/Training*
3. *Single Adult Ministries Journal*

Please find an extra copy of this Rocket on page 243 to use when planning with your leadership team.

Soon, several of us began to meet and pray. Those months of prayer provided the launch pad for what would later become Vacations with a Purpose, a short-term mission program that became one of the most exciting ministries with which I have ever been involved.

Several practical steps exist to help you create a launch pad of prayer for new and exciting ministries:

1. Ask yourself what needs exist in the world around you.
2. Make a commitment to pray about them often.
3. Research those issues.
4. Talk to friends about your concerns.
5. Gather others together who are interested in the same issues.
6. Pray together.

When you do not establish your ministry on a solid foundation of your prayer, that ministry is weakened. This weakened ministry contains two common characteristics:

■ Leadership is never precisely clear as to why this ministry exists.
■ Leadership is not sure what needs are being met.

THE FUEL

Needs are the fuel that power your Rocket toward your target. They are the catalysts that propel you toward intentional and effective ministry.

Needs are the "why" of ministry. Once you know the needs, you can clearly identify the intention of your ministry. Take time to thoroughly assess the needs you may wish to address. Divide the process into physical, relational, spiritual, and community needs. Examples of these areas of needs include the physical need to actually "be around" someone; the relational need to develop friendships; the spiritual need to learn about God and tell others about Him; and the community need to support and be supported by those around you. Faith is lived out in community.

Some needs will overlap. Categorizing needs is not as important as recognizing as many needs as you can.

Recognizing Needs

The first Vacation with a Purpose trip to Mexico involved eighteen people from University Presbyterian Church's singles department. After this initial team returned, several of the key participants discussed what needs we could meet by offering this experience to others. We thought about physical, relational, spiritual, and community needs to fuel this potential ministry. The needs we recognized included:

1. Some Christians need to test whether they have a genuine call to the mission field.

2. People need to build relationships with each other and with other peoples of the world.
3. People need to be challenged to stewardship.
4. The gospel needs to be shared.
5. World poverty needs to be addressed.

I was asked once to work with a singles ministry in a local church. I agreed to meet with the single adults. After introductions, I asked, "Why does your singles ministry exist? Why do you have one?" The room was silent. Nobody was sure why the group was meeting. I asked them, "What would you like to be meeting for?" They quickly livened up and answers began to fly one after another—"fun," "friendships," "spiritual growth," "reaching out to others," and so on.

The next day, I met with the leadership. We debriefed about my meeting with the single adults. I asked them what needs they felt were being addressed in the group. They were unsure. I asked them about their own needs. They responded with answers of friendship, social needs, and the need to understand the Bible and live according to its direction. At this point, I said, "Your needs are the same as their needs."

We tempt ourselves to minister to others with "their" problems. In truth, however, ministry touches the basic needs that we all have. If you are a single adult, your needs are similar to all single adults. If you are a single parent, you have similar needs to all single parents. We all have needs for friendship, support, and love. Discovering a group's needs begins with asking what needs exist. We can accomplish this through practical steps:

1. Ask questions or conduct surveys. (Two surveys you can use in your ministry appear in chapter 14, pages 229 and 232.)
2. Meet with people and ask them to list their needs. For example, ask a single parent to lunch to learn that person's spiritual, social, educational, and relational needs.
3. Drive around your community and see what needs exist.
4. Hire a professional to survey and document the demographics of your church's community.
5. Look at the U.S. Census Bureau statistics for your area.
6. Ask a clerk or official at city hall what needs you might address in your city. Many city governments have volunteer coordinators or a list of organizations that regularly need volunteers and other help.

Failure to recognize needs can drastically weaken your ministry. A weakened ministry in this area has the following characteristics:

■ Too "me" focused. Involved only in meeting, not in meeting needs.
■ The people involved in this ministry will say their own needs are not being met.

Once you have built a foundation of prayer and collected fuel for the ministry Rocket, you are prepared to map out a mission.

THE MISSION STATEMENT

NASA does not launch a space shuttle without a specific purpose in mind. The purpose may be to launch a satellite or set a planetary mission in motion. The shuttle may carry hundreds of scientific experiments to be conducted at zero-gravity. Whatever the reason, NASA launches each shuttle to accomplish a specific mission, an intentional mission. Indeed, NASA often refers to the shuttle's "mission" when discussing a particular voyage.

We do the same when we launch an intentional ministry. We don't take off until we have determined our specific mission. A mission statement has these characteristics:

- A mission statement tells people who you are, stating the reasons you feel called and qualified by God to address these needs.
- A mission statement reflects your overall purpose for existing as a ministry. Remember, you are in ministry to build people, not programs. Your mission statement, then, should clearly state how you plan to serve people.
- A mission statement tells the direction you are headed. This should be generally stated in two to three sentences. Stated directions not only tell others where you are headed, but also help keep you on track. With a focused direction, you can more easily say no to distractions that tend to draw you away from the stated course.

Once the Vacations with a Purpose core team had developed a foundation of prayer and identified the needs they would try to address, they were ready to establish a mission statement. Notice how their statement reflects the team's needs addressed earlier:

We intend to give singles the opportunity to gain a world view and to respond to the world's needs in experiences that foster relationships with each other and with those to whom they go. It is our goal to share the gospel and ourselves in ministry.

Practical Steps for Creating a Mission Statement

1. List all the needs you identified earlier. Now write two to three sentences using these needs to describe your intentions. Start the first sentence with "We intend to" or "We exist to."

2. Take your time. If possible, get away with your team members for a day or weekend to a relaxed setting where you can thoughtfully prepare your mission statement.

3. Make sure your mission statement is easy to understand. Make it simple, not long and complex. Don't use words that no one understands or language that only your church community understands. For example, avoid words and phrases such as

redeeming, fellowship, or *share the gospel*. Instead use words and phrases such as *lovable, friendship*, and *tell people about Jesus*.

4. Create your own mission statement. You may have seen one you like, so why not copy it? Don't. You and your ministry are in a different setting, and you are unique people.

5. Don't be satisfied with a mission statement just because it sounds good. Make sure you understand and believe it.

6. Change your mission statement when you or your ministry change. Don't feel like it's forever cast in stone. It's meant to serve you, not box you in. When you decide you want to try some new direction, rework your statement. That way you are being thoughtful and intentional about your ministry. Do this with the help of other team members and keep others informed. (Chapter 14 contains a worksheet that will help you and your team develop a mission statement. See page 234.)

> *Discovering a group's needs begins with asking what needs exist. . . . Failure to recognize needs can drastically weaken your ministry.*

Ministries that lack a ministry statement are weakened and bear the following characteristics:

- The ministry has no clear direction.
- Leadership cannot articulate the ministry's focus.
- People don't know why the ministry exists.

THE TARGETS

Once you have built a solid launch pad of prayer, determined the needs to fuel the ministry, and created your mission statement, you are now ready to aim your ministry toward more specific targets.

Targets should be broad enough to permit you flexibility in designing your ministry, yet specific enough to provide guidance. For example, in the early sixties, we all heard that the United States was "going to the moon." Most of us didn't care if it was the dark side or the light side; we just wanted to get there! The same applies to single adult ministries—people just want to get there; they aren't as concerned about specific programs as they are with the fact that a singles ministry is in existence.

One of the targets in my own ministry Rocket is leadership training. As a target, it is not so specific that it can be measured. Its breadth allows me to participate in and develop many specific programs that would constitute leadership training, yet it provides a target for my ministry so I will not be pulled off course. With leadership training as a target, I can ask myself at each new juncture, "Will this new program train leaders?"

Identify five to ten targets for your single adult ministry. (Begin with a few. You can always add more later.) Seriously contemplate the targets that will provide direction for your ministry.

Setting Your Targets

People going through divorce have unique needs that must be effectively met. They need acceptance, a listening ear, and assurance that the church is going to stand by them, others have made it through this experience, God still loves them, and they still have an important role in society and the church.

The best way to determine needs is to simply ask the singles involved in your divorce recovery ministry. You can also ask counselors about the needs they perceive. Check with the bureau of information—the U.S. government often does research on issues such as divorce. Examine your church records to see how many divorced people attend. Check with the statistics bureau to see how many divorced people live in your community. Ask yourself how well your ministry meets the short- and long-term needs of those going through divorce.

I have seen seemingly successful divorce recovery programs that are just meetings. They exist only to meet short-term needs. As Terry mentioned in the first chapter, the church should not be a hospital emergency room where the professional only stops the bleeding. The church must be a center that focuses on short-term needs (stopping the bleeding) as well as long-term needs (a place for healing, teaching, and counseling) so that people can be "released" to help others.

After you have determined needs, think of five to ten targets to help you meet the needs. For example, sponsor monthly seminars followed by small group discussions, weekly fellowship events, and ongoing counseling opportunities. A divorce recovery ministry that strongly meets needs will hit important targets.

Small groups in your singles ministry can hit a variety of targets: to have everyone in small groups of eight people; to help people study the Bible; to develop small group study guides; to help people support one another; to help people strengthen their leadership skills; to help people recover from addictive behaviors; and so forth. Identifying these targets dictates what type of small groups you'll establish.

Other target areas in single adult ministry may include single parents; young single adults; older single adults; social, educational, and relational ministry; seminars; children of divorce; and others. Several years ago, our single adult ministry decided on five target areas:

- Classes for different age groups (forty-plus, thirties, and twenties).
- Divorce recovery workshop.
- Missions.
- Resource center for single parents.
- Quarterly magazine for singles.

We established several targets for the Vacations with a Purpose program:

- Short-term mission trips to Haiti.
- Short-term mission trips to Mexico.
- Short-term mission trips to our church's missionaries around the world.
- Short-term mission training curriculum.
- Short-term local mission experiences.

Notice that targets are broad enough to leave flexibility, yet specific enough to focus your efforts. Be creative. Targets can be anything you want as long as they meet needs.

Practical Steps for Choosing Targets

1. Establish multiple targets (at least five to ten). If you have only one target, you may be tempted to fall out of balance and fail to address certain needs. When you aim toward several related targets, you are less likely to develop tunnel vision.

2. Choose targets that maximize your resources and efforts. Be selective rather than random in choosing targets.

3. Targets must be born out of your mission statement. They cannot be abstract. Our mission will be carried out through these commitments. Through targets, we can measure our effectiveness.

I spoke recently with a single adult pastor whose mission statement concentrated on reaching unchurched singles. A target suggested by her leadership team was to hold a large retreat with other church single adult groups in the area. After discussion, the leadership team members determined that this retreat did not fit the purposes outlined in the mission statement, so they eliminated that target as being inappropriate for reaching unchurched singles.

4. Targets should be functional. These targets must be specific enough to take you somewhere and intentional enough to keep you motivated.

5. Start with only a few targets, then add more later.

6. Avoid dangerous targets. For example, avoid being self-centered in the selection of targets, aiming only to meet your own needs.

Targets tell us where to invest our time, energy, and resources. They define where we are going to concentrate our efforts and who is going to do the work. Targets are critical for focusing an intentional ministry.

Without targets, the ministry is weakened and takes on each of these three characteristics:

- The ministry tries to do everything.
- Few people feel the ministry addresses their particular needs.
- Leaders are burned out.

DREAM DESTINATIONS

In his book *Young Adult Ministry*, Terry writes about the concept of the "dream session." This is the time to be creative, to sit back and let yourself imagine. Look within each target area and try to picture the nearly unimaginable destinations for your ministry.

Ask yourself: "In terms of each target, if nothing were impossible, what would I like to see happen?" Don't worry about the feasibility or even the rationality of the dreams shared.

Even though there are few rules for holding a dream session, some guidelines exist:

Each dream must be measurable. "I want single adults in this church to be appreciated" is a good dream, but it isn't measurable. "I would like to see single adults involved at all levels of church leadership" is a measurable goal.

Don't stop to discuss or rationalize. Dreams are intellectual power in action. I have seen many dreams squelched by negative comments. The four words *We can't do that* can cause a dream to be lost forever. Remember, power can't be limited, only stopped. There is no such thing as a bad dream. People can be full of creative ideas, especially when they're encouraged. When people say "We can't do that" or "That won't work," ideas come to a stop—end of conversation.

While sitting in on a leadership core team meeting for a single adult ministry recently, I observed as the leader started the meeting: "Let's just dream for a while. What could we do to turn this ministry around?" One person responded, "We can't do anything. It won't work. No one in the church will let us do anything (meaning the pastor)." A second top leader added, "They never let us try anything new." Imagine being on that team—a place where people have allowed themselves to feel like victims. We are not victims. We have power in our ability to imagine how to do things. Don't let others stop you. Keep thinking. Keep dreaming.

The Vacations with a Purpose core team produced three pages of dreams. We wanted to someday dig wells in Haiti, send medical teams to Mexico, and build medical clinics in rural villages. Remember, there is no such thing as a bad dream. This is the time to dream, not evaluate.

Another single adult leadership team came up with the dream of getting every single adult involved in weekly small groups where people would read the Bible, pray, and share their own stories.

Practical Steps for Planning Dream Destinations

1. Set the ground rules for a dream session: (a) There is no such thing as a bad dream or idea, and (b) Don't respond, "We tried that before."

2. Take a night or longer to pray about the dreams and think them over.

3. List dreams on paper. Post them on the wall to look at and think about.

4. Choose three to five dreams on which you want to work. (These chosen dreams will become the goals you work on later in the Rocket process.) Attach people's names to the dreams. These people will be responsible to make sure the dream is accomplished by getting the group together to do it or choosing a team of people who will complete the task.

Ministries that are weak in dreaming take on the following characteristics:

■ The people involved in the ministry feel that no one cares about their ideas.

■ Seldom will fresh, new, exciting things happen.

METEORITES

As we attempt to meet needs, we will run into obstacles or potential problems. We call these meteorite showers, which can be damaging, costly, and dangerous. Sometimes you can anticipate and avoid them, but at other times you must meet them head on. When planning your Rocket, think about potential meteorites that might adversely affect your plan. By thinking about potential meteorites, you can anticipate possible problems and address them before they damage your plan.

Potential meteorites in a single adult ministry include a church that is uneducated about singles, a pastor who thinks all singles are losers, an unsupportive staff, and singles in the church who don't feel a need for singles ministry.

The Vacations with a Purpose core team identified the following potential meteorites:

1. The quality of each trip would be compromised if we attempted too many trips each year.
2. Trips would suffer if we couldn't find people to own them.
3. We might not raise the money needed to finance the trips.
4. Poorly selected team members might diminish the quality of each team and the program as a whole.
5. Mission agencies may not want short-term teams working with them.

Some of these meteorites presented more challenges than others, but each one helped us think before acting. This process gave us a chance to address any potential problems. Your ministry, too, can identify meteorites by following these practical steps:

- List all potential problems you may encounter.
- List all restrictions your church may give you.
- List people who may pose potential problems.
- List any legal limitations.

When your ministry does not identify potential meteorites, you can be bogged down by having to deal with contingencies that arise but weren't foreseen. Leaders then become frustrated and begin to feel that the ministry is destined for failure.

MISSION SUPPORT

The next step in the Rocket process is to identify available resources to support your mission. For every astronaut who is sent into space, hundreds of other individuals provide technical and emotional support. In addition, the astronauts rely on vast resources of technical and scientific expertise that have been developed throughout the history of air and space travel. In the same way, you have resources you can call upon for your intentional ministry.

When we started Vacations with a Purpose, we identified the experts in our midst as part of our planning. We didn't have to look far; our mission pastor was the former president of a world relief agency. We discovered many who had been on past mission trips. They, in turn, pointed us toward agencies in the United States and contacts in foreign countries. It also didn't take long to find people in our midst who spoke other languages who would help prepare our mission teams to communicate when in different countries. In the end, the high impact of the Vacations with a Purpose program was due in large part to many wonderful people in our own church body.

We also discovered several other resources while establishing our short-term missions program. Creative fund-raising options were available. Other churches offered themselves as resources. The library, the airline company, pharmaceutical companies, area hospitals, and countless other sources had knowledge and resources that were helpful to us in planning mission trips.

Several resources are available to single adult ministries, including:

■ National Association of Single Adult Leaders
■ *Single Adult Ministries Journal*
■ *National Single Adult Ministries Resource Directory*
■ Singles Ministry Resources Leadership Training Group

The final section of this book offers additional resources for single adult ministry. Check the resources section on page 253 for addresses.

When identifying possible support and resources for your mission, follow these practical steps:

■ Identify the experts you can call upon.
■ Identify resource agencies such as other churches and community agencies.
■ Identify untapped resource people in your church.
■ List the programs or procedures already in place in your ministry or church that will facilitate this mission.

When your ministry fails to identify mission support, you waste valuable time and energy "reinventing the wheel," rather than gleaning the insights learned by others. Your ministry also tends to rely heavily on a small group of experts, leaving them overtaxed, while other experts are under-utilized.

MISSION GOALS

This next stage is primary to your success. The right goal at the right stage of your ministry's development will help you achieve your purpose and your dreams. If you try to achieve too much too soon, you will usually cause burnout. If you move too slowly, you can produce frustration, along with a loss of interest.

Mission goals are not the same as mission statements, target areas, or dreams. Compare their definitions:

■ Mission statement—your ministry's purpose.
■ Targets—objectives that help focus your ministry.
■ Dreams—the sky is the limit approach to your ministry. You list all dreams, then choose three to five on which you want to work.
■ Goals—chosen dreams from your dream session; the feet that carry out your mission statement.

An example will clarify the differences. I was in Atlanta working through the Rocket process with the head of a national organization. As we worked on the mission statement, he handed me a file that had several mission statements from other Christian organizations. Some were wonderfully written, but what struck me was that none included accompanying organizational goals. Mission statements are only a part of the process; you also need goals to carry out the mission statement.

Your mission goals are not targets, either. Targets are bigger, less specific. Earlier, I used Americans' desire to go to the moon as an illustration of a target. In that case, the moon was the target, but NASA had several mission goals it had to reach before it could successfully land astronauts on the moon.

In the Rocket, you'll see that the establishment of mission goals involves several phases: three-month goals, six-month goals, nine-month goals, and twelve-month goals.

Practical Examples
The Vacations with a Purpose team listed the several mission goals and named the individuals responsible to see they were carried out (see next page). Remember, these individuals don't do it alone. They are responsible to get others to work together to accomplish the goal.

In another example, a core team discovered single parents had a need for low- or no-cost medical help. Their target was to organize a single parent resource center to help meet that need. From their dream session, they came up with several ideas to develop this resource center. They then established the following goals:

Three-month: Create a brochure to send to health care professionals such as dentists and doctors to outline the need for low-cost help for single parents. Publicize in the church bulletin the idea of establishing a single parent resource center.

Six-month: Mail the brochure to doctors, dentists, and other health care professionals in the church and community. Publicize the resource center with single parents. Begin to recruit resource people. Begin to identify single parents and their needs.

Nine-month: Match resources according to single parents and their needs.

Twelve-month: Begin a single parent support group. Maintain an ongoing single parent resource center.

MISSION GOALS AND PERSON RESPONSIBLE FOR EACH

Phase One: Three-Month Goals	Person(s) Responsible
1. Pray regularly	Rob
2. Meet with resource people	Rob and Kim
3. Hold a dream session	Kim and Jerry

Phase Two: Six-Month Goals	
1. Pray regularly	Jim and Nancy
2. Hold bi-weekly leadership core team meetings	Kim and Jerry
3. Gather information about potential sites	Traci, Vikki, and Jeff
4. Choose a potential site	Entire committee

Phase Three: Nine-Month Goals	
1. Pray regularly	Jim and Nancy
2. Send two people to check out the site	Traci and Jim
3. Begin to select the mission team	Linda, Rob, Nancy

Phase Four: Twelve-Month Goals	
1. Pray regularly	Jim and Nancy
2. Train the team	Kim and Jerry
3. Send the team on the short-term mission	Mission team
4. Evaluate the experience	Leadership core team and mission team

---

In both of these examples, the groups took these practical steps to establishing mission goals:

- Make sure your goals are specific enough to accomplish.
- Make sure you have given yourself plenty of time.
- Attempt to accomplish only a few goals in each phase.

When a ministry does not set mission goals, the ministry tries to accomplish too many goals in a three-month period and, therefore, fails to set or meet other goals. Ministries also fail in this area when they list goals, but not the person who is ultimately responsible to see that the goals are met and tasks completed.

UPDATING THE ROCKET

The Rocket process provides a way to be intentional about your single adult ministry. It provides direction and focus for your ministry, and keeps you from being distracted. The Rocket, however, is only as good as your commitment to use it and keep it updated with new dreams and new directions.

Once you create your Rocket, update it on a regular basis. If your team members serve one-year terms, update the Rocket every six months; if they serve six-month terms, update the Rocket every three months. Add new goals that have arisen, and delete other goals that are no longer pertinent. Discuss the Rocket with new leadership. Review with all leadership core team members to keep your ministry on target and focused.

TROUBLESHOOTING

When I present the Rocket to various groups, a few questions continually surface:

What if we don't meet all of our three-month goals? That's okay! You may choose to push them to the next three months, or they may no longer be important. Remember that goals, like every step in the Rocket, are meant to guide you, not confine you.

What if the group changes leadership drastically in the next three months? Make sure all incoming leaders understand the Rocket and agree with the ministry's direction. The old leaders can explain each step of the Rocket to the newcomers. Not only will this educate the new leaders, but it will affirm the old leaders and the process they undertook to arrive at their current ministry. Whenever you have major leadership changes (for example, if more than half of the leaders are new), hold a leadership retreat to work through the Rocket process with both old and new leaders. (See suggested retreats in chapter 12 and seminars in chapter 13.) The new Rocket should reflect the input and personality of this new corps of leaders.

> *Whenever you have major leadership changes . . . hold a leadership retreat to work through the Rocket process with both old and new leaders.*

What if our mission statement is not the same as our church's mission statement? A distinctive mission statement is okay as long as it is not in opposition to your church's mission. A single adult ministry's mission statement is usually more specific than the church's statement. However, if your statement contradicts the church's, rework it after discussing the differences with the church leadership.

University Presbyterian Church has a concise mission statement: "Every member a minister: sharing, caring, shaping, going." The single adult ministry's mission statement is several paragraphs long, yet it corresponds nicely with the church's mission statement. It reads in part:

> We believe that each member is a minister and it is our primary goal to equip the ministers by helping to deepen each one's personal relationship with God. We seek to develop more intimate relationships of discipleship, accountability, and support with one another. Finally, we seek to further each one's responsibility to the work of Christ in the form of outreach, mission, education, and giving.

REFLECT AND REVIEW

Think about the material in this chapter, then answer the following questions. Remember, don't try to do the ministry alone. Whenever possible, discuss these questions with your single adult leadership team.

1. Take a look at your current singles ministry. Is the planning unintentional or intentional? Do you hit targeted needs, or do you try to do everything?

2. Focus your ministry by using the Rocket planning process and the Rocket Checklist found on page 228. Go through the steps with an already-established core team or other interested individuals. Check off each step as you complete it:

❑ Launch pad of prayer and research

❑ Fuel: Determining needs

❑ Map out a mission statement

❑ Establish your targets

❑ Host a dream session

❑ Identify meteorites—potential problems

❑ Identify mission support—resources

❑ Establish specific mission goals

TAKING CARE OF YOURSELF

Chapter 10: Small Groups: Being in Community (page 149)
This chapter portrays community, a place where single adult leaders find care and encouragement. Learn about our need for community, the importance of small groups, and obstacles that get in the way.

Chapter 11: Learning to Say No (page 159)
This chapter stresses the benefits to our health as leaders when we balance time with others and time alone through Sabbath—saying no, taking care of ourselves, and setting boundaries.

MEMO

TO: Karen

FROM: Rich and Terry

RE: Chapter 10: Small Groups:
     Being in Community

So far we've talked about building a solid foundation for single adult ministry. We've read about key
ingredients to building a core team of leaders. Now
we want to hear about ways to take care of ourselves. Why is it important for leaders to share in
small groups? To be in community?

- What are small groups?
- Why do we need community?
- How do we promote and model community?
- What obstacles get in our way?

CHAPTER TEN

Small Groups: Being in Community

Karen Butler

We live in a world that places a premium on independence. It seems that "making it on our own" is a sign of success today. Nothing could be farther from the truth. We were created not to be alone, but to be in community. So we live with a tension: We believe that we can make it alone, but we need one another. As leaders, what can we do to live with that tension?

One of the most effective ways to live with that tension is, simply, to be in a small group. "Wait," you might say, "I'm already spending time with a leadership core team, isn't that enough?" No, it's really not.

While your leadership team is a small group, its mission or purpose goes beyond simply supporting and caring for one another. Supporting and caring for one another are certainly integral parts of your mission, but additional tasks have brought you together. Healthy leadership teams become community, but you need another small group of people around you to support and care for you as well.

What do I mean by small group? I mean a group of people who intentionally come together to study, pray, and share their lives. Called *covenant groups, discipleship groups, support groups*, or *small groups*, they share the same purpose: To help members grow in Christ and in Christian community. In the process, we find family—a place where we belong in the Christian community.

THE NEED FOR COMMUNITY

I became convinced of my own need for community on the first team mission trip I took with a group from our church. Our assignment was to work at an orphanage in Baja California, Mexico, for several days and then vacation and debrief for two days on a nearby beach. We first trained for four weeks; language studies, cultural lessons, and team-building exercises designed to help us to begin to become community.

The first night I attended our team meeting I thought, "This is one odd assortment of people!" I could not imagine how so many radically different people could possibly get along in close quarters when we were out of our comfort zone. I was comforted knowing that at least I had a couple of friends in the group who I knew were like me. At the end of the training, we left for Mexico and our community experience.

What I learned over that week about community and my own need for those around me was astonishing. I was in a group of people who were so different from me and from each another, yet we got along great. Two were recently divorced, a few more had just ended serious relationships, one was a recent widow, and a few others were floundering with questions of what to do with their lives. But that week, despite many differences, we were in it together as a team. We worked together, played together, laughed and cried together. We experienced some of the saddest times we would ever go through, and were there to catch the tears of one another.

When I came home from the trip, I went into what I call "community withdrawal." Back in the "making it on my own" mode, I went to work and got together with my friends and my small group, but I just could not communicate exactly what happened in me during that experience. Because it was difficult to explain, I could not get that community feeling back again.

For a week I was depressed and sad, saying, "Where are all those people who cared about me, with whom I shared my days, nights, tears, and laughter?" I did not feel connected in that same way with anyone else. What had happened between that first team meeting where I thought we would never make it and that first week back home when I thought I couldn't go on without my community?

I had experienced true community in a group setting. That experience went beyond all of my preconceived notions about community and my teammates in particular. During our time together in Mexico, I experienced a group of people spending time working and playing together, but also getting to know one another in a close context. Our devotional times led to our helping one another to process some of the cross-cultural and other faith-challenging issues we experienced. We allowed others to witness our own personal and spiritual growth. We were able to say "I'm hurting" and know that we'd find a place where people cared for us. This helped us to open up. As we became more comfortable, we opened up not only about our experiences during the week but also about what we had come from at home or what we were going back to. By the end of the week, we were a group of people who loved, cared for, and served one other.

When we returned home, I discovered I wasn't the only one who experienced "community withdrawal." Other mission team members did as well. Our first reunion was wonderful. We gathered to relive our experiences via photographs and stories, but also to catch up on what coming home was like and what lay ahead. New friendships had begun and many continue today.

Since my first great community experience, I have become more convinced of my own need for community—a place where I can come with my heart brimming full or torn open and bleeding. When I come to my community, in whatever state, I know I will be loved and forgiven because my community is a group of people who are committed to Christ and to one another. Because I am taking care of myself in this community, I am able to empower others to minister as well.

EFFECTIVE LEADERS NEED COMMUNITY

Leaders need to experience community—the support and care of small groups—for various reasons. Here are just a few.

God created us to be in relationships. Leaders aren't exempt. Everyone needs each other. God says in Genesis 2:18, "It is not good for the man to be alone." In Acts 2:42-47, we see the early fellowship of believers as being a devoted, teaching, sharing, praying, and worshiping community. Even Jesus gathered a small group about Him in Mark 3:13-19. He "called to him those he wanted, and they came to him . . . that they might be with him and that he might send them out" (verses 13-14). Jesus, our model leader, was a part of a small group, a community.

We need support in the midst of ministry. A few years ago as an intern at a large church, I was not involved in a small group. In fact, I had just come out of a small group which had not gone so well, so I was hesitant to get involved again for fear that I would waste my time again. The pastor for whom I was an intern, however, told me that I needed to be in a small group to build a support system for myself in a smaller version of the Christian community. He was right, but who would I ask to join me in a small support group?

I remembered having had a five-minute conversation with four women over lunch at an all-day planning meeting a few months earlier. I had enjoyed the women, who were leaders in the same ministry, but barely knew them. I was positive they were already plugged into fellowship with their own friends. They wouldn't want to be in one more group on one more night out, would they? The more I thought about it, though, I couldn't think of anyone else to ask to be in a small group, so I called them.

I happened to contact two of them with the first call. One was at the other's house—a fact that I found somewhat intimidating since that showed me they were already friends. I worried that I'd be an outsider. When I asked one of them to be in a small group, she got so excited that she couldn't talk and put the other one on the phone. They didn't even think about it; they just said yes. That was promising, so I called the other two, who said they would be in a group too.

We gathered, some knowing one another and some not. All of us were too busy with our leadership responsibilities and everything else in life to be in a group, but for two-and-a-half years we met weekly to share, pray, and sometimes study. The

---

EFFECTIVE LEADERS NEED COMMUNITY

1. God created us to be in relationships.
2. We need support in the midst of ministry.
3. We need to help others and to be helped ourselves.
4. We don't make major decisions alone.

group turned out to be one of the two best small groups I have ever experienced. We supported each other through relational issues such as broken engagements, ex-boyfriends dating and marrying someone else, job and family issues, and ministry frustrations. We even occasionally fought with one another. Through it all, we had community. We accomplished our goal to grow in Christ and in Christian fellowship and support. We no longer meet because a couple have moved away and the rest of us have other commitments, but we are still close friends and intend to remain that way for a long time.

The pastor had basically required me to be in a small group during my internship. He was smart. I needed it. I still need it and believe I always will. He knew I needed a support system—a place where I wasn't just ministering, but was ministered to as well. As leaders, we often give without taking time to receive. This is unhealthy. The healthy leader not only has places to give, but places to be supported as well.

We need to help others and to be helped ourselves. Christian communities free others to live. In John 11, Jesus raised Lazarus from the dead, but after doing so, said to those around Him, "You unwrap him," telling them to take off the grave clothes and free him. As He did with Lazarus, Jesus works in us, but we are still bound by our own grave clothes. He says to those around us, "You unwrap him or her." Community is a place where we help each other out of the binding grave clothes, now that we have been given new life.

> *As leaders, we often give without taking time to receive. This is unhealthy. The healthy leader not only has places to give, but places to be supported as well.*

We don't make major decisions alone. Community, whether a small group or a leadership core team, is a place where we can bounce ideas off each other, be accountable to each other, and give one another perspective. As leaders, we aren't to operate out of a vacuum. Small groups, or community, help us to operate in a healthy way.

EFFECTIVE LEADERS PROMOTE COMMUNITY

Leaders not only need community, but are aware that they are not alone in this need. We all need community, whether we are leaders or not. As leaders, we can promote community for single adults and others in our ministry. Here are some ways to do this:

Make small-group opportunities available. Let people know it's okay to need each other. As leaders, we frequently have the inside information on small groups, fellowship, and other opportunities, whether in our churches or elsewhere. Make that information available. Find the places around us where community is happening and where some of the people in our ministries can plug in. When we are aware of people's needs, we can meet their needs. This task is not just the responsibility of pastors, but all of us.

Involve others in small groups with us. We give others a great gift when we allow or enable them to minister to us. This can be difficult. It's easier to minister and have control over the relationship as a "leader," than to be the recipient of ministry by others. We are all in this together, though, regardless of roles or control games. Others need us, but we need them too. We promote community by modeling it with the people around us.

Teach small groups and community. Instruct others about the meaning of being in a small group, the universal need for community, and the elements of community, such as care for one another, vulnerability, forgiveness, love, and service to one another. Learning consists of experience and information. This is the purpose of new members classes. They tell inquirers about the church and the benefits of becoming a member of the community. Many tools for instructing others about small groups exist. Your church may have a staff person to do this. In most cases, this won't be true— so check the resources at your library. Also, see the bibliography for a list of helpful books about small groups.

EFFECTIVE LEADERS MODEL COMMUNITY

When we understand the characteristics of community, we can better model it—not just by being in a small group (where no one but the five or six other people in the group know what goes on in our lives), but every day in the midst of relationships. To model community, however, we must know what it is. Here are some characteristics of community:

Community is a place of vulnerability. One of the most difficult aspects for us to model in community is vulnerability. When we are vulnerable with those around us, we give them potential power over us. I was joking recently with a friend on the telephone about all the items he knows that could anger or hurt me. This friend has known me for a long time and knows my weak points. After joking about it that day, I realized how vulnerable I am to this friend. Should he choose to do so, he could hurt me with just a few words. Being vulnerable means I trust this friend not to choose to abuse the information and consequent power he has in our relationship.

Vulnerability—opening ourselves to the possibility of being wounded—is not a weakness, but a strength. When we allow others to see our need for them in our lives, we give power away and trust that they will not abuse it. Our trust is an act of love. Healthy relationships in community do not abuse our vulnerability.

We fool ourselves if we think community happens without risk of vulnerability. Even in the church, community is a risk. Keith Miller, in his book *The Taste of New Wine*, says:

> Our churches are filled with people who outwardly look contented and at peace but inwardly are crying out for someone to love them . . . just as they are—confused, frustrated, often frightened, guilty, and often unable to communicate even within their own families. But the other people in the church

look so happy and contented that one seldom has the courage to admit his own deep needs before such a self-sufficient group as the average church meeting appears to be.[1]

By modeling vulnerability, we will show others in our single adult ministry that it's okay for them to be vulnerable as well.

Community is a place where we share and encourage dreams. When I am in a healthy community, my dreams are encouraged and taken seriously. When we began a young single adult group several years ago, my involvement escalated because a few people listened to and encouraged my dreams. Terry and Rich, the other authors of this book, are great examples of what it means to encourage dreams. They understood my dreams for ministry and encouraged me through support and dreams of their own.

Community is a place where we are accountable to one another. We can be held accountable for numerous things. Within a small-group context, I am held accountable to be growing in my spiritual walk and to be praying, studying, and learning. Within a leadership core team, I am accountable to others to play as a team member. If I am treating someone unfairly, I am accountable to the team for it. If I am doing too much work, I count on them to hold me accountable to have a balanced life outside of this ministry. They hold me accountable to act with integrity, direction, and God's leading.

Community is a place where we grow together and individually. When I am in a community that requires me to risk, I grow. When my fellow leaders challenge me to go outside my comfort zone to try something new, I grow. When the people around me want to get to know me, I also grow. We tell our stories to one another—where we have come from, who we are, and where we dream we are going.

OBSTACLES TO COMMUNITY

As with all good things, we occasionally have difficulty living out our lives in the optimum fashion. Being in community is a must for leaders, but it is not always easy. Here are some things to watch out for:

Lone Rangers looking for Tontos. The Lone Ranger had a great companion and right-hand man in Tonto, but he was far from a "team player." Jennifer James, a Seattle columnist, said this about the Lone Ranger:

> He rides into town, grandstands like Donald Trump with the white horse and silver bullets, and then leaves before anyone can resolve the events he stirred up. Lone wears a mask all the time because he has not cleared up his personal problems and therefore has to hide his identity. . . . We learn nothing about Lone before he leaves because he doesn't like to communicate. We have no idea of the nature of his relationship with Tonto. Tonto doesn't talk, so we don't know if he's being exploited or not.[2]

In the context of Christian community, we should beware of men and women wanting to be the "big cheese" at the expense of others. Community is not one leader finding a bunch of people who will do what he or she says. Community is men and women working together.

Community gluttons. Community is needed by all of us, but we are also called to balance in our lives. If we are so entrenched in community that we do not spend time alone with God or take time to do what we need, perhaps we should look at our need for community and see how much is a convenient distraction and how much is really necessary. For those of us who are extroverts, this is particularly true, since we may not feel such a great need to be alone as the introvert. Community is important, but so is individual growth. Taking time for ourselves means that we have more to give. (Chapter 11 tells more about taking time for yourself.)

> ***Community is a place where other people take care of me, not in a dependent way, but with my consent.***

Codependency. In any community, we can find problems that need to be fixed. But we are not in community to fix each other, we are here to walk alongside until God does the fixing. We can help, but we are not responsible for others' problems.

Insecurity. We are all insecure in some ways, but overt insecurity that gets in the way of how we treat others is an obstacle to community. Community is not the place where we simply gather people around us who will tell us we are great until we can believe it ourselves. We can give each other the grace to accept ourselves as human (insecurities and all), and we are called to treat ourselves and each other with respect and integrity.

Cliquishness. As we make community available to others, we open our scope of friends and teammates to new relationships. Cliquishness—keeping our own group for ourselves and excluding others—only hurts that concept and does not promote community or growth.

Hierarchical attitudes. A healthy community enables others to give the ministry away. In a community setting, whether a team or a small group, one person setting himself or herself above the others as hierarchically superior is destructive and does little to aid in the fellowship of believers. Our task is to empower each other in community.

Competitiveness. Competitiveness can take the form of game-playing, stemming from insecurity. In community, if we are encouraging one another's growth and growing together as believers, we don't compete, but applaud others' successes.

Lack of appropriate confidentiality. Confidentiality is a must in the context of community. What we are willing to share about others may not be what they want us to share about them. Therefore, if we want to have rich, meaningful, vulnerable community experiences, we must observe an agreed-upon confidentiality. This comes only from healthy communication within a group.

Lack of direction. With a leadership core team or a small group, community suffers when we don't know where we are going and why. Some would say, "That's

---

OBSTACLES TO COMMUNITY

- Lone Rangers looking for Tontos
- Community gluttons
- Codependence
- Insecurity
- Cliquishness
- Hierarchical attitudes
- Competitiveness
- Lack of appropriate confidentiality
- Lack of direction

---

why I should be the leader!" Wrong. A group consensus can help bring direction. Without a clear purpose, we will flounder, lack enthusiasm, and usually fail. Discuss the purpose up front and evaluate it periodically to ensure that you are moving along the path you have chosen together. Use the Rocket planning process outlined in chapter 9 to help develop group direction and facilitate community at the same time.

THE BENEFITS OF COMMUNITY

Community is a place where other people take care of me, not in a dependent way, but with my consent. Community is a series of relationships that don't start and stop at a meeting time or location. Community is a small group of three to twelve peers and friends with whom I am in ministry. In my community, I come weary from battle with myself, others, and the world, or I come full of joy from successes or great things that have happened for me, those around me, or the world in general. Regardless of my condition when I approach my relationships in community, I know that I am loved and forgiven by those around me—because we are committed to one another. We are in this together for the long haul. In community, I am blessed with a number of great models for healthy relationships.

REFLECT AND REVIEW

Think about the material in this chapter, then answer the following questions. Remember, don't try to do the ministry alone. Whenever possible, discuss these questions with your single adult leadership team.

　　1. Are you taking care of your need for community? Are you involved in a supportive small group? If not, how can you do it?

　　2. How can you promote community in your singles ministry? What opportunities are available?

3. What are you currently doing to promote and instill community with the singles ministry leadership team in your church? What are the biggest hindrances?

4. Which of the following aspects of community are the most difficult for you to do? Think about your small group. How are you doing as a group in each of these areas?

    a. Be vulnerable.

    b. Share dreams.

    c. Encourage dreams.

    d. Be accountable to others.

    e. Grow together.

    f. Grow individually.

5. Review the list of obstacles listed on page 157. Which ones hinder you from experiencing true community?

MEMO

TO: Terry

FROM: Rich and Karen

RE: Chapter 11: Learning to Say No

We've talked a lot in this book about boundaries, or learning to say no, which is not easy. Somehow the church system mitigates against healthy boundaries. So how can we stay sane? How can we learn to say no?

- Give us some insight into the process of setting boundaries and self-care.
- Tell about our need for a time to ourselves.
- Help us know what Sabbath looks like.

Learning to Say No

Terry Hershey

His response still troubles me. The pastor of a fairly large suburban church had asked my opinion about the most essential next step for the associate minister, now responsible for beginning a single adult ministry.

I told him, "Make sure he has a Sabbath day."

The pastor responded, "You know, all of our staff get one day off per week. But I'm proud to say that none of the staff take them."

This approach to ministry is all too common. For paid staff and lay workers alike. The tireless laborer working for the Kingdom of God, sprinkled with a liberal dose of uneasiness, reminding us that somehow in our flurry of activity we are still not meeting all of the needs of the community. Consequently, in the name of sincerity and Christian care, we push ourselves to the breaking point. In the end, we too often splinter, tear, or crash.

With such an approach to ministry and life in general, I'm convinced that no "essential next programming steps" will make a difference.

I know. Some may think I'm being naive. After all, we live in a fast-paced world, and those who lag behind get devoured. Calendars are unyielding. Crises are inopportune. Needs must be met. If that pressure is not enough, you can be assured in church work there's always someone ready to tell you there's something you're not doing!

Unfortunately, more is never enough.

We in the church have been co-opted by a system that sacrifices people in favor of productivity. We've been convinced that success is tied to exploits and conquests. We've bought the cultural tape that says we achieve distinction and prominence through being spectacular and entertaining. We believe that reputation is essential and tied to the number of trinkets we collect. Somewhere in the back of our mind, we think that God believes the same.

An exaggeration? Perhaps, but I don't think so.

LEADERSHIP AS SELF-CARE

The difficulty lies in the fact that change begins with us. This reminder takes us back to the first chapter, where we premised that effective leadership is self-responsibility. It means confronting those obstacles in our lives that continually tempt us to give in to ministry modes of hurriedness, performance, and entertainment.

Anne Wilson Schaef and Diane Fassel, writing in *The Addictive Organization*, say leadership is not control (or, we can add, performance, entertainment, or being powerful). It is first and foremost a model of self-responsibility. "Leaders' power would come from their honesty and from their willingness to live their own process and respect the process of other persons."[1]

It does not matter whether you are a full-time, part-time, or an every-now-and-then leader. It does not matter whether you are paid, not paid, or ill-paid. It does not matter whether you work exclusively in single adult ministry or are a jack-of-all-trades. The principle applies to all: Only as we are changing and growing can our ministry change and grow. Ministry flows from a real life—a life that practices self-care. Effective ministry is modeled. As the old adage says, it is caught, not taught.

The theology of self-care is about the theology of "Sabbath." By Sabbath, we do not refer to the age-old argument about the correct day for worship. We adhere to Jesus' practice of regular rest, of times of stopping. Ironically, we do not reflect our theology of Sabbath in our statement of faith, but on our calendars. Our calendars betray what we believe about boundaries, time for rest, and time for friends and family.

This subject often puts us on the defensive. It confronts our difficulty with discipline and the ways we're convinced we "should" be different. It confronts our need to blame ("I'm so busy!") and get our self-worth from what we do and how we perform ("But so many great things are happening!"). Pascal, a seventeenth-century French mathematician and theologian, was right when he said that by means of a diversion, people can avoid their own company twenty-four hours a day!

Sabbath is God's call for us to learn to stop, learn to receive, and begin to understand what it means to "be at home."

THE CALL FOR SABBATH

Church representatives often ask me, "What seminars can you do for us?"

"I have a new one on Sabbath," I reply.

"That won't sell. How about one on intimacy or sex? Or something on guaranteed program ideas? Or best singles curriculum?"

We are continually tempted to "do something." We've heard the challenge about our need to stop. Now, O teacher, give us three to five easy steps. With our continual need for control, we seek programmatic containment for life, significance, fulfillment, and purpose and identity. If we have a problem, let's do something!

A visiting minister asked a monk at Saint Andrew's Priory (a benedictine monastery), "What do you do?"

"We pray," responded the monk.

"Why?" asked the visitor. "I mean, what is the reason for your prayers? What do you accomplish when you pray?"

"It is enough," the monk assured him, "just to pray."

Our Western mind-set translates all of life into pragmatic components. Our potential value is measured by our ability to produce, create, or generate. We determine our existence by doing. (How many programs? How many people? How many events on the calender?) Consequently, Sabbath is a foreign concept to most of us. For Sabbath is not doing at all.

What is "Sabbath"? And why is it so important to us? It may be best to begin with a glimpse of our misunderstandings and misconceptions.

Sabbath does not equal a day off. A day off is a utilitarian invention. We say, for example, "This is a good idea; so if I take a day off, it will make me work better." Or our pious side says, "Therefore, taking a Sabbath will make me a better leader, or a better Christian."

> *The plain and simple fact is, Sabbath is not what you do, it is what you don't do.*

Nor is it the day in which we can do all the little things that couldn't get done last week.

Nor is it always Sunday (or Saturday), for many of us work on that day, and it's the craziest day in the week.

No doubt many of you think this is a strange subject for a book about giving the ministry away. I understand the suspicion. I also know that without this reminder, "ministry" is reduced to keeping busy by keeping a group of people occupied. Such activism only serves to short-circuit any renewal. For the plain and simple fact is, Sabbath is not what you do, it is what you don't do.

Sabbath means to quit. Stop. Rest. Take a break. In fact, there is nothing particularly devout, holy, or Christian in the word Sabbath. What you do with the concept of Sabbath makes it holy or special. The implication of this concept is what we would call a "waste of time." We North Americans hear Sabbath and ask "Why?" "There's got to be a measurable reason," our pragmatic mind wants to argue. "We'll try it if there's a payoff," we tentatively agree.

I have often wondered why it is that we're the only culture who goes on vacation—and when we return people ask, "What did you do?" Or when we return from a weekend retreat we're asked, "Was the retreat of value?" Or, "Did you have fun?"

I believe we are afraid to waste time. I am. On one of my first trips to a monastery in the high desert of Southern California for an overnight retreat, I carted an arm load of books, Bibles, and study manuals because I wanted to be "successful"—my time was going to be productive and significant.

When I came to the dinner table, I felt somewhat chagrined, embarrassed, and guilty. I told one of the monks so. When he asked why, I responded, "Because I failed my Sabbath."

"How could you fail a Sabbath?" he asked, surprised.

"Well, I went to my room late morning, laid down on the bed, and woke up ten minutes before dinner!"

His rejoinder surprised me. "I didn't know that Sabbath was a test. Perhaps sleeping was best for you. With your personality, maybe it was the only way for you to stop long enough for God to talk to you. When you're awake and busy, you're probably in too much of a hurry to do things with God, and you don't really listen."

Henri Nouwen, in his book *Lifesigns*, tells the story about his time with Jean Vanier, a founder of homes for adult mentally handicapped persons:

> When you see the many small homes for the handicapped, you wonder if Jean and his co-workers could not use their time and energy more efficiently. While the needs of the world clamor for our attention, hundreds of capable, intelligent men and women spend their time, often all of their time, feeding broken people, helping them walk, just being with them, and giving them the small comfort of a loving word, a gentle touch, or an encouraging smile. To anyone trying to succeed in our society, which is oriented toward efficiency and control, these people are wasting their time. What they do is highly inefficient, unsuccessful, and even useless. Jean Vanier, however, believes that in this useless work for the poor the truth of God's perfect love for all people is revealed.[2]

PRACTICING SABBATH

The first step in practicing Sabbath is to unlearn our misconceptions about Sabbath. This process confronts our fears about wasting time, being nonproductive, and dreading solitude.

The next step is to hear a new definition of Sabbath. Sabbath is taking the time to quiet the internal noise and separate ourselves from the people who cling to us and the routines to which we cling. Keith Clark puts it this way in *Make Space Make Symbols*:

> If we are going to hear him knocking, we will have to make space amid the clutter and clatter of our lives. A knock at our door won't be heard if the din within is all-consuming of our attention. Making space means to be quiet— not just the kind of quiet that comes from removing sounds which beat against our eardrums. It means stilling the noise of our own thoughts and concerns and preoccupations. But it starts by removing the external noise.[3]

Perhaps the best definition I read, however, was on the counter of a Wendy's restaurant the week before Thanksgiving: "Wendy's will be closed on Thanksgiving so that employees may spend time with their families."

What is Sabbath? It is the sign around my neck that says, "Terry will be closed today so he can spend time in self-nurture."

The fact is simple: If we do not quit working one day a week, we take ourselves far too seriously—I repeat, far too seriously. Someone gave me a coffee mug that made the point bluntly: "Who voted you Messiah today?"

Okay, we're convinced. But just how do we apply this?

"Give us something to do!" the pragmatist in us shouts.

Single adult ministry is by its very nature busy, hectic, spur-of-the-moment, and fast-paced. We can easily derive our significance from our busyness. If we are indispensable, we assume everyone else is irresponsible. To be most effective at whatever we do, we need down time, renewal—Sabbath. The alternative is emotional and spiritual suicide, burnout, and resentment.

At the same time, we must avoid the temptation to simply outline an agenda for how to spend our Sabbath time. Exactly how our Sabbath time looks will vary from person to person. For some, it will be a full day; for others, twenty minutes. For some it will be relational; for others, complete solitude. No matter the specifics, some basic principles apply to all of us.

Sabbath Is Grace

If you're at all like me, this idea of Sabbath makes you feel guilty. It seems as if I can't do enough. Any attempts to make retreats, prayer time, or devotional life don't measure up. That's when I need to hear that above all else, Sabbath time is grace.

Sabbath declares that renewal begins with God's Word about us, not our word about God. Sabbath is grace. In other words, I can stop because I am loved. Where do we see God's Word about us? In the person of Jesus. In *Confessions of a Parish Priest*, Andrew Greeley writes:

> Who was the God revealed in the parables? He was the father of the prodigal son who welcomed back a ne'er-do-well and dishonest son, the crazy farmer who paid loafers a day's wage when they had worked only half an hour at the most, the judge who dismissed a case against an adulterous woman who had not even expressed guilt—a God of exuberant love who had been so captivated by His creatures that His behavior by human standards seemed mad.
>
> What kind of a God is it who falls passionately in love with His creatures, especially creatures who seem so inherently unlovable as we are?
>
> A God who is almost too good to be true.
>
> The Good News seems too good to be true.[4]

Frederick Buechner, in *Telling the Truth*, adds:

> God is the comic shepherd who gets more of a kick out of that one lost sheep once he finds it again than out of the ninety and nine who had the good sense not to get lost in the first place. God is the eccentric host who, when the country-club crowd all turn out to have other things more important to do than come live it up with him, goes out into the skid rows and soup kitchens and charity wards and brings home a freak show. The man with no legs who sells shoelaces at the corner. The old woman in the moth-eaten fur coat who

makes her daily rounds of the garbage cans. The old wino with his pint in a brown paper bag. The pusher, the whore, the village idiot who stands at the blinker light waving his hand as the cars go by. They are seated at the damask-laid table in the great hall. The candles are all lit and the champagne glasses filled. At a sign from the host, the musicians in their gallery strike up "Amazing Grace." If you have to explain it, don't bother.[5]

Before I get worked up about the myriad of details that remain undone for the next event on the calendar; before I give in to the tyranny over how my reputation will suffer from the drop in attendance; before I beat myself up for not doing enough for needy people, maybe I need to hear the good news. Amazing grace, my identity and worth are not predicated on my performance, résumé, or calendar of events.

Sabbath Is Listening Versus Doing
Sabbath is the permission to begin to see God incognito in the ordinary rhythm of life.

During another visit to the Benedictine monastery, my spiritual director suggested that I complete a listening exercise: "Take an empty pad of paper, sit alone in the garden, and write whatever God tells you."

Unaccustomed to such direct, divine dispatches, I was skeptical at best about this exercise. After thirty awkward and discomfiting minutes, I returned with my notepad, simply containing four words: "Dry cleaning. Call Tom." Some spiritual experience, I thought. My spiritual director didn't suppress his grin. "What did you expect?" he wondered, "an epistle? That you would have flowery dictums? Just because your pad contains ordinary things, you automatically assume it is not of God. Who are you to tell God He can't be involved in your laundry and your friendships?"

In *Letters to an American Lady*, C. S. Lewis writes about this difficulty in listening:

> We all go through periods of dryness in our prayers, don't we? I doubt . . . whether they are necessarily a bad symptom. I sometimes suspect that what we feel to be our best prayers are really our worst; that what we are enjoying is the satisfaction of apparent success, as in executing a dance or reciting a poem. Do our prayers sometimes go wrong because we insist on trying to talk to God when He wants to talk with us? Joy tells me that once, years ago, she was haunted one morning by a feeling that God wanted something of her, a persistent pressure like the nag of a neglected duty. And till mid-morning she kept on wondering what it was. But the moment she stopped worrying, the answer came through as plain as a spoken voice. It was "I don't want you to do anything. I want to give you something"; and immediately in her heart was peace and delight. St. Augustine says, "God gives where He finds empty hands."[6]

Sabbath Is Intentional Versus Spontaneous
We are not victims of the Sabbath. It is a choice. Ministry is not just those things to which we say yes, but to which we say no. Ministry is an aerobic sport; it takes time and practice.

Choices are never easy. I can relate once again to Keith Clark, who in thinking about making space for God conjured up images of walking in a serene garden, reading, and speaking softly with others. Yet he recalls:

> I don't remember such a day! I don't like gardening; I'm a poor reader; I usually talk loud. I'm usually too busy with things far removed from the natural and the humane. My life is filled with telephones, machines that don't work right, deadlines that have just passed without the job being finished, people who want to talk, cars that are a thousand miles past due for a tune-up, airplanes to catch or which haven't arrived on time, conventions to attend, interviews to conduct, talks or papers to be written, people to visit. Making space in the midst of all that is a trick. Space doesn't happen.[7]

> *Sabbath means . . . giving up the excuse that we are victims of the Day-Timer. In fact, the most practical advice I can give is to buy a red pen, take out your calendar, and put an X somewhere on your weekly schedule. The X says, "I'm closed here."*

Sabbath means being intentional with our calendars, giving up the excuse that we are victims of the Day-Timer. In fact, the most practical advice I can give is to buy a red pen, take out your calendar, and put an X somewhere on your weekly schedule. The X says, "I'm closed here."

"I don't see how it's possible," responded one woman at a recent leadership training conference. "I mean, it sounds like a good idea, but it doesn't fit reality. I'm a nurse and work nights. My husband works days. We pass like ships in the night. We have one child with another on the way. I work every other Saturday. And the pastor asked us to teach the singles' Sunday school class. So how can we do this red X?"

Her scenario is not that uncommon—people up to their ears in commitments and obligations. I affirmed her for even being at the conference and then suggested respectfully, "I believe in starting slow and small. I recommend that you teach the class three Sundays out of the month. On the fourth Sunday, have the class teach themselves or have one of the class members teach. You and your husband hire a baby-sitter and the two of you go play."

Her comment was immediate, "But what will the pastor think?"

"I hope he thinks he has very wise leaders," I told her. "The alternative is that in nine months he will have two very overworked, burned out, and 'crazy' leaders."

Effective ministry begins when we admit that we are not indispensable, which is not always fun, because it means saying no to a lot of good things. We say no for the sake of personal sanity, for emotional and spiritual health.

Sabbath Is Centering Versus Excessive Activity

Centering is not a cosmic trance. Nor is it an emptying of the mind. It simply means to be focused. The alternative is to have our attention—mind, heart, and soul—diverted in many directions. When we give our attention to the "many things," we suffer from the "Martha Syndrome." We find the story in Luke's gospel—Jesus gently scolding Martha, "You worry and fuss about a lot of things."[8] In contrast, we are told that Mary has chosen the most important thing. She was centered, not pulled in many directions. Being centered is difficult because we too easily find our identity in the many things.

Sabbath is a divine reminder. A reminder of who owns us. A reminder that life is lived from the inside out. A reminder that God is ultimately in control.

Whenever I lecture on this subject, there is a lingering confusion. Now what does he really mean by Sabbath? What is or isn't allowed?

Is it devotions? It can be, but then not every devotional time is a Sabbath.

Is it doing a hobby? Maybe, if the hobby allows you to be in a posture where you listen.

Is it time off? Yes, but not for utilitarian reasons.

Is it resting? Yes, but not just to catch up with life.

Is it Sunday? It can be, but it need not be confined to that one day.

Should this be a religious activity? Can God possibly speak to you if you are not consciously thinking about Him? Here's where we face a misconception. For Sabbath is essentially not a religious event. It is a non-event.

"But what activities are allowed?" our mind asks, still wanting closure. Can we listen to music? Watch television? Just sit? Go to a movie? Read a book? Work in the garden? Take a walk? Take a nap?

I can't answer those questions for you. The answers will vary from person to person. I do know that the following questions are helpful for me in determining my "red-X" time for Sabbath:

- Does the time remind me of grace?
- Does it let me receive?
- Does it let me be quiet?
- Does it take me off the rat-race wheel?
- Does it let me be centered, focused on the most important things?
- Does it remind me that I am not God?
- Does it help me break down the wall between sacred and secular?

I realize that I can't resolve all the questions for you. (But remember, the Jewish leaders tried to do just that and ended up with reams of laws—not to mention headaches—about what was or was not allowed on Sabbath.) There's even a good possibility that I have raised more questions than I have answered. But this much I do know emphatically: Sabbath is a must for emotional and spiritual sanity. I've seen too many people—working diligently and faithfully and caring in single adult ministry—end up resenting the very people with whom they minister. Because they were never given the permission to stop. To refuel. To be nurtured.

But my theory about what you should do is not nearly as important as that you do it! Practice it. Try it. Take out your red pen and place some X's on your calendar. Let it become a habit. Then you can give each other permission to practice—and stop.

REFLECT AND REVIEW

Think about the material in this chapter, then answer the following questions.

1. What are our fears about taking a regular Sabbath. (Fears about wasting time? Being nonproductive? The dread of solitude?)

2. Reread this new definition of Sabbath: "It is quieting the internal noise. It is the time necessary to separate ourselves from the people who cling to us. It is the time necessary to separate ourselves from the routines to which we cling." What does this mean to you?

3. Sabbath means being intentional with our calendars. Buy a red pen, take out your calendar, and put an X somewhere on your weekly schedule. The X says, "I'm closed here."

4. Can you think of a time that . . .

   a. Reminded you of grace?

   b. Let you receive?

   c. Let you be quiet?

   d. Took you off the rat-race wheel?

   e. Let you be centered?

   f. Reminded you that you are not God?

   g. Helped you break down the wall between sacred and secular?

Try a Sabbath!

IDEAS AND RESOURCES FOR RELATIONAL SINGLE ADULT MINISTRY

Chapter 12: Team-Building Retreats (page 171)
This chapter provides agendas for one-, two-, and three-day retreats,
including suggestions for using this book's material. Learn why these retreats
are great ways to train leaders and build communication
and fellowship within teams.

Chapter 13: Leadership Training Seminars (page 187)
This chapter offers schedules for either a six-week or one-day seminar to train
single adults and equip them for leadership. Seminar schedules include
suggestions for using this book's material.

Chapter 14: Leadership Training Tools (page 199)
This chapter contains worksheets for teams to use to work through the material
in this book. The worksheets cover every phase of the process described for
"giving the ministry away."

Following chapter 14, you'll find other resource materials—answers to
some **Tough Questions** in chapter 15 (page 244), a **Glossary** (page 247),
Notes (page 251), and a **Bibliography** (page 253).

MEMO

TO: Karen

FROM: Rich and Terry

RE: Chapters 12: Team-Building Retreats

We've covered a lot of material about building teams, communication, self-care. Earlier we mentioned that retreats are helpful. Can you give us some guidelines for developing an effective retreat?

CHAPTER TWELVE

Team-Building Retreats

Karen Butler

A popular trend today is building teamwork through outdoor experiences. These programs promote communication and teamwork amid a challenging outdoor experience. While we may not go to the extremes of having teams take "death walks" on a narrow board several feet off the ground, relying on their teammates for support, we do believe in gathering people for an annual team-building retreat.

GUIDELINES FOR TEAM-BUILDING RETREATS

What Is a Team-Building Retreat?

A team-building retreat is a gathering of leaders for a time of personal and corporate growth and vision. The purposes for a team-building retreat are many:

1. To build a sense of teamwork for those involved in the ministry.
2. To train leaders.
3. To provide ongoing support through networking various ministries together.
4. To share a common vision to accomplish ministry goals.
5. To dream about individual areas of ministry and how our ministries can interact with the rest of the community and the world.

Why Have a Team-Building Retreat?

Team-building retreats provide time for instruction and training of leaders. During this time, new recruits, as well as veteran leaders, develop vision for the singles ministry and for their personal ministry roles. These retreats offer a time for leaders to develop friendships and to give an assessment of the team and where it's going. Retreats offer leaders time to step back from daily routines and rekindle long-term visions for ministry. Finally, team-building retreats give us time to celebrate, have fun, enjoy free time, laugh a lot, and take a breather. We need it.

Who Is Involved in a Team-Building Retreat?

Invite current, past, and potential future leaders in your ministry. Many team-building retreats include members of other ministries that may benefit from networking as well as from their own team building. Other retreats can be smaller with just one leadership core team.

For a single adult ministry team-building retreat, your invitation list may simply be your singles leadership core team or a group of young adult leaders, divorce recovery leaders, and single parents. You will need to make that decision, depending on the nature of your ministry. If you choose to hold a team-building retreat with related ministry teams, I'd recommend meeting six months later with just your small team for more intimate team building.

What Do We Do at a Team-Building Retreat?

Part of our time together is spent reporting and finding out where the ministry has come from and where it is headed. During this time, review the previous year's Rocket (see chapter 9). This is a great opportunity to reflect on the milestones, where God has brought us during the past year. In addition, use your team-building time to develop short- and long-range goals and develop a new planning Rocket.

In the retreat outlines, we list possible presentation ideas with points for the speaker to highlight. You may want to delete one of these presentations and have your retreat participants take the Team-Building Assessment or the Role Preference Test (both found in chapter 14). This depends on your situation and what you would like to accomplish at the retreat.

How Often Do We Have Team-Building Retreats?

The frequency of team-building retreats depends on the makeup and terms of your leadership team. If new team members commit to serve for one year, you could have a three-day team-building retreat at the beginning of the term year—a great time to "pass the baton" between the former leadership team and the new team. Hold a short, one-day retreat mid-year as an enthusiasm-builder, then have another three-day retreat at the end of the year as new team members begin their leadership. If your team members serve six-month commitments, host a longer retreat at the beginning and end of the term, with a one-day retreat in the middle of the term. Again, the frequency of team-building retreats depends on your group.

Who Leads the Team-Building Retreat?

Leadership of team-building retreats depends on the retreat. For a small group that works together as one leadership core team, the retreat may be led by the team or pastoral leader. For a larger group made up of several ministry teams, the retreat may run more smoothly when led by a committee composed of one member from each ministry team.

The person to whom the leadership team is accountable—leader, pastor, staff member—must take some form of leadership at the retreat. That means that the staff member responsible for the leadership team may be the speaker, or may arrange for an outside speaker. The staff member should be on hand during the weekend and, at the minimum, should conduct the welcome, introduction, and affirmation of leaders. Involvement of staff members affirms the retreat participants and shows them how important their leadership is to the overall church ministry.

The team-building retreat includes two essential ingredients:

■ An understanding that nothing is impossible.
■ A spirit of fun and laughter.

This usually is the only time during a year when team members come together to play as well as dream, and we firmly believe that both add to a spirit of teamwork and sense of community.

HOW TO USE THIS CHAPTER

The following one-, two-, or three-day team-building retreat agendas can be adapted for use by your particular group. The retreats are written to handle several ministry teams. If you plan a retreat for one small leadership core team, simply conduct the activities together rather than dividing into small groups.

Determine which retreat you want to plan for your team. Go to that section and glance over the agenda. Note that you will need to choose some options ahead of time. The most basic instruction is to plan ahead! Choose a retreat agenda, pick options, and decide who and what you will need to get the most out of the retreat.

In keeping with our philosophy of "giving the ministry away," remember not to plan this retreat all by yourself. If you anticipate a small group of participants (under ten members), ask at least one other team member to help you organize it. If you anticipate a medium-size group of participants (ten to twenty members representing more than one

> *In keeping with our philosophy of "giving the ministry away," remember not to plan this retreat all by yourself.*

ministry), have four or five people work together on planning the retreat. If you anticipate a large number of participants (fifty or more members representing many ministries), ask eight to ten people to work together with you in an advisory role. Pages 203-208 in chapter 14 list job duties for various retreat planning team members. Use the list to help you plan the retreat.

Once you determine your group size and who is going to help plan, consider these items together:

Supplies
Ensure supplies are on hand for whatever you do. If you post a discussion question on the wall, are you going to post it on a large sheet of paper or on an overhead projector? Is there an overhead projector available? If you are having people settle into

cabins or rooms for the overnight retreat, do you need maps? Where can you get them? What instructions do you want to have written for the participants? For refreshments, are you going to ask each participant to bring his or her favorite food, or are you going to supply it?

Other supplies you'll need for the retreat include paper, pencils, songbooks, extra Bibles, copies of worksheets from this book (see page 199), information to be handed out to new recruits, supplies for musicians to lead singing, supplies for the team-building activities, and so on. Read through each step of the agenda to decide what you will need to bring and who will bring it. Also, tell participants what they need to bring—sleeping bag, towels, Bible, notebook, etc.

A Goal for the Retreat
State the goal up front, for all the retreat participants to see or hear—it tells people why they are there. This goal may be amended to best suit your group, depending on whether they are veteran leaders, newcomers, a small group, a large group, etc. Here's an example of a retreat goal:

> We come together as a team for strategy, relationship, and renewal. We come here to step back and look at what we are doing in ministry, to develop new plans together, to get to know each other more, to have fun together, and to celebrate the great things God is doing in and through His people.

At the end of the retreat, ask the participants to reflect on the following questions:

- Have we strategized? (Do we know where we are going?)
- Have we built relationships? (Do you know others better than when you arrived?)
- Have we been renewed? (Have we had fun, laughed, or relaxed in any way?)

Get-Acquainted Time
This introductory period poses many alternatives. Some groups, especially when members don't know each other well, need a structured activity or discussion questions to facilitate introductions. Others prefer to just place their things in their rooms and return to start the retreat right away. Each group is unique. I've been in many groups where all that was needed to get acquainted was a table full of junk food—the grazing automatically stimulated conversation! Another get-acquainted idea is to write a question on newsprint and post it on the wall. For example, "Why are you involved or interested in single adult ministry?" Encourage people to mingle and discuss their answer to the question. The idea you use will depend on your group members, so think about how to make this introductory time easiest for them.

Presentations and Speakers
Before the retreat, think of these questions: Do you want to have someone come speak to your group, or do you plan to do this yourself? Do you want to share it with other

group members? Part of this decision will depend on your budget. The presentation materials shown in the retreat agendas are suggestions. If you have never planned a retreat before, the agendas will give you guidelines for presentations, including scripture references and topics from this book. Experienced speakers can use these ideas to coincide with their own materials, or they can develop their own presentations altogether. These agendas are suggestions, not requirements.

Discussion Starters

To facilitate conversation in the small-group sessions, start with a discussion starter to warm everybody up. Here are some ideas of questions to ask group members to discuss with the person sitting next to them:

1. What is something crazy you did in high school?
2. What is something you've always wanted to do?
3. How do others know when you are happy?
4. What has been your favorite vacation?
5. If you could pick only one luxury to have in your home, what would it be?
6. What is one thing you respect most in a family member?

Team-Building Activities

These light, fun activities enable your group members to get quickly acquainted with one another. Plan ahead for these activities. Remember to bring the supplies and/or have the participants bring what they'll need. In addition to the activities listed in the retreat agendas (see pages 178, 180, 183), here are some other options.

Line-Up Race. The purpose of this activity is to have light fun while people are meeting one another, possibly for the first time. Divide large groups into fifteen-member teams. Have the teams race to arrange themselves in alphabetical order by their mother's maiden name, in order of birthdays, and finally, in order of weight at their birth.

Baby Pictures. Use this with a group of people who already know each other well. Ask each participant to bring a baby picture, and then put the pictures on the wall. Have people guess who's who.

Famous Persons Game. On each participant's back, place a name tag with the name of a famous personality written on it (Mother Teresa, the president, an actor, a cartoon character, etc.). Participants ask yes-or-no questions of each other and try to guess the name on their back. (Am I a male? Am I an author? Am I living?) Once they have guessed the identity correctly, they move their name tag to the front of their shirt.

Various activities exist to help participants mingle and get to know one another. Use the ideas listed above or check out books at the library. Use your imagination when deciding on activities to use with your group.

Dream Sessions

The retreat agendas tell you to divide up into ministry teams (see page 178). If several ministry teams are attending the retreat, divide into teams to work through the dream session. If this retreat is for your own small core team, simply do this exercise as a group.

ONE-DAY RETREAT

(8:00 a.m. to 5:00 p.m.)

8:00-8:30   Registration/Get Acquainted

8:30-8:40   Introduction and Singing
Retreat Goal: "We come together as a team for strategy, relationship, and renewal. We come here to step back and look at what we are doing in ministry, to develop new plans together, to get to know each other more, to have fun together, and to celebrate the great things God is doing in and through His people."

8:40-9:30   First Presentation: Developing Vision—How and Why
Highlight these points in the presentation:
1. Who God is and who we are. See chapter 4, pages 49-50. Also see John 10:11-18 (the Good Shepherd) and John 15:1-18 (the vine and the branches).
2. Our essential aim—the gospel. See chapter 4, pages 48-49. Also see 2 Corinthians 5:17-20.
3. How we minister to others through:
    a. Loving the people around us. See chapter 7, pages 93-96. Also see John 13:1-17 (Jesus washing the disciples' feet).
    b. Finding a place where we want to be and ministering there. See chapter 8. Remember that ministry is fun, so find something to do that you love, and do it.

9:30-10:15   Small Groups
Form groups of four to six people. Post these questions on the wall and encourage small groups to answer them.
   Discussion Starter, see page 176.
1. Describe the most positive experience you have ever had with a Christian group.
2. What (or who) has God used in your involvement in the group to change your life (i.e., relationship, prayer, learning to trust, etc.)?
3. Describe how God is changing you personally (for example, handling money/stewardship, dealing with moral issues, attitude in ministry/humility).
4. What would you like to see happen in your group (that is not happening now) that would meet one of your needs?
5. If you had to leave your present place of ministry, what would you want in another place of fellowship?

10:15-10:30   Break

10:30-11:00   Second Presentation: Review Your Philosophy of Ministry
Distribute copies of your philosophy of ministry, then ask the following questions in the large group:
1. In what ways has our picture of God and His role in this ministry been evident in the past six months?
2. In what ways is what we believe about Scripture evident?
3. What does our ministry say about how we feel about other people in this ministry?
4. Are there patterns or priorities evident in how we have been ministering in the past six months? If so, what are they?
If you don't have a philosophy of ministry, use this time to develop one (see chapter 7, pages 95-96.) The worksheet on page 209 provides questions for your team to work through.

11:00-12:00   Case Studies
Complete exercise A in the case studies in chapter 14, pages 236-237. Work through the case studies in small groups according to the instructions.

☞

12:00-1:00   Lunch

1:00-2:00   Team-Building Activity: Journey of Faith
    1. Give each person a piece of paper and a pencil. Have participants draw a diagram, picture, time line, chart, or whatever they wish to depict their own journey of faith—the journey that has taken them from first knowing there was a God who knew them by name up until the present.
    2. Encourage creativity.
    3. When people are finished preparing the journey stories, have them share one by one. Listen and affirm God's working in their lives and His faithfulness over time.

2:00-2:15   Break

2:15-2:25   Singing

2:25-3:00   Third Presentation: The Vision for the Future
Include these points in the presentation:
    1. God's concerns; humanity's needs. See Mark 6:34-44 and John 3:16-17.
    2. Encouragement for the future from Scripture. See John 14:15-21 (Jesus promises the Holy Spirit) and John 17:20-26 (Jesus' prayer for all believers).
    3. Where do we go from here? We start by:
        a. Building our own relationships with God. Include personal time of prayer, study, meditation—refer to Sabbath described in chapter 11.
        b. Being in leadership together, building relationships with one another. (See chapter 7, page 96, about team communication.)
        c. Finding your right fit in ministry—where God leads you. (See chapter 8.)

3:00-3:45   Dream Session
Ask participants to sit with their ministry teams. Have the teams discuss these questions and write the answers on a piece of paper. When they are finished, post the paper on the wall.
    1. What do you feel are some unaddressed needs for your ministry? Which do you feel strongest about (i.e., they make you "want to pound your fist on the table")?
    2. If everything were possible, what would you like to see happen to address these needs?
    3. How can we make these ideas measurable? Make a list.

3:45-4:45   Rocket Time
Ask the teams to choose one or two dreams they want to develop into ministry goals. The teams can begin developing their own planning Rocket for these dreams (see chapter 9). The teams won't have time to finish their Rockets. Schedule a future meeting to finish planning—on a Saturday morning or a weeknight no later than two to three weeks following this retreat. Allow two to three hours for this follow-up meeting.

4:45-5:00   Closing
End the retreat on a positive note by:
    1. Asking two or three people to share spontaneously what dreams or plans they are most excited about.
    2. Thanking those who planned the retreat and people for coming.
    3. Praying together. Thank God for each participant and his or her dreams and goals for the ministry.

TWO-DAY RETREAT

(One evening and one full day)

7:00-7:30 p.m. Registration/Get Acquainted
Post this question on the wall: "What do you hope to accomplish during this retreat?"
Encourage people to register, then get acquainted by mingling and discussing answers to the
question.

7:30-7:45   Introduction and Singing
Retreat Goal: "We come together as a team for strategy, relationship, and renewal. We come
here to step back and look at what we are doing in ministry, to develop new plans together, to
get to know each other more, to have fun together, and to celebrate the great things God is
doing in and through His people."

7:45-8:15   Team-Building Activity
Choose from the ideas on pages 179-180.

8:15-9:00   First Presentation: Developing Vision—How and Why
Highlight these points in the presentation:
   1. Who God is and who we are. See chapter 4, pages 49-50. Also see John 10:11-18
      (the Good Shepherd) and John 15:1-18 (the vine and the branches).
   2. Our essential aim—the gospel. See chapter 4, pages 48-49. Also see 2 Corinthians
      5:17-20.
   3. How we minister to others through:
      a. Loving the people around us. See chapter 7, pages 93-96. Also see John
         13:1-17 (Jesus washing the disciples' feet).
      b. Finding a place where we want to be and ministering there. See chapter 8.
         Remember that ministry is joyful, so find something to do that you love, and do it.

9:00-10:00   Team-Building Activity: Journey of Faith
   1. Give each person a piece of paper and a pencil. Have participants draw a diagram,
      picture, time line, chart, or whatever they wish to depict their own journey of faith—
      the journey that has taken them from first knowing there was a God who knew them
      by name up until the present.
   2. Encourage creativity.
   3. When people are finished preparing the journey stories, have them share one by one.
      Listen and affirm God's working in their lives and His faithfulness over time.

SECOND DAY

8:00-9:00   Breakfast

9:00-9:15   Singing

9:15-10:00   Second Presentation: Who Are Ministers, and What Is Our
**   Ministry Vision?**
Highlight these points in the presentation:
   1. Who does God call to minister? See chapter 4, pages 52-54. Also see 1 Peter 2:4-12.
   2. What is ministry? See chapter 4.
   3. What is our ministry vision?
      a. Open hearts and minds to God. We are ministering because of God, who has
         called us to ministry and leads us in it. This means we pray and study, drawing
         closer and relying on Him for guidance.

      b. Care for others (see chapter 7, page 94). Both fellowship and encouragement are essential for caring for others.

      c. Taking appropriate action to meet needs (see chapter 3, pages 37-41).

10:00-10:45   Small Groups

Form groups of four to six people. Post these questions on the wall and encourage small groups to answer them.

    Discussion Starter, see page 176.

    1. Describe the most positive experience you have ever had with a Christian group.

    2. What (or who) has God used in your involvement in the group to change your life (i.e., relationship, prayer, learning to trust, etc.)?

    3. Describe how God is changing you personally (for example, handling money/stewardship, dealing with moral issues, attitude in ministry/humility).

    4. What would you like to see happen in your group (that is not happening now) that would meet one of your needs?

    5. If you had to leave your present place of ministry, what would you want in another place of fellowship?

10:45-11:00   Break

11:00-11:30   Third Presentation: Review Your Philosophy of Ministry

Distribute copies of your philosophy of ministry, then ask the following questions in the large group:

    1. In what ways has our picture of God and His role in this ministry been evident in the past six months?

    2. In what ways is what we believe about scripture evident?

    3. What does our ministry say about how we feel about other people in this ministry?

    4. Are there patterns or priorities evident in how we have been ministering in the past six months? If so, what are they?

If you don't have a philosophy of ministry, use this time to develop one (see chapter 7, pages 95-96.) The worksheet on page 209 provides questions for your team members to work through.

11:30-12:15   Case Studies

Complete exercise A in the case studies in chapter 14, pages 236-237. Work through the case studies in small groups according to the instructions.

12:15-1:00   Lunch

1:00-2:00   Team-Building: Body Parts

Give each person a piece of paper and a pencil. Ask group members to answer these questions then discuss with each other:

    1. If you were to attach a physical body part to help you in your ministry, what would it be? Write it down or draw it. For example, a hand to help me with all my duties, an ear to listen to others, a smile to keep me happy and to help me encourage others.

    2. What is one area of personal need for you, and why? For example, an arm to hug me when I feel discouraged.

    3. List and share one quality you appreciate in each group member. List the qualities each person said he or she appreciates about you.

2:00-2:15   Break

2:15-2:25   Singing

2:25-3:00   Fourth Presentation: The Vision for the Future
Include these points in the presentation:
    1. God's concerns; humanity's needs. See Mark 6:34-44 and John 3:16-17.
    2. Encouragement for the future from Scripture. See John 14:15-21 (Jesus promises the Holy Spirit) and John 17:20-26 (Jesus' prayer for all believers).
    3. Where do we go from here? We start by:
        a. Building our own relationships with God. Include personal time of prayer, study, meditation—refer to Sabbath described in chapter 11.
        b. Being in leadership together, building relationships with one another. (See chapter 7, page 96, about team communication.)
        c. Finding your right fit in ministry—where God leads you. (See chapter 8.)

3:00-3:45   Dream Session
Ask participants to sit with their ministry teams. Have the teams discuss these questions and write the answers on a piece of paper. When they are finished, post the paper on the wall.
    1. What do you feel are some unaddressed needs for your ministry? Which do you feel strongest about (i.e., they make you "want to pound your fist on the table")?
    2. If everything were possible, what would you like to see happen to address these needs?
    3. How can we make these ideas measurable? Make a list.

3:45-4:45   Rocket Time
Ask the teams to choose one or two dreams they want to develop into ministry goals. The teams can begin developing their own planning Rocket for these dreams (see chapter 9). The teams won't have time to finish their Rockets. Schedule a future meeting to finish planning—on a Saturday morning or a weeknight no later than two to three weeks following this retreat. Allow two to three hours for this follow-up meeting.

4:45-5:00   Closing
End the retreat on a positive note by:
    1. Asking two or three people to share spontaneously what dreams or plans they are most excited about.
    2. Thanking those who planned the retreat and people for coming.
    3. Praying together. Thank God for each participant and his or her dreams and goals for the ministry.

THREE-DAY RETREAT

(Friday night through Sunday afternoon)

FIRST DAY

7:00-7:30 p.m.   Registration/Get Acquainted

7:30-7:45   Introduction and Singing
Retreat Goal: "We come together as a team for strategy, relationship, and renewal. We come here to step back and look at what we are doing in ministry, to develop new plans together, to get to know each other more, to have fun together, and to celebrate the great things God is doing in and through His people."

7:45-8:15   Team-Building Activity: Interview Partners
The purpose of this activity is to have fun while people are meeting one another, possibly for the first time. Have people find one person they don't know and sit down and interview them, finding out as much as possible about each other in five minutes (two and a half minutes each). Call time after the five minutes expires and have each person introduce his or her partner to the rest of the group.

8:15-9:00   First Presentation: Developing Vision—How and Why
Highlight these points in the presentation:
1. Who God is and who we are. See chapter 4, pages 49-50. Also see John 10:11-18 (the Good Shepherd) and John 15:1-18 (the vine and the branches).
2. Our essential aim—the gospel. See chapter 4, pages 48-49. Also see 2 Corinthians 5:17-20.
3. How we minister to others through:
   a. Loving the people around us. See chapter 7, pages 93-96. Also see John 13:1-17 (Jesus washing the disciples' feet).
   b. Finding a place where we want to be and ministering there. See chapter 8. Remember that ministry is fun, so find something to do that you love, and do it.

9:00-10:00   Team-Building Activity: Journey of Faith
1. Give each person a piece of paper and a pencil. Have participants draw a diagram, picture, time line, chart, or whatever they wish to depict their own journey of faith— the journey that has taken them from first knowing there was a God who knew them by name up until the present.
2. Encourage creativity.
3. When people are finished preparing the journey stories, have them share one by one. Listen and affirm God's working in their lives and His faithfulness over time.

SECOND DAY

8:00-9:00   Breakfast

9:00-9:15   Singing

9:15-10:00   Second Presentation: Who Are Ministers, and What Is Our Ministry Vision?
Highlight these points in the presentation:
1. Who does God call to minister? See chapter 4, pages 52-54. Also see 1 Peter 2:4-12.
2. What is ministry? See chapter 4.
3. What is our ministry vision?
   a. Open hearts and minds to God. We are ministering because of God, who has

called us to ministry and leads us in it. This means we pray and study, drawing closer and relying on Him for guidance.

b. Care for others (see chapter 7, page 94). Both fellowship and encouragement are essential for caring for others.

c. Taking appropriate action to meet needs (see chapter 3, pages 37-41).

10:00-10:45   Small Groups
Form groups of four to six people. Post these questions on the wall and encourage small groups to answer them.
Discussion Starter, see page 176.
1. Describe the most positive experience you have ever had with a Christian group.
2. What (or who) has God used in your involvement in the group to change your life (i.e., relationship, prayer, learning to trust, etc.)?
3. Describe how God is changing you personally (for example, handling money/stewardship, dealing with moral issues, attitude in ministry/humility).
4. What would you like to see happen in your group (that is not happening now) that would meet one of your needs?
5. If you had to leave your present place of ministry, what would you want in another place of fellowship?

10:45-11:00   Break

11:00-12:00   Personal Devotion/Prayer Time

12:00-1:00   Lunch

1:00-2:00   Team-Building: Body Parts
Give each person a piece of paper and a pencil. Ask group members to answer these questions then discuss with each other:
1. If you were to attach a physical body part to help you in your ministry, what would it be? Write it down or draw it. For example, a hand to help me with all my duties, an ear to listen to others, a smile to keep me happy and to help me encourage others.
2. What is one area of personal need for you, and why? For example, an arm to hug me when I feel discouraged.
3. List and share one quality you appreciate in each group member. List the qualities each person said he or she appreciates about you.

2:00-3:00   Case Studies
Choose any exercises and accompanying case studies in chapter 14. Work through the case studies in small groups according to the instructions.

3:00-3:45   Recreation

3:45-4:15   Third Presentation: Review Your Philosophy of Ministry
Distribute copies of your philosophy of ministry, then ask the following questions in the large group:
1. In what ways has our picture of God and His role in this ministry been evident in the past six months?
2. In what ways is what we believe about Scripture evident?
3. What does our ministry say about how we feel about other people in this ministry?
4. Are there patterns or priorities evident in how we have been ministering in the past six months? If so, what are they?
If you don't have a philosophy of ministry, use this time to develop one (see chapter 7, pages 95-96). The worksheet on page 209 provides questions for your team members to work through.

4:15-5:00   Case Studies
Complete exercise A in the case studies in chapter 14, pages 236-237. Work through the case studies in small groups according to the instructions.

5:00-6:00   Dinner

6:00-6:15   Singing

6:15-7:00   Fourth Presentation: The Vision for the Future
Include these points in the presentation:
1. God's concerns; humanity's needs. See Mark 6:34-44 and John 3:16-17.
2. Encouragement for the future from scripture. See John 14:15-21 (Jesus promises the Holy Spirit) and John 17:20-26 (Jesus' prayer for all believers).
3. Where do we go from here? We start by:
   a. Building our own relationships with God. Include personal time of prayer, study, meditation—refer to Sabbath described in chapter 11.
   b. Being in leadership together, building relationships with one another. (See chapter 7, page 96, about team communication.)
   c. Finding your right fit in ministry—where God leads you. (See role preferences in chapter 8, page 112-116.)

7:00-7:30   Dream Session
Ask participants to sit with their ministry teams. Have the teams discuss these questions and write the answers on a piece of paper. When they are finished, post the paper on the wall.
1. What do you feel are some unaddressed needs for your ministry? Which do you feel strongest about (i.e., they make you "want to pound your fist on the table")?
2. If everything were possible, what would you like to see happen to address these needs?
3. How can we make these ideas measurable? Make a list.

7:30-10:00   Evening Activity/Entertainment
Host an award ceremony and affirm each individual leader for his or her contribution to the ministry. This is a great opportunity to treat those who have given so much for the ongoing cause of the ministry. Give small gifts such as Mars bars for "out-of-this-world ideas" or Snickers bars for an "always smiling and upbeat personality."

You could also hold a concert, a dance, ice cream social, or any other activity you think your leaders will enjoy as a time of fun and affirmation together. One of the funniest events is a talent show. There's no predicting the ingenious talents your group members have hidden.

THIRD DAY

8:00-9:15   Continental Breakfast and Personal Prayer Time

9:15-10:15   Worship
Include singing, prayer, and an opportunity for personal sharing facilitated by the presentation speaker. Come together to worship with a spirit of thankfulness for the fellowship and guidance God has given you for the weekend. Make that your tone for the morning.

10:15-10:30   Break

10:30-11:30   Rocket Time
Ask the teams to choose one or two dreams they want to develop into ministry goals. The teams can begin developing their own planning Rocket for these dreams (see chapter 9). The teams won't have time to finish their Rockets. Schedule a future meeting to finish

planning—on a Saturday morning or a weeknight no later than two to three weeks following this retreat. Allow two to three hours for this follow-up meeting.

11:30-11:45   Closing

End the retreat on a positive note by:

1. Asking two or three people to share spontaneously what dreams or plans they are most excited about.
2. Thanking those who planned the retreat and people for coming.
3. Praying together. Thank God for each participant and his or her dreams and goals for the ministry.

11:45-12:45   Celebration Brunch

CHAPTER THIRTEEN

Leadership Training Seminars

Karen Butler

You've read this book, enjoyed the materials, and now want to move quickly into action. You want your leaders to know what "giving the ministry away" is all about. You want to use the tools found in this book to develop your single adult leaders. Where do you start? You could start by buying copies of this book for each of your leaders and insist they read it, but that's not always a practical idea. Another alternative is to choose one of the following seminar outlines and lead your leaders through this book's material. Sound good? Let's get started. You should take several things into consideration when planning a seminar.

SEMINAR FORMAT

Decide what seminar format you want to use. Can your team of leaders commit to six weeks of training for about two hours each week? They will need to attend each week to get the full picture of "giving the ministry away." If you think this approach will work, use the seminar schedule on pages 190-194. If your team members are already overcommitted and can't fit another night into their schedule, try a one-day seminar. Use the schedule on pages 195-198.

Do not try to cover all of this material in a half-day seminar. You realistically cannot cover what you need in that amount of time. If your training time is limited, here are a couple alternatives:

Plan two half-day seminars. For example, one Saturday from 9:00 a.m. to 12 noon, cover the morning material outlined in the one-day seminar schedule (pages 195-196.) The following Saturday during the same time period, cover the afternoon material outlined on pages 197-198.

Schedule a half-day seminar to cover specific areas such as the Rocket planning process (chapter 9), role preferences (chapters 8 and 14), or team building (chapters 7 and 14).

TEAM PLANNING

Plan your seminar with a team. In keeping with our philosophy of "giving the ministry away," don't organize this seminar all by yourself. If you anticipate a small group of participants (under ten members planning to attend the seminar), ask at least one other team member to help you organize it. If you anticipate a medium-sized group of participants (ten to twenty members representing more than one ministry), have four or five people work together on planning the seminar. If you anticipate a large number of participants (fifty or more members representing many ministries), ask eight to ten people to work together, with you in an advisory role.

Supplies

Ensure supplies are on hand for whatever you do. If you post a discussion question on the wall, are you going to post it on large paper or on an overhead projector? Is there an overhead projector available? What instructions do you want to have written for the participants?

Other supplies you'll need for the retreat include paper, pencils, songbooks, extra Bibles, and copies of worksheets from this book (see page 199). Read through each step of the schedule to decide what you will need to bring and who will bring it.

Get-Acquainted Time

This introductory period poses a lot of alternatives. Some groups, especially when members don't know each other well, need a structured activity or discussion questions to facilitate introductions. Each group is unique. I've been in many groups where all that was needed to get acquainted was a table full of junk food—the grazing automatically stimulated conversation! Another get-acquainted idea is to write a question on newsprint and post it on the wall. For example, "Why are you involved or interested in single adult ministry?" Encourage people to mingle and discuss their answer to the question. The idea you use will depend on your group members, so think about how to make this introductory time easiest for them.

Presentations and Speakers

Do you want to have someone come speak to your group, or do you plan to do this yourself? Do you want to share it with other group members? Part of this decision will depend on your budget. The presentation materials shown in the seminar schedules are suggestions. If you have never planned a seminar before, the schedule will give you guidelines for presentations, including scripture references and topics from this book. Experienced speakers can use these ideas to coincide with their own materials, or they develop their own presentations altogether. These agendas are suggestions, not requirements.

Discussions

During discussion time, divide into groups depending upon the number of participants. If the seminar is for your own leadership core team only, discuss the questions together. If several ministry teams are attending the seminar, gather people with their specific team to discuss the questions.

Recap Section

During this time, review the pertinent topics taken from the book. Summarize the main points of each topic—in most cases, one sentence will do. Use your notes to help you recall and recap the main points. Schedule your time wisely, because you have so much material to cover in a short time. The recap session should be short on review and long on discussion, making it more interesting and giving leaders a "hands-on" learning experience. The seminar schedules offer specific time suggestions.

Adjust Your Schedule

Adjust the seminar schedules to fit your needs. You may want to spend more time on team communication, preferred roles, or the case studies found in chapter 14. If so, vary the schedule by skipping a certain topic or discussion on a given questions. Adjust the schedules to fit your team's needs.

SIX-WEEK LEADERSHIP TRAINING SEMINAR

WEEK ONE: Chapters 1-2

Get Acquainted (15 minutes)
Use ideas listed on page 188, or have participants find a partner to discuss their answers to this question: "What is something crazy you did in high school?"

Recap by Leader (20 minutes)
Facts About Single Adults
1. Expect transition, page 17.
2. Single adult ministry is not youth ministry, page 17.
3. Single adults cannot be "lumped together," page 18.
4. Many people in the church have misconceptions about (and are threatened by) single adults, page 18.

Myths About Single Adults
1. Single people have more time than married people, page 18.
2. Single people are less committed, page 19.
3. All single people are hurting, page 20.
4. All single people are looking for a marriage partner, page 20.

Discussion Questions (35 minutes)
Develop an evaluation based on the self-evaluation on page 12. Have team members take the test, then discuss their answers to the questions.
1. What words or phrases come to mind when you hear the phrase *single adult*? (Leader: Write these words and phrases on a poster board, flip chart, or a chalkboard for everyone to see.)
2. How many of these descriptions are negative? Positive?
3. What do we learn from these answers about our preconceived notions about single adults?

Recap by Leader (20 minutes)
Leadership—A New Definition
1. Relational leadership is a foundational assumption. See page 27.
2. Some other terms to know, see page 21.
   a. Empower
   b. Personal boundaries
   c. Self-responsibility

Becoming an Effective Minister
1. Every Christian is a minister, page 30.
2. Effective ministries are owned by the people, page 30.
3. Effective ministries empower others, page 30.
4. Effective ministries are built on a foundation of self-care, or self-responsibility, page 31.
5. Effective, successful ministries produce healthy relationships, not just predetermined goals, page 31.

Discussion (30 minutes)
1. What are some characteristics of a dominating leader?
2. What are some characteristics of a leader who delegates?
3. Is it possible to be a good leader without being absorbed by the job, without having to be all things to all people? Explain.

☞

4. What are some effective ways to combat our fear that others can't do the job as well as we can?

5. What is the best aspect about relational ministry?

WEEK TWO: Chapters 3-4

Get Acquainted (15 minutes)

Use ideas listed on page 188, or have participants find a partner to discuss their answers to this question: "What is something you've always wanted to do?"

Recap by Leader (20 minutes)

Obstacles to Effective Leadership

1. We take ourselves too seriously, page 35.
2. We assume all problems are "fixable," page 41.
3. We misunderstand success, page 42.
4. We assume people are irresponsible, page 43.
5. We have a faulty perception of leadership, page 44.

Discussion (35 minutes)

1. What are some of your personal obstacles to effective leadership? (Have everyone take the self-quiz on pages 44-45.)
2. How would you define success?
3. What are some ways in which you tend to assume people are irresponsible?
4. What are some tangible ways we can overcome those obstacles individually and as a ministry team?

Recap by Leader (20 minutes)

Characteristics of an Empowered Leader

1. An empowered leader knows to whom he or she belongs, page 49.
2. An empowered leader is self-responsible, page 51.
3. An empowered leader is a wounded healer, page 52.
4. An empowered leader knows how to play, page 54.
5. An empowered leader creates a nurturing environment, page 55.
6. An empowered leader sees beyond the immediate to the potential, page 55.
7. An empowered leader is patient, page 57.
8. An empowered leader is willing to give ministry away, page 58.

Discussion (30 minutes)

1. Why is it sometimes easy to forget who we belong to?
2. What does it mean to be self-responsible? Describe an unhealthy example and a healthy example.
3. Why is play important in the life of a leader?
4. What does it mean to give ministry away?

WEEK THREE: Chapters 5-7

Get Acquainted (15 minutes)

Use ideas listed on page 188, or have participants find a partner to discuss their answers to this question: "How do others know when you are happy?"

☞

Recap by Leader (20 minutes)
Team Selection and Time with the Team
1. Hierarchical ministry versus relational ministry, page 64.
2. Building a core team.
   a. Selecting a few, page 68.
   b. Spending time with a few, page 69.
   c. Continue development as you give leaders ownership, page 71.
3. The Jesus model, page 80.
4. When your leaders seem to fail, page 80.
   a. Clearly define the job, page 81.
   b. Make sure the task is appropriate for the leader, page 83.
   c. Have teammates to help, page 84.
   d. Establish accountability, page 85.
   e. Affirm the leader, page 85.

Discussion (35 minutes)
1. What difficulties stand in the way of building a core team of leaders and sharing ownership?
2. What are the hazards of working with volunteer leaders versus selected leaders?
3. How do we select leaders? (Where can we find them?)
4. How do we spend time with leaders?
5. How do we develop new leaders?
6. How did Jesus model leadership selection and team building?
7. Are our own jobs well-defined, or are we setting ourselves up for failure?

Recap by Leader (20 minutes)
Team Communication
1. What teams are, page 91.
2. Characteristics of effective, healthy teams.
   a. Fellowship, page 93.
   b. Encouragement, page 94.
   c. Strategy, page 94.
   d. A philosophy of ministry, page 95.
3. Procedures to help your leaders do their best, pages 96-97.
4. Principles of team membership, page 100.

Discussion (30 minutes)
Using the worksheet on page 209, have team members begin to work on a philosophy of ministry. Afterward, discuss:
1. Who do we believe God is? What role does He have in this ministry?
2. What role does Scripture play in the ministry?
3. What role do people play in the ministry?
4. How do people do ministry?

Write the answers on an overhead project or large sheet of paper, or chalkboard. Go back through the words as a group, and circle important words and phrases. Select one or two people to write a sample philosophy for review later (not in the seminar).

You can allow extra time during this meeting to complete the Team-Building Assessment found on page 220 (recommended for leaders who have been working together for at least six months), or send it home with the leaders as "homework" and schedule an additional time to go over it.

WEEK FOUR: Chapter 8

Get Acquainted (15 minutes)
Use ideas listed on page 188, or have participants find a partner to discuss their answers to this question: "What has been your favorite vacation?"

Recap by Leader (30 minutes)
Team Roles
    1. Why role preferences? How can they help us? See page 115.
    2. The four roles.
        a. Creator, page 116.
        b. Developer, page 118.
        c. Caretaker, page 120.
        d. Participant, page 121.

Discover Your Role Preference (25 minutes)
Take the Role Preference Test beginning on page 224, regardless of the length of the leaders' service. Allow twenty minutes for the test, a few minutes for scoring, and then facilitate discussion.

Discussion (35 minutes)
    1. What role preference did you select?
    2. Do you believe this assessment is accurate?
    3. How is this role manifested in your ministry today?
    4. If it is not manifested, what would you really like to do?

WEEK FIVE: Chapter 9

Get Acquainted (15 minutes)
Use ideas listed on page 188, or have participants find a partner to discuss their answers to this question: "If you could only pick one luxury to have in your home, what would it be?"

Recap by Leader (30 minutes)
Taking Aim
    1. The Rocket, page 132.
    2. The launch pad of prayer and research, page 132.
    3. The fuel: needs, page 134.
    4. The mission statement, page 136.
    5. The targets, page 137.
    6. Dream destinations, page 139.
    7. Meteorites: potential problems, page 141.
    8. Mission support: resources, page 141.
    9. Mission goals, page 142.

Discussion (60 minutes)
Use the Rocket Checklist on page 228. Begin to work through this process. The teams won't have time to finish their Rockets. Schedule a future meeting to finish planning. Allow two to three hours for this follow-up meeting.

WEEK SIX: Chapters 10-11

Get Acquainted (15 minutes)
Use ideas listed on page 188, or have participants find a partner to discuss their answers to this question: "What is one thing you respect most in a family member?"

Recap by Leader (20 minutes)
Small Groups—Being in Community
    1. Defining small groups, page 150.
    2. Our need for community, page 152.
    3. Promoting community, page 153.
    4. Modeling community, page 154.
    5. Obstacles to community, page 155.

Discussion (30 minutes)
    1. What is a small group? Are you in one?
    2. Is there a group of people who support you?
    3. Are small groups available to those in our ministry? If not, how could you make them more available?
    4. Which aspect of community is most difficult for you?
    5. Which obstacles to community come up most often in your life?

Recap by Leader (20 minutes)
Learning to Say No
    1. Leadership as self-care, page 161.
    2. The call for Sabbath, page 161.
    3. Practicing Sabbath, page 163.

Discussion (30 minutes)
    1. What is self-care?
    2. Why have Sabbath? What is its value?
    3. What are some things that keep you from taking Sabbath?
    4. What do you enjoy most about it when you make Sabbath a part of your week?

Note: This is a lot of material for six weeks. If your group is agreeable, meet for one additional session to wrap up and address additional questions and concerns, or finish any tasks such as the Rocket or the Team-Building Assessment.

ONE-DAY LEADERSHIP TRAINING SEMINAR

Note: You cannot squeeze all the book's material into one day without losing something. Since a one-day seminar may be easiest for some small groups, however, we have mapped out a sample agenda. We suggest starting at 8:00 a.m. and ending at 4:00 p.m., since attention spans have a tendency to dwindle with more time than that.

8:00-8:10   Introductions, Overview of Agenda

8:10-8:30   Recap by Leader
Facts About Single Adults
    1. Expect transition, page 17.
    2. Single adult ministry is not youth ministry, page 17.
    3. Single adults cannot be "lumped together," page 18.
    4. Many people in the church have misconceptions about (and are threatened by)
       single adults, page 18.

Myths About Single Adults
    1. Single people have more time than married people, page 18.
    2. Single people are less committed, page 19.
    3. All single people are hurting, page 20.
    4. All single people are looking for a marriage partner, page 20.

8:30-8:50   Discussion Questions
Develop an evaluation based on the self-evaluation on page 12. Have the team members take the test then discuss their answers to the questions.
    1. What words or phrases come to mind when you hear the phrase *single adult*?
       (Leader: Write these words and phrases on a poster board, flip chart, or a chalkboard
       for everyone to see.)
    2. How many of these descriptions are negative? Positive?
    3. What do we learn from these answers about our preconceived notions about
       single adults?

8:50-9:00   Break

9:00-9:20   Recap by Leader
Leadership—A New Definition
    1. Relational leadership is a foundational assumption. See page 27.
    2. Some other terms to know, see page 21.
       a. Empower
       b. Personal boundaries
       c. Self-responsibility

Becoming an Effective Minister
    1. Every Christian is a minister, page 30.
    2. Effective ministries are owned by the people, page 30.
    3. Effective ministries empower others, page 30.
    4. Effective ministries are built on a foundation of self-care, or self-responsibility,
       page 31.
    5. Effective, successful ministries produce healthy relationships, not just predetermined
       goals, page 31.

9:20-9:45   Discussion
    1. What are some characteristics of a dominating leader?
    2. What are some characteristics of a leader who delegates?
    3. Is it possible to be an effective leader without being absorbed by the job or having to be all things to all people? Explain.
    4. What are some effective ways to combat our fear that others can't do the job as well as we can?
    5. What is the best aspect about relational ministry?

9:45-10:00   Break
Use this time to get better acquainted. Use ideas listed on page 188, or have participants find a partner to discuss their answers to this question: "What is one thing you respect most in a family member?"

10:00-10:20   Recap by Leader
Characteristics of an Empowered Leader
    1. An empowered leader knows to whom he or she belongs, page 49.
    2. An empowered leader is self-responsible, page 51.
    3. An empowered leader is a wounded healer, page 52.
    4. An empowered leader knows how to play, page 54.
    5. An empowered leader creates a nurturing environment, page 55.
    6. An empowered leader sees beyond the immediate to the potential, page 55.
    7. An empowered leader is patient, page 57.
    8. An empowered leader is willing to give ministry away, page 58.

10:20-10:45   Discussion
    1. Why is it sometimes easy to forget who we belong to?
    2. What does it mean to be self-responsible? Describe an unhealthy example and a healthy example.
    3. Why is play important in the life of a leader?
    4. What does it mean to give ministry away?

10:45-10:55   Break

10:55-11:15   Recap by Leader
Team Communication
    1. What teams are, page 91.
    2. Characteristics of effective, healthy teams.
        a. Fellowship, page 93.
        b. Encouragement, page 94.
        c. Strategy, page 94.
        d. A philosophy of ministry, page 95.
    3. Procedures to help your leaders do their best, pages 96-97.
    4. Principles of team membership, page 100.

11:15-12:00   Discussion
Using the worksheet on page 209, have team members begin to work on a philosophy of ministry. Afterward discuss:
    1. Who do we believe God is? What role does He have in this ministry?
    2. What role does Scripture play in the ministry?
    3. What role do people play in the ministry?
    4. How do people do ministry?

Write the answers on an overhead projector, large sheet of paper, or chalkboard. Go back through the words as a group, and circle important words and phrases. Select one or two people to write a sample philosophy for review later (not in the seminar).

If your team has served together for six months, send the Team-Building Assessment home with them as "homework," and schedule an additional time to go over it together.

12:00-12:30   Lunch
Continue discussing philosophy of ministry with one another over lunch.

12:30-12:40   Break

12:40-12:45   Check In
How are we doing? Ask another get-acquainted question. Use ideas listed on page 188, or have participants find a partner to discuss their answers to this question: "How do others know when you are happy?"

12:45-1:10   Recap by Leader
Team Roles
    1. Why role preferences? How can they help us? See page 115.
    2. The four roles.
        a. Creator, page 116.
        b. Developer, page 118.
        c. Caretaker, page 120.
        d. Participant, page 121.

1:10-1:30   Take the Role Preference Test on page 224

1:30-1:45   Discussion
    1. What role preference did you select?
    2. Do you believe this assessment is accurate?
    3. How is your role preference manifested in your ministry today?
    4. If it is not manifested, what would you really like to do?

1:45-1:50   Break

1:50-2:45   Taking Aim
Use the Rocket checklist on page 228 and begin to work through each phase, recapping each Rocket phase as you complete it. You won't have time to complete the Rocket. Schedule a separate follow-up meeting to complete the planning process.
    1. The Rocket, page 132.
    2. The launch pad of prayer and research, page 132.
    3. The fuel: needs, page 134.
    4. The mission statement, page 136.
    5. The targets, page 137.
    6. Dream destinations, page 139.
    7. Meteorites: potential problems, page 141.
    8. Mission support: resources, page 141.
    9. Mission goals, page 142.

2:45-3:05   Recap by Leader
Small Groups—Being in Community
    1. Defining small groups, page 150.
    2. Our need for community, page 152.

3. Promoting community, page 153.
4. Modeling community, page 154.
5. Obstacles to community, page 155.

3:05-3:20   Discussion
1. What is a small group? Are you in one?
2. Is there a group of people who support you?
3. Are small groups available to those in our ministry? If not, how could you make them more available?
4. Which aspect of community is most difficult for you?
5. Which obstacles to community come up most often in your life?

3:20-3:40   Recap by Leader
Learning to Say No
1. Leadership as self-care, page 161.
2. The call for Sabbath, page 161.
3. Practicing Sabbath, page 163.

3:40-3:55   Discussion
1. What is self-care?
2. Why have Sabbath? What is its value?
3. What are some things that keep you from taking Sabbath?
4. What do you enjoy most about it when you do make Sabbath a part of your week?

3:55-4:00   Close/Wrap up/Prayer

Leadership Training Tools

T his chapter contains worksheets and checklists to help you and your leadership core team "give the ministry away." These tools are divided according to the chapters in which they are described.

Conditional permission is given to copy the pages in this chapter for use with your single adult ministry leadership groups. You may copy pages 201-243 for actual preparation for each leadership group with which you work. No pages in any other part of the book may be copied for any reason without permission.

Here is a quick index to help you find each of the leadership training tools in this chapter.

TOOLS FOR CHAPTER 8: TEAM ROLES

Role Preference Test, page 224

TOOLS FOR CHAPTER 9: TAKING AIM

Rocket Checklist, page 228
Single Adult Survey 1: Tell Us About You, page 229
Single Adult Survey 2: Tell Us What You'd Like, page 232
Map Out Your Mission Statement, page 234
Extra Planning Rocket, page 243

TOOLS FOR CHAPTER 12: TEAM BUILDING RETREATS AND TOOLS FOR CHAPTER 13: LEADERSHIP TRAINING SEMINARS

Case Studies, page 235

CERTIFICATE OF APPRECIATION

FIRST

You are
a winner!

To: _____

For: _____

We appreciate your help with:

Signed: _____

Date: _____

JOB DESCRIPTION

Position Title: _____

General Description and Purpose for Position: _____

_____

Position Responsibilities:

    1. _____

    2. _____

    3. _____

Reports to: _____

Provides Information for/Receives Information from: _____

_____

Works Closely with: _____

Gifts/Skills Required: _____

Expectations/Standards: _____

Three Measurable Goals for Term:

    1. _____

    2. _____

    3. _____

Term of Position: from _____ to _____

Date of Evaluation: _____

Assigned Person's Signature: _____

Date Signed: _____

SAMPLE JOB DUTIES
FOR A RETREAT PLANNING TEAM

Following are sample job duties for a retreat planning team coordinator and various team members. Use the descriptions as a guide for preparing your own planning teams and members job descriptions.

Retreat Coordinator

You are responsible for working with a church staff member to ask several single adults to serve on the retreat planning team.

It is the duty of the retreat committee to organize the retreat and to make sure it runs smoothly.

It is your duty to nurture the committee while that process takes place. Say "thanks," "good job," and "I appreciate your efforts" often. Choose your "battles" carefully. If the issue is not crucial to the success of the retreat, let it go.

Beyond the selection and nurture of the planning team, you and your team will need to:

1. Develop and adhere to a budget in close cooperation with the church staff person.

2. Assign one team member to coordinate the development of a publicity flyer. This team member will ask other single adults to help him or her create the flyer (a mini-committee). The flyer should be started three months before the retreat.

3. Develop a retreat schedule. Usually two schedules are used—a "technical" schedule, which is detailed and used by the retreat committee throughout the planning process, and a "general" schedule for publication in the participants' registration packet.

4. Explain to the retreat planning team the various areas of responsibility (job descriptions) and allow the members to choose, according to their commitment level, the areas in which they would like to be involved. These then become mini-committees. They should have co-facilitators to bring progress reports back to the larger retreat planning team. Most committees should have approximately five members. People often like to work on more than one area, especially if the areas are closely related.

5. Meet with the various mini-committees as your time allows to encourage them. Be careful not to intrude.

6. Contact the music committee chairperson early. He or she needs the themes for each presentation, as well as the schedule to determine the length of the singing time. Give the music committee a technical schedule as soon as you can.

7. Develop a retreat evaluation form. Determine how you want to distribute and collect it at the retreat.

8. By looking at the grounds and a map, designate a quiet room for the weekend. Announce the location of the quiet room at the retreat and make sure the room is adequately identified.

9. Make sure the retreat planning team acts as its own small group during the retreat. At least once during the retreat, take time to be together, give feedback, and pray.

10. Should handicapped persons wish to go on the retreat, contact the church staff person about getting them a sponsor for the weekend.

11. Schedule a retreat planning team meeting for the week immediately following the retreat to get feedback and congratulate each other on a job well done.

Publicity Flyer Coordinator
You will work closely with the retreat planning team coordinator. Choose several single adults to help you create and distribute a flyer to promote the retreat.

The flyer should be mailed five to six weeks prior to the retreat. Allow three weeks for printing, addressing, etc., between the time you design the flyer and the time you drop it in the mail. So you should start on the flyer ten to twelve weeks before the retreat.

1. Design the flyer. Make sure it includes:
   a. Dates of retreat
   b. Cost of retreat
   c. When registration starts/ends
   d. Time the retreat starts/ends
   e. What to bring
   f. Directions to the camp
   g. Speaker's name and brief biography
   h. Speaker's subject
   i. Retreat sponsors
   j. What the Saturday night activity will be, if possible
   k. Registration fee is non-refundable
   l. Registration is not allowed at the retreat, advance registration only
   m. Registration form, including:
      ■ Registrant's name, address, and phone number
      ■ Housing: male/female
      ■ Can they provide transportation for others? If so, how many?
      ■ "Mail to" address (usually the church, c/o the singles department)
      ■ Deadline for mail-in registration
   n. Name of contact person(s) on retreat planning team and their phone numbers. Do not use the singles department for contact.

(TIP: When designing the flyer, remember that whatever you put on the back of the registration slip is going to be torn off and returned. So be careful what you place there. For example, don't put the directions to the camp on the back of the registration slip.)

2. Before having flyer printed, get approval from a church staff person and the retreat planning team coordinator.

3. Get flyer typeset—see if someone at the singles department can do it on the computer—allowing ample time. Then, print, fold, and mail the flyers.

☞

Retreat Registrar

You work closely with the retreat planning team coordinator. Choose other single adults to help you with this registration process.

Your job entails two parts: registering people on Sunday mornings, starting one month prior to the retreat; and checking in people at the retreat.

People who did not previously register generally are not allowed to attend the retreat, but use your discretion.

Sunday Mornings

1. Have registration slips (extra copies of the registration slip on the flyer) ready for people to complete.

2. Make a list of those who volunteer to drive others, including the drivers' names and phone numbers. People who need a ride can look at the list and make their own contacts.

3. Do not accept registrations without full payment.

4. Direct all scholarship requests to the assigned church staff person, who will contact the planning team about approved requests. These requests are confidential.

5. Consider making up to ten spots available for Saturday only (charging these people fifteen to twenty dollars less). Reserve these spots for single parents who cannot afford a baby-sitter for the entire weekend.

6. Contact the singles department about what to do with the money you collect.

7. Choose someone to collect registrations that arrive at the church during the week.

8. Develop a letter acknowledging payment received. Leave copies of the letter with the singles department to send to mail-in registrants.

9. Assign people to cabins.

At the Retreat

1. People will check in at an area you designate. You will give them a registration packet, which should contain their room and small-group assignment, and a name tag. (See the job duties for the registration packet coordinator.)

2. Arrive at the retreat site early to set up.

3. Have the check-in site prepared and occupied for people who will arrive at the retreat on Saturday morning.

Registration Packet Coordinator

You will work closely with the retreat planning team coordinator and the retreat registrar. Choose several single adults to help you create and organize a packet of registration materials to give retreat participants. Registration materials are those sheets of information given to the registrants as they arrive at the campgrounds.

These materials should be completed three weeks before the retreat for the registration planning team, who will then create cover sheets with people's names, cabin numbers, and small groups.

☞

Registration packets generally include:
      1. Cover sheet for name, cabin, small group.
      2. Letter of greeting.
      3. Schedule.
      4. Small-group questions. (If these are coming from the speaker, request them early. Otherwise, contact the small-group committee.)
      5. Quiet time questions, if applicable.
      6. Map of grounds.

Responsibilities include:
      1. Designing the material into an easy-to-use, attractive packet.
      2. Getting these materials typeset. (Check with the singles office. Usually someone can do this on the computer, but give them ample time.)
      3. Have the church photocopy, collate, and staple the materials, allowing a couple days.

Small Groups Coordinator
You will work closely with the retreat planning team coordinator. Choose several single adults to work with you on a committee to organize the small-group time for the retreat. Your duties include:
      1. Develop small-group questions, if they are not supplied by the speaker. As soon as possible, get the questions to the people developing the registration materials, so they can incorporate the questions into the registration packet.
      2. Locate facilitators and alternate facilitators for the small groups. Do not use anyone from the retreat planning team because they'll be busy with other retreat duties.
      3. Hold one training session for the facilitators before the retreat. If possible, give them the small-group questions at the training session.
      4. Small groups should be eight to ten people in size. Arrange for one facilitator per small group.
      5. Obtain the names of the registrants from the registration planning team. Assign them to small groups.
      6. Number or name the small groups. Have the registration packet coordinator list the small-group names/numbers in the registration packet for each registrant.
      7. Organize a way for the people at the retreat to locate their small group and facilitator. (You could assign a color for each small group. Make one group's name tags red, another group's blue, etc.)
      8. Ask the small groups to meet in the facilitator's cabin. This way the retreat planning committee can locate the small groups, if needed.
      9. Give a master list of all the small groups to the retreat planning team.

Friday Night Activities Coordinator (not including registration)
      1. People start arriving around 6:00 p.m., with the majority arriving around 9:00 p.m. People are tired, but nervous and sometimes fidgety. Plan activities that are highly participatory, not sitting and listening.

☞

2. Plan activities that let participants mingle and get to know each other.

3. Choose activities that will introduce people to their small group (coordinate this with the small-group committee).

4. Consider substantive snacks that will be supper for many. Coordinate food with the food committee.

5. Aim for lights out around 11:00 p.m. and enforce it. When people mill around for hours, they can disturb people who are trying to sleep nearby. If weather permits, arrange for late-night talks, walks, etc., prior to lights out.

Saturday Afternoon Activities Coordinator

1. Remember, it always rains . . . .

2. Try to have a lot of indoor and outdoor options available, so everyone has a choice. Avoid trying to coordinate one major activity for everyone.

3. Here are some ideas: aerobics, football, volleyball, basketball, nature hike, board games, relay races, tug-of-war.

4. Distribute a flyer at lunch with times, places (map if needed), and nature of events available for the afternoon.

Saturday Night Activities Coordinator

This is the big social event of the weekend. Keep in mind . . .

1. Usually more women than men attend, so be careful of pairing people into couples, causing many women to be left over and feel uncomfortable.

2. Plan highly participatory events in which everyone can get involved.

3. Food can help people mix (for example, an ice cream sundae bar with different toppings on different tables).

4. This event usually lasts two to three hours (from 8:00 to 11:00 p.m.).

5. Coordinate food choices/purchasing with food committee.

6. Try to keep the event to the stated time limit in consideration of the people who may be trying to sleep nearby. Possibly plan an outdoor activity (maybe around a campfire) to move the late-nighters away from those who would like to sleep.

7. Stick to the budget allowed by the retreat coordinator.

Food Coordinator

You will work closely with the retreat coordinator and committees to purchase food items beyond what is supplied by the camp. Ask several single adults to work with you on a food committee. You will purchase, transport, and serve the items. Your duties include:

1. Make snacks available Friday evening, Saturday afternoon, and Sunday. Usually Friday evening snacks must be fairly substantial, because these snacks are supper for many people.

2. Purchase communion supplies.

3. Purchase a major dessert for Saturday night's main event.

4. Purchase supplies for a Sunday continental breakfast.

5. Determine how much money has been budgeted for food, and help the various committees find treats for their events to fit in that budget.

6. Request funds from the church a week or so in advance of the day you will make your purchases.

7. Arrange for food storage at the camp. Many facilities do not have freezers or refrigerators, usually just a sink.

8. Mark the kitchen door "Retreat Planning Team Only" to avoid late-night raids that leave short supplies for upcoming snacks and refreshments.

9. Determine when foods will be served, and how.

10. Make lists of the events using foods and post them in the kitchen. For example:

Friday	Saturday
Lemonade	Apple juice
Popcorn	Carrots
Apples (half of supply)	Apples (half of supply)
Candy	Celery and peanut butter

Other Retreat Duties

People will be needed for these other duties to help make the retreat a success:

Creative announcements. Develop two to three creative, high-energy, fun announcements that sell the retreat. Tell the church office which Sundays you'll announce the retreat, beginning six weeks in advance. No skit/announcement should last more than five minutes. Announcements in the bulletin and newsletters should also start six weeks before the event. Use bright banners with the retreat theme hung above the registration table to advertise the retreat. Take the banner to the retreat and hang it there as well.

Video or tape recording. Work with the retreat coordinator to make sure that all sessions are video or tape recorded and that the tapes get to the church so people will be able to check them out.

Care of speaker. The person responsible for arranging for a speaker should also arrange the speaker's transportation and lodging. A Sunday lunch during the retreat is an effective way to structure time for the speaker to be with the retreat planning team.

Music. Work with retreat and music team members to prepare a good music program for the retreat. If necessary, create overheads or song sheets. Arrange for musicians as necessary.

Equipment. Determine the type of equipment needed, including a PA system, overhead projectors, screens, movie projectors, and sports equipment. Reserve equipment as soon as possible. Check out equipment, transport it to the retreat, set it up, then make sure it is promptly and safely returned. Make sure you know how to operate any special equipment safely and properly.

Signs. Contact the retreat planning team to determine what signs are needed. See that the necessary signs are made, posted, and then taken down after the retreat. Signs are necessary for the restrooms and are useful for setting the mood around the retreat site (for example, write the retreat theme or upbeat messages on them). Other useful signs include directions and activities. Use your imagination.

DEVELOP YOUR
PHILOSOPHY OF MINISTRY

1. Write the ideas you have in response to the following questions.

   a. Who do we believe God is? What role does He have in this ministry?

   b. What role does Scripture play in the ministry?

   c. What role do people play in our ministry? How do we see them as "players"? What are their various responsibilities?

   d. How do people do ministry? Do they do programmatic ministry? Do they spend time with people? Do they do "big events" ministry?

2. Circle important words or phrases above that you want to emphasize in your philosophy of ministry.

3. Combine the thoughts into one or two short paragraphs. Write it below.

DETERMINING YOUR TEAM'S NEEDS

The following three worksheets help you and your team members build communication. This first worksheet helps you determine needs. You can also use the Team-Building Assessment found on page 220. Here are questions for you and your team members to answer. Refer to the pages if necessary:

1. What is our philosophy of ministry? (Read pages 95-96.) The philosophy reminds us why we operate as we do.

2. What is our goal? (This question can be easily answered if the team has worked through the Rocket material in chapter 9.)

3. Are people supporting our efforts? (Are singles showing up at our activities?)

4. Do team members feel supported, affirmed, and encouraged in their efforts?

5. Are people complaining about our ministry?

6. Is there a lack of interest in what we are doing?

7. Are decisions made that cause confusion?

8. Are team members experiencing unresolved conflicts with each other? (Read pages 97-99 and 212.)

9. Are team members taking risks? Are they being imaginative?

10. Is our single adult ministry moving ahead, maintaining, or disintegrating?

11. Are team members serving in roles they truly enjoy? (Read about role preferences in chapter 8. Take the Role Preference Test found on page 224.)

After you determine needs by answering the above questions, move to the next step—determining existing problems. Use the following worksheet.

DETERMINING PROBLEMS

The Team-Building Assessment on page 220 helps you determine problems as well as needs. You can also check the health of your leadership style with the following test. Rate yourself on each aspect of leadership from 1 to 5 (1=I have a problem with this; 5=I do well with this).

1. I am careful to communicate my expectations and dreams, and I take time to listen to my teammates' expectations and dreams.   1   2   3   4   5

2. I'm not concerned about my ego. I'm not overambitious. I don't want to win at all costs to the detriment of the rest of the team.   1   2   3   4   5

3. I'm sensitive to people's feelings or needs.   1   2   3   4   5

4. I am able to delegate.   1   2   3   4   5

5. I don't criticize others to make myself feel or look good.   1   2   3   4   5

6. I don't betray my teammates. (I don't go behind their back or betray a confidence.)   1   2   3   4   5

7. I have a vision for the future.   1   2   3   4   5

8. I have a warm, caring personality.   1   2   3   4   5

9. I encourage the training and equipping of others for ministry.   1   2   3   4   5

10. I come alongside and support teammates as fellow ministers.   1   2   3   4   5

11. I'm not lazy. I work as hard as other teammates.   1   2   3   4   5

12. I am able to ask for help when I need it.   1   2   3   4   5

Add up your score. A score of forty-five points or more means you are leading with the right motives in mind. Keep up the good work! A lower score means you may need to examine your motives for ministry. Pray for guidance as you learn to let go and give the ministry away.

RESOLVING CONFLICT

If you and your teammates have taken the Team-Building Assessment and have determined needs and problems, use the discussion questions provided in the assessment to help you resolve conflict and meet needs.

Another way to do this is to read through the following ideas. Review them with your team. These guidelines will help you and your teammates communicate to resolve problems and function in a healthy way.

1. *Hear feelings, not words.* Attempt to be empathetic. During conflict, people often say things that hurt others. When this happens, stop and ask yourself, "What is this person really feeling?"

2. *Be congruent.* Be in touch with your feelings and, therefore, responsible for them. If you are angry with a person or upset with a situation, ask yourself, "What am I really feeling? Why am I so angry about this? What's going on that this is so important to me?"

3. *Avoid you messages.* You messages cause others to be defensive. Use I messages, instead. For example, don't say "You make me so mad when you always criticize my ideas." Instead say, "I feel hurt when I offer an idea and it's criticized and not considered."

4. *Don't use* **never** *or* **always***.* Avoid generalizations.

5. *Be ready to forgive and ask for forgiveness.* Real empathy brings genuine apologies and repentance that will soften hearts and free us from the slavery of bitterness, hostility, and vindictiveness.

6. *Be responsible for personal change.* Do not take the responsibility to change another. Read Matthew 7:3: "Why do you look at the speck of sawdust in your brother's eye and pay no attention to the plank in your own eye?"

7. *Stay with one issue at a time.* Don't be tempted to bring up past grievances that may or may not be connected with the current issue.

8. *Call time when the discussion becomes destructive.* The person who calls time is responsible for arranging a new time (preferably within twenty-four hours) to discuss the matter further, once the feelings have been tempered.

9. *Stay with the here and now.* Avoid bringing up the past or referring to the future.

10. *Avoid "below-the-belt" remarks.* Do not make remarks such as, "I can see why you have problems at home." These remarks are insignificant to the issue; they are only designed to hurt. They also abuse a confidence. Attack the problem, not the person.

11. *Address the conflict yourself, when possible.* Approach the one, and only the one, with whom you have the conflict. If that person is unable or unwilling to hear, meet with a referee (preferably a mutually agreed-upon person). Finally, approach with a group. Jesus offers this approach in Matthew 18:15-17. (A word of caution: Approach as a group only as a last resort. This is often used as a power move, not as a healing tool. People in the small group must be committed to confidentiality, the restoration of the person, and the moving forward in restored relationship.)

☞

12. *Avoid blaming, placating, and distracting.* Instead, attempt to be adult. Attempt to resolve the situation. Hear feelings. Be rational, logical, and intelligent.

13. *Above all, be loving.* Show love that is accepting, supportive, and caring.

14. *Learn to clarify.* Since most problems arise out of misunderstandings, this is one of the most helpful steps to remember in resolving conflicts. Once we clear up misunderstandings within the team, moving forward becomes easier.

TEAM MEMBERS COVENANT

1. When I can't attend a leadership meeting, I will contact my team facilitator/leader to let him or her know. If I must miss a meeting, I am responsible to find out what happened in my absence and what decisions were made. My absence indicates my approval of the suggestions made there.

2. I will make sure dates for all events are cleared with the church staff person in charge of singles ministry.

3. I am responsible for monies requested and spent in my area. I will follow existing procedures to request money and account for all funds at the end of each event.

4. I will meet at least monthly with the leaders of my ministry area to encourage and support them.

5. I will recruit my own successor. The leadership team and church staff must approve the person I suggest as a leader.

6. If a person in the ministry is causing a major problem, I will discuss what to do at our next leadership meeting. I will alert the staff to problems.

7. If I have a complaint, I will write it down and put it in an envelope. I will put the envelope in my clothes dresser. In a week or two, I will pull it out and see if the issue is still a problem of major importance. If so, I will bring it to the next meeting.

Name: _____

Signed: _____

Date: _____

TEAM MEMBERSHIP PRINCIPLES

Always be willing to do more than your share.
>   *Everyone works less hard.*

Refrain from saying uncomplimentary things about other team members behind their backs.
>   *This is destructive and undermines trust and respect.*

Accept reality.
>   *All members do not have the same duties, experience, and ability. Each person is gifted in different ways.*

Participate in team activities even when it is inconvenient to do so.
>   *Participation facilitates mutual respect, which is important to team development.*

Confront your conflicts.
>   *It is emotionally less expensive. Resolved conflicts strengthen relationships.*

Don't be late or absent for trivial reasons.
>   *To do so is unfair to your teammates who must carry your load.*

Be involved, concerned, and active in your personal growth.
>   *Team development and personal growth cannot be separated. When we are growing, our team benefits as well.*

Contribute to other team members' personal growth whenever it is appropriate.
>   *Share resources and information. Remember not to be an advice-giver or fixer.*

TEAM REPORT

Name: _____

Area: _____

Date: _____

1. I need decisions from you for the following items:

2. I am having a problem with the following:

3. I am planning to:

4. I am making progress in the following areas:

5. I would rate my personal happiness factor at (1=suicidal, 100=best I've ever been):

   I say this because:

6. Please pray for me in the following areas:

EVENT FINANCES WORKSHEET

Event Name: _____

Location: _____

Date: _____

Coordinator: _____

Phone Number (Day): _____ (Evening): _____

Event Price: _____

Event Capacity: _____

Possible Income: _____

Income	Past	Projected	Actual
Number of Paid Participants			
Number of 50% Participants			
Total Income (number paid x price)			
Expenses			
Facility			
Transportation			
Speaker Honorarium			
Adult Leaders Honorarium			
Printing/Publicity			
Food/Refreshments			
Other			
Total Net Cost			
Net Cost Per Participant			
# Scholarship (including staff)			
$ Scholarship (# x cost per)			
Total Cost			
TOTAL PROFIT			

ACTIVITY REQUEST FORM

Event Coordinator: _____

Phone (Home): _____ (Work): _____

Address: _____

City and Zip: _____

Event Name: _____

Event Date: _____ Event Place: _____

Statement of Purpose: _____

_____

_____

_____

Team Members	Day Phone	Evening Phone
Contact Person: _____		
Promotion: _____		
Registration: _____		
Setup: _____		
Decorations/Supplies: _____		
Cleanup: _____		
Other (specify): _____		
_____		

Promotion Plan (include specific steps you will use to publicize this event. Include dates for proposed bulletin inserts, mailings, posters, etc.): _____

_____

_____

_____

_____

Event Schedule: _____

_____

_____

_____

Does this event have a budget? ❏ Yes ❏ No
(If yes, budget must accompany this request.)

Approved by:_____ Date approved: _____

TEAM-BUILDING ASSESSMENT
(See next page)

If team members serve one-year terms, take the test after you have served together for at least six months, so you know each other better and have worked together for a while. (If you serve six-month terms, take it after serving together for three months.) Following the initial test, the group can retake it at approximately three-month intervals. As a group, you will answer, "How are we doing?" Use this assessment as a tool for the team-building retreats in chapter 12 and the leadership training seminars in chapter 13.

Group Leader Instructions

1. Hand out copies of the test to each group member.

2. Explain that group members are to complete each question by reading the statement and filling in a number from one to five before the statement (one=strongly agree; five=strongly disagree). The numbers are shown on the test as well.

      1=strongly agree
      2=agree
      3=have no opinion
      4=disagree
      5=strongly disagree

3. Once members finish answering the questions, each person evaluates his or her own test by using the instructions found at the end of the test. (If time allows, go over the instructions for scoring the test.)

4. After group members have tallied their own scores, facilitate a discussion regarding their own assessment of how they are doing as a team. Lead members (including yourself as an equal member) in the discussion using the following questions. Remember, your vulnerability will set the stage for the rest of the group.

- What do you think of the test? Does it seem to accurately depict what is going on in us and within our team?
- How do you think you, personally, are doing? (Where did you score high? Low?)
- How are we doing in encouraging one another? Do all members feel encouraged and appreciated?
- Is there anything going on in your personal life that is negatively affecting your ministry role? If so, how can we help?

5. Remember, this test is not meant to tear down teams or members, but to build them up. If someone is not feeling supported, or doesn't appreciate your leadership, find out why, so that the team can be built up. Be willing to discuss your own disappointments and appreciation as well.

6. List positive steps for improvement. These steps may be a reaffirmation of what is already going well, or some practical ways you can better work together as a team. Make sure the steps are positive, that everything decided upon is said in terms of what "we can do," rather than "what so-and-so shouldn't do." Read chapter 7 to help in this evaluation process.

7. End your discussion in prayer. Thank God for each person and his or her gifts.

8. One final note: If you would prefer to have a pastor or staff member sit in on the evaluation time with you, that's fine. Sometimes it helps to have another person (someone not too intimately involved with the team dynamics) facilitate a discussion on how you are doing.

TEAM-BUILDING ASSESSMENT

Please complete this assessment by filling in a number from one to five beside each statement.

>   1=strongly agree
>   2=agree
>   3=no opinion
>   4=disagree
>   5=strongly disagree

I. Goals

_____A. My team has operated under a common goal for the past six months.
_____B. I personally understand that goal.
_____C. As a team, we are reaching that goal.
_____D. I have personally contributed to the reaching of that goal.
_____E. My teammates have personally contributed to the reaching of that goal.

II. Ideas

_____A. I feel free to contribute ideas to my team.
_____B. My ideas are heard when I share them.
_____C. All of my teammates share ideas and are heard.
_____D. I am able to be creative within my team.
_____E. My team does a good job of implementing ideas.

III. Personal Growth

_____A. I believe I am growing in leadership skills.
_____B. I am being challenged spiritually.
_____C. I feel that I have a balanced workload in my leadership responsibilities.
_____D. I feel that the team as a whole has balanced workloads too. We're all doing our share in facilitating the ministry.
_____E. Personal dreams of mine have been or are being fulfilled in this ministry experience.
_____F. I have dreams for the next six to twelve months of this ministry.

IV. Team Dynamics

_____A. I feel like I am able to be myself with the team.
_____B. I share personally with my teammates.
_____C. If I have a personal problem, I can bring it to one or more of my teammates.
_____D. I am close to at least one of my teammates.
_____E. When I share personally, my teammates listen to me.
_____F. My teammates do specific things that make me feel cared for.
_____G. My teammates and I have worked through and resolved conflicts to our satisfaction.
_____H. There are no ongoing unresolved conflicts within the group.
_____I. The team interacts well with the leader.
_____J. I appreciate (value, respect, admire) our leader.

☞

V. Ministry Roles

_____A. I have a specific, clearly defined area of responsibility/ministry on this team.
_____B. I feel supported in my ministry. Other members are encouraging me.
_____C. I think the work is generally well-distributed among team members.
_____D. I am supporting others in their ministry.
_____E. Enthusiasm for the ministry is growing.
_____F. New leadership is being recruited and developed.

❖ ❖ ❖

Evaluation
Instructions: Add the scores of each section and place them below:

I. Goals   _____ (Score from 5-25)

II. Ideas   _____ (Score from 5-25)

III. Personal Growth   _____ (Score from 6-30)

IV. Team Dynamics   _____ (Score from 10-50)

V. Ministry Roles   _____ (Score from 6-30)

Total Score   _____ (Score from 32-160)

Total Score 32-63: You are doing exceptionally well as a team. You feel supported and encouraged, and the team is working together. Sharing your positive feelings with the rest of the team is important. Your positive assessment may be an encouragement to others who may not feel as positive as you do about the ministry and your leaders.

Total Score 64-82: You personally feel encouraged about the team. Look at the areas where you answered a 3 or greater, and think about how you can improve in these areas—either personally or in your relationships with others. As a team, compare the total scores for each section to see if everyone scored the same areas high. As a team, discuss both the positive areas and the areas with room for improvement.

Total Score 83-107: Overall, you are doing fairly well. You could stand to feel/do better in certain areas. Do you need more encouragement? Are you feeling overworked? Do you get along with your teammates? Take time to think about how to improve in the weaker areas—either personally or in your relationships with others. As a team, look at the total scores of each section and see if some of your higher scores were in the same areas. Perhaps you are personally struggling in a particular area, but your teammates are not (for example, personal growth). Be open with your teammates about these areas.

Total Score 108-132: Generally, you are not feeling really great about this ministry opportunity. Are you under a lot of stress or bored? Is there a conflict with the group? Are other things going on in your life that hinder your involvement with the ministry? Look at those areas and discuss the areas that involve your team, as well as the personal areas. Your teammates will probably be more than willing to help you.

☞

Total Score 133-160: Either you had a bad day when you took this test or you are having a difficult time with this ministry. Are you taking this test at the beginning or end of a term of ministry? If so, give yourself a break! You may be tired, scared, or nervous. Are you involved in a conflict with the group? Read chapter 7 for ideas on resolving conflict, or talk with your facilitator or staff person about it. Are you experiencing difficulties in your life apart from ministry (for example, depression, financial problems, relationship struggles, or other failures) that are coloring your perception? Or are you just simply discouraged, burned out, or having a rotten time? As difficult as it may be, discuss this with your team. Others may be feeling discouraged, too, or may be wondering what's wrong with you. You can make it clear to your team that this is not a time to fix you, but that you want them to know your situation. Do not drop out of leadership (if you scored in this range, you have probably thought about it!) without working on some of these issues. If, when your term is up, you still feel this way, make sure you have some support and accountability system in place for yourself.

ROLE PREFERENCE TEST
(See next page)

Although not the most comprehensive test possible, the Role Preference Test is quick, easy to use, and gives team members a general indication of their preferred ministry roles. Use this test either in a group setting or individually. It can be taken at any time. You don't have to be a leader to take it. Anyone can take the test to learn more about his or her preferred roles in ministry.

Group Leader Instructions

1. Briefly describe the following role preferences:

- Creator—dreams of new ministries and innovative ideas for existing programs.
- Developer—applies practical thoughts to dreams. Knows how to "make it happen."
- Caretaker—senses needs and sees they are met. Provides encouragement to people and programs.
- Participant—observes programs and roles therein. Participates within a limited ministry role.

After describing general roles, tell your group members they'll take this test to discover their own preferences.

2. Hand out copies of the test to each person.

3. Tell group members to answer each question as it best describes their preferences at the current time. Answer by circling the appropriate letter.

4. Once they are finished answering the questions, have each person score his or her own test by using the instructions found at the end of the test. (If time allows, go over the instructions for scoring the test.)

5. When your group members discover their current preferred ministry roles, read the role descriptions and characteristics found in chapter 8.

6. Brainstorm about their preferred roles. Do they seem accurate? Are some preferences inconsistent with what those people are currently doing? What other activities would they like to be doing? Talk about these preferences. Encourage them to understand their own roles better and learn to understand each other's as well.

ROLE PREFERENCE TEST

Instructions
This test will help determine which of the following four ministry roles you prefer:

- Creator—dreams of new ministries and innovative ideas for existing programs.
- Developer—applies practical thoughts to dreams. Knows how to "make it happen."
- Caretaker—senses needs and sees they are met. Provides encourage ment to people and programs.
- Participant—observes programs and roles therein. Participates within a limited ministry role.

For each question circle the selection that best describes your preference at this time. Note that at any time your role preferences may change, so this is not intended to label you for life.

Once you have completed your test, score it by using the instructions found at the end of the test.

When you have discovered your current preferred ministry role, read the role descriptions and characteristics described in chapter 8.

Think about your role preference. Does it seem accurate? Does it seem consistent or inconsistent with your current ministry role? In what other activities or areas of ministry would you like to be involved? Based on this test, are there other ministry areas for which you might be better suited?

Talk with a friend or fellow minister about your role preference. Does he or she also see you this way? Would you like this person's help in finding ways to exercise your role preference?

Experiment! If you haven't already done so, plug in to the ministry with a job you enjoy doing that fits your ministry role preference.

Section One
An obvious need has been discovered affecting many single adults in your church. Individuals are needed to develop a project or ministry to meet that need. Answer questions one through five concerning this particular situation (select only one answer).

1. In this project, which of these tasks would you most like to do?
   a. Come up with a creative idea to meet that need.
   b. Take an idea and make it work.
   c. Use methods and controls to keep the project going once it is in place.
   d. Participate in the program once it is running.

☞

2. Concerning your involvement in the above project, which would be most
   important to you?

   a. That my conceptual idea is the answer to meet the need.
   b. That my practical ideas make the concept work.
   c. That the project runs smoothly and needs are met.
   d. That I am a part of the project.

3. How would you want others to perceive you in this project?

   a. A creative genius, the mastermind.
   b. The one who made it work.
   c. The one that people feel free to go to with their needs/problems.
   d. A dependable supporter and a potential resource where needed.

4. What would most drive you crazy about this project?

   a. In implementing the project, the creative flair behind it was lost.
   b. Those involved had no real direction.
   c. There was too much risk or change.
   d. There was no clear leadership to follow.

5. How long would you generally want to be involved in a single large project
   such as this one?

   a. A limited time—basically just long enough for me to get the idea worked
      out and developed.
   b. Six months to a year—just long enough to get the project up and running
      so I could then move on to something else.
   c. At least one to three years—I could really dig in and help out in a long-
      term, committed way.
   d. Indefinitely—as long as I am needed.

Section Two
Answer the next five questions in conjunction with your current experiences in
ministry:

6. Which of the following needs concerns you most?

   a. A stagnant, dead-end ministry.
   b. A good program or idea that is not working.
   c. Details and/or people falling through the cracks.
   d. Not having a place where I fit in.

7. Which of the following would be your highest priority?

   a. Freshness/newness in ministry.
   b. A well-run ministry.
   c. Handling crises or needs as they arise.
   d. Being a follower or part of a group led by someone other than myself.

8. In which of the following ways would you prefer to get things done?

   a. On my own.
   b. Working with an idea person and developing a team to implement the
      idea in a practical, workable way.
   c. Attending to details and needs as they arise.
   d. As a follower or part of a group led by someone other than myself.

☞

9. Which of the following relationships do you most prefer?
    a. Working only with those of like mind and talent.
    b. Leading a team of people in a particular direction.
    c. Being a helper to someone who needs it.
    d. Following others' leadership. I fit in wherever.

10. Which of the following tasks would you most like to do?
    a. Design something that's never been done before.
    b. Figure out who and what is needed to reach a goal.
    c. Help someone solve a conflict, resolve a problem.
    d. Explore all the opportunities before me.

Section Three
For 11 through 15, select one word that represents the greatest motivation for you at this present time.

11.   a. Vision
      b. Application
      c. Need
      d. Participation

12.   a. Creativity
      b. Goals
      c. Detail
      d. Support

13.   a. Theory
      b. Practice
      c. Efficiency
      d. Assistance

14.   a. Problem-solving
      b. Team-building
      c. Serving
      d. Learning

15.   a. Pioneer
      b. Delegator
      c. Encourager
      d. Recruit

Scoring Your Test
Go back over the answers for sections one, two, and three, and total the number of times you selected each letter A through D:

        A _____
        B _____
        C _____
        D _____

☞

If you have selected:

- Twelve to fifteen of any one letter, you show a high preference for the roles shown below.
- Ten to twelve answers in any one area, you have a moderate tendency toward a particular role.
- Six to eight answers in two roles at the same time, you probably prefer a combination of those two roles, such as a creator/developer or developer/caretaker.
- Four to six answers, you have a slight interest in a particular area.
- Zero to three answers, you have a low interest.

> A=Creator
> B=Developer
> C=Caretaker
> D=Participant

Remember, your role preference can and will change from time to time as you move from one ministry experience to another and as you continue to grow and change spiritually.

ROCKET CHECKLIST

Date: _____

Use this checklist to help you and your team members establish your goals using the Rocket. If team members serve one-year terms, evaluate and update your goals every six months. If team members serve for six-month terms, evaluate and update your goals every three months.

❏ Established a launch pad of prayer and research.
  ❏ Asked what needs exist.
  ❏ Researched needs and prayed about them.
  ❏ Gathered others around who are interested in the same needs. Prayed about them.
❏ Determined needs—the fuel for our ministry.
  ❏ Used a survey, asked others, researched through community agencies. (See sample surveys on pages 229 and 232.)
  ❏ Determined physical, relational, spiritual, and community needs.
❏ Mapped out a mission statement. (Use the worksheet on page 234.)
  ❏ Wrote two to three sentences that state our purpose.
  ❏ Statement begins with "We exist to . . ." or "We intend to . . ."
  ❏ Statement is easy to understand.
  ❏ Statement is ours and not someone else's.
  ❏ We change our statement when we change.
❏ Aiming our ministry toward targets.
  ❏ Targets are objectives that address our needs.
  ❏ Broad areas help focus our ministry.
  ❏ Started with a few targets, then added more later.
  ❏ Made sure our targets are consistent with our mission statement.
❏ Held a dream session.
  ❏ Asked: "In terms of our targets, what would we like to do if nothing were impossible?" Listed all dreams, realizing there's no such thing as a bad dream.
  ❏ Took a night or longer to pray and think about them.
  ❏ Looked through the list and chose 3 to 5 dreams on which we wanted to work.
❏ Identified potential problems—the meteorites that could damage our mission.
  ❏ Listed all potential problems we may encounter.
  ❏ Listed all restrictions our church may give.
  ❏ Listed people who may pose potential problems.
  ❏ Listed any legal limitations.
❏ Identified resources to support our mission.
  ❏ Identified the experts in our church and community whom we could call upon.
  ❏ Identified resource agencies.
  ❏ Listed the programs or procedures already in place in our church or community that will facilitate this mission.
❏ Developed specific goals.
  ❏ The goals came from our dream session. They are specific enough to accomplish.
  ❏ Established three-, six-, nine-, and twelve-month goals—a few goals per phase. Gave ourselves plenty of time.
  ❏ Attached a name to each goal. This person doesn't do it alone, he or she is responsible to see that others help to accomplish the goal.
❏ Update the Rocket on a regular basis.

SINGLE ADULT SURVEY 1

Tell Us About You!

Thanks for taking a few moments to complete this survey. Your answers will help us program to better meet your needs.

Name: _____

Address: _____

Telephone (Home): _____ (Work): _____

Sex: ❑ Male   ❑ Female

1. Occupational field (check one):

    ❑ Skilled trade (specify)_____

    ❑ Service (specify)_____

    ❑ Business (specify)_____

    ❑ Homemaking

    ❑ Professional (specify)_____

    ❑ Management (specify)_____

    ❑ Student (specify field and present level)_____

    ❑ Other (specify)_____

2. Current status:
    ❑ Never been married
    ❑ Single parent
    ❑ Widowed
    ❑ Separated
    ❑ Divorced

3. Check as many as apply:
    ❑ I live alone.
    ❑ I live with my child/children who are ages_____.
    ❑ I live with my parent(s).
    ❑ I live with one friend.
    ❑ I live with two or more friends.
    ❑ I live in a retirement home.

4. Age category:
    ❑ 65+
    ❑ 50-64
    ❑ 35-49
    ❑ 25-34
    ❑ 18-24

5. For transportation, I:
    ❑ Use public transportation
    ❑ Drive my own car

☞

6. Health condition:
   - ❏ I am in good health.
   - ❏ I can get out with assistance.
   - ❏ I am unable to get out.

7. What kinds of activities would you like our church to provide?
   - ❏ Study and discussion around issues and concerns related to single adults. Please list the top three issues in which you would be interested:

       a. _____

       b. _____

       c. _____

   - ❏ Bible study and discussion
   - ❏ Social gatherings to get to know others
   - ❏ Recreation
   - ❏ Trips and tours
   - ❏ Interest groups (art, crafts, music, drama)
   - ❏ Activities that include children of single parents
   - ❏ Retreats for singles
   - ❏ Programs and activities with other congregations
   - ❏ Other (specify)_____

8. Church participation:
   - ❏ I am a member of this church.
   - ❏ I regularly attend this church.
   - ❏ I am a member of an adult class.
   - ❏ I do not attend a church.
   - ❏ I am interested in being more involved; please contact me.
   - ❏ I am interested in receiving more information about the church and the single adult ministry.

9. If you have attended one of our single adult groups or functions, what have you enjoyed most about them?

10. What have you liked the least?

11. If you could change one thing about the group you attended, what would you change?

12. If you haven't been to a single adult function in a while, would you tell us why you have chosen not to return?

13. What could we add, change, or delete that would encourage you to come again?

14. What do you think the purpose of a single adult ministry should be?

15. We are currently meeting on _____ nights. Is this a convenient night? What night would you prefer? Why?

16. Any other comments or insights you feel we could benefit from as we plan the single adult programming and group structuring with your needs in mind?

17. Would you bring a friend to a single adult function? Why? Why not?

Please return the questionnaire to the single adult ministries office.
Thanks for your time!

SINGLE ADULT SURVEY 2

Tell Us What You'd Like!

Thanks for taking a few moments to complete this survey. Your answers will help us program to meet your needs.

❑ Male   ❑ Female

1. Current status:
   - ❑ Single parent
   - ❑ Widowed
   - ❑ Separated
   - ❑ Divorced
   - ❑ Never been married

2. Age category:
   - ❑ 65+
   - ❑ 50-64
   - ❑ 35-49
   - ❑ 25-34
   - ❑ 18-24

3. How long have you attended our church?
   - ❑ 0-3 months
   - ❑ 4-12 months
   - ❑ 1-2 years
   - ❑ 3-4 years
   - ❑ 5 years plus

4. What have you enjoyed most about the singles program in the past two months?

5. What have you liked the least?

6. If you could change one thing about our program, what would you change?

☞

7. Please check the five topics you would most like to see presented and discussed. Add any of interest that we didn't include. (Please choose only five.)
- ❑ Tax planning and preparation
- ❑ Remarriage
- ❑ Nutritional health
- ❑ Goal setting/life planning
- ❑ Success
- ❑ Time management
- ❑ Personal financial planning
- ❑ Transition/handling change
- ❑ Relationship issues (specify)_____
- ❑ Elder care: Parenting our parents
- ❑ AIDS education
- ❑ Job search skills/career moves
- ❑ Sexuality
- ❑ Stress treatment
- ❑ Divorce recovery
- ❑ Self-esteem/identity
- ❑ Effective parenting for (specify):
  - ❑ preschool   ❑ elementary   ❑ teenage years
- ❑ Intimacy
- ❑ Leadership skills
- ❑ Other (specify)_____

8. Would you bring a friend to our program? Why, or why not?

9. Any other comments or insights you feel we could benefit from knowing as we plan the single adult programming and group structuring with your needs in mind?

Please return this to the singles office or a singles officer. Thank you for your time!

MAP OUT YOUR MISSION STATEMENT

List your needs:

Write your mission statement (begin with "We exist to . . ." or "We intend to . . ."):

Check each of these if they apply:
- ❏ Do you use simple words and phrases?
- ❏ Is it short and concise?
- ❏ Does it tell people where you're headed?
- ❏ Does it tell people who you are?
- ❏ Does it reflect your overall purpose?
- ❏ Do you understand it and believe it?
- ❏ Does it complement your church's mission statement?
- ❏ Does it cover the existing single adult needs?

CASE STUDIES
(See the following pages)

All leaders must make decisions that affect the people and programs within their ministry. Some of those decisions will be simple, guided by beliefs, experience, and available options. Other decisions, however, will be difficult—falling into that "gray area" of judgment calls, or unpopular ones that nobody wants to make.

The exercises and accompanying case studies in this section give you and your leaders hands-on practice in making decisions. They present typical problems that many leadership core teams face. By working through them, you and your team can examine your feelings about the issues and determine reasons behind your decision-making.

Here's how to use the material:

1. Read pages 236-242. The four exercises are written so your leadership team (of under ten members) can work through the accompanying case studies. Instructions are included to help your team members work through the case studies and determine "What would we do if we were faced with similar situations?"

■ Exercise A uses case studies 1-3 and copies of the philosophy
   of ministry.
■ Exercise B uses case studies 4a-4b.
■ Exercise C uses case study 5.
■ Exercise D uses case study 6.

2. Schedule regular decision-making practices for your leadership core team. For example, once a month at a team meeting, work through an exercise and its accompanying case studies.

3. Use the case studies at team-building retreats (chapter 12) or leadership training seminars (chapter 13). Choose the exercises on which you want to work, or use the ones suggested in the retreat and seminar schedules.

4. Each exercise includes time suggestions, preparation needs, and directions for using the case studies with your team. Read the exercise so you are prepared before you use it with your team.

EXERCISE A

Estimated Time: Twenty-five minutes.

Preparation: You'll need copies of your philosophy of ministry (or the one provided below) and copies of case studies 1-3 found on page 237.

Directions: Give each person a copy of the philosophy and a copy of the three case studies. Then, divide your leadership core team into three smaller groups (pairs or trios). Assign one case study to each group. Let them use the discussion question listed on their case study handout to talk about their respective problems.

After about fifteen minutes, gather everyone together. Ask a spokesperson from each small group (one at a time) to report how his or her partners used the philosophy of ministry to solve the assigned problem.

Philosophy of Ministry
The starting point of our ministry is God.
The guide for our ministry is the Bible.
The focus of our ministry is people, not programs.
The environment of our ministry is teamwork, not individualism.

☞

CASE STUDY 1

Your leadership core team has one dominant leader. Team members feel unimportant as decisions are made for them. Instead of dreaming and planning for the ministry themselves, the team members await instructions from the dominant leader. The only person with a sense of ownership is this dominant leader. The remaining team members feel inadequate, powerless, and frustrated. They are thinking of dropping off the leadership core team since it seems to be a waste of time for them. How do you solve this using your philosophy of ministry?

CASE STUDY 2

A leader on your core team is using his leadership role to meet, date, and become involved with members of the opposite sex, leaving a trail of bad relationships and hurting people in his wake. How do you solve this using your philosophy of ministry?

CASE STUDY 3

One of the leadership core team members likes to drink heavily on weekends and is frequently up front on Sunday mornings with a hangover. This person jokes about it with friends inside and outside the church. How do you solve this using your philosophy of ministry?

EXERCISE B

Estimated Time: Twenty-five minutes.

Preparation: For half of your team members, make copies of case study 4a; for the other half of your team, make copies of case study 4b.

Directions: Divide your core team in half. Give copies of case study 4a to the first group; copies of case study 4b to the second group. Allow ten minutes for them to work through their respective problems using the discussion questions on their case study handout.

Then gather everyone together. Tell the entire team that they worked on the same problem, but case studies 4a and 4b contained different sets of information. Have the team members "re-solve" the problem using the combined sets of information. Did viewing the problem from a different perspective change the decisions that were made? Why, or why not?

☞

CASE STUDY 4a

You are members of your single adult ministry leadership core team. Since you are committed to giving the ministry away, you have encouraged ownership in potential leaders who are not on the leadership core team. You have specifically asked a small group of people to put on a New Year's Eve party for the single adults. You have given them some guidelines that include:

- No alcohol is allowed at the party.
- The party will run no later than 2:00 a.m.
- The facilities where the party will be held are from another denominational background. They allow no dancing.
- The cost for attending the party should not exceed twenty-five dollars per person, including a sit-down dinner.

You left the party at about 1:00 a.m. and went home. At 3:30 a.m., you received a phone call. The person on the other end of the line asked if you were a leader with your group. You answered yes, and then the person became irate and told you that the party was still going on, there was drinking and dancing, and the place was a mess. It would easily cost three thousand dollars to repair the physical damage.

You remember your credo of giving the ministry away and are angry that it apparently failed. The next day, you call the leadership core team and those who planned the party together and confront the issue. How will you resolve this conflict?

☞

CASE STUDY 4b

You are   team, but you were
asked b   ults. The leaders
gave yo

[handwritten note:] Need Ordered and 13 copies Made of this page

other

enty-five dollars

and h   id not supply alcohol
Every   her entertainment.
                                                    bang.
                                                    someone angrily
confr   way, and you did not
see anything else for about ten minutes, when the p_____ le back in and ordered
everyone out of the room. People who were still at the party at this time were
confused and felt that they were treated rudely by this person. After all, they were
just having a good time on New Year's Eve.

The next day you received a call from a leadership core team member who
said there was a problem with "your party" and asked if you could meet with them.
You thought you had been given responsibility for the event and did not understand
why the leader was coming back to you now, after the party was over, to discuss
problems. How will you resolve this conflict?

Estimated Time: Twenty minutes.

Preparation: Each team member will need a copy of case study 5.

Directions: Distribute a copy of case study 5 to each team member. Work through the problem together by reading the situation and then answering the questions.

CASE STUDY 5

Your leadership team is no longer functioning properly. No one seems to know what happened. For a long time, the team worked and shared well together. Each person knew the struggles that were going on in the other persons' lives. The team had become a supportive, caring group of close friends.

Suddenly, however, no one talked about his or her needs. Instead of sharing what was going on and how they could be prayed and cared for, people suddenly shared someone else's need or simply reported on their schedule. Depersonalizing began to grow in the sharing time.

Individually, you have become frustrated with the lack of support you are experiencing and sad that you no longer feel close to this group. This support was important for you in this ministry. It was crucial that you receive the support so you didn't feel like a Lone Ranger in your area of ministry. At the same time, you enjoyed the sense of others helping to carry your burden and encourage you. Now you don't know what to do.

You have decided to approach this problem in your leadership meeting, because, frankly, if you don't start feeling supported you would rather serve in another area of ministry where you know you will be supported. When you mention this at the meeting, you find that everyone else feels the same way. Now you need to decide, as a group, what the problem is and how to remedy it. You decide as a group that each person will share how he or she has contributed to this downward process, by answering the following questions:

1. What actions have you taken which may have led to the lack of sharing and vulnerability?
2. Where have you decided to remain aloof or distant? Why?
3. In what ways have you been dysfunctional in what was originally a functional group?
4. What are the strengths and weaknesses you bring to the group individually?

Now, in your own group, give possible answers to the questions—sharing only for yourself, stating how you possibly contribute to similar problems and what you can do to remedy it. Once each group member has given individual answers, work together as a group to resolve the problems so you function as the supportive, caring body you once were.

EXERCISE D

Estimated Time: Twenty minutes.

Preparation: Each team member will need a copy of case study 6.

Directions: Give each person a copy of case study 6. Work through the situation together by answering the questions listed on the handout.

CASE STUDY 6

Each person on your leadership core team has a specific area of responsibility that he or she delegates to a group of volunteers outside of your leadership core team. Two team members have come to your leadership meeting particularly frustrated with their areas of ministry and the people with whom they are working.

One leader is coordinating small groups and has developed a team with whom she works. That small group team is coordinated by one volunteer. The leader is frustrated because the coordinator is doing all the work and not delegating it to his fellow volunteers. The other volunteers feel like their time is being wasted and are beginning to drop out of this ministry, while the dominant coordinator is complaining of having to do all the work himself. Your leadership core team member oversees the ongoing work of the small group ministry, and is worried about the effect the coordinator is having not only on the ministry of the other volunteers, but on the small group ministry as a whole.

The second leadership core team leader is frustrated with an opposite problem. This leader is responsible to get people together to plan social events. The Christmas party is upcoming, and a group of volunteers are ready and willing to plan it. Unfortunately, the coordinator of this group of volunteers has done and continues to do nothing at all—even though he says he will get the group together to discuss plans, arrange for the location, date, and details for the party. Your leadership core team member is concerned because he knows that last-minute planning will not only be less effective, but will also lead to burnout for everyone involved.

As a group, your job is to decide what to do with these two volunteers. They seem to have leadership potential, but their actions (or lack of actions) are inconsistent with your philosophy of ministry. You recognize you have a problem. Work through these questions:

1. How do you encourage ministry and develop leadership skills, but not give up on the work you have done and continue to do?
2. Where does "giving the ministry away" enter into the equation? You have recruited these people for specific tasks. How do you keep them on track and teach them to work with you, as leaders, and with the teams of volunteers they are to coordinate?

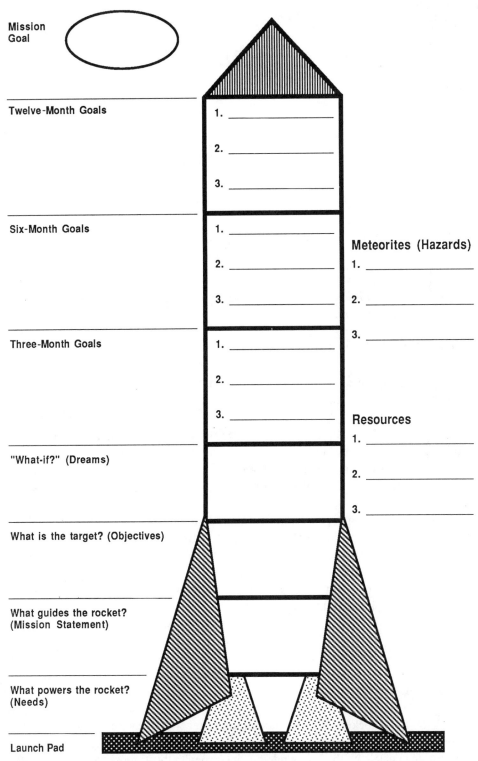

Mission Goal

Twelve-Month Goals

1. _____
2. _____
3. _____

Six-Month Goals

1. _____
2. _____
3. _____

Meteorites (Hazards)

1. _____
2. _____
3. _____

Three-Month Goals

1. _____
2. _____
3. _____

Resources

1. _____
2. _____
3. _____

"What-if?" (Dreams)

What is the target? (Objectives)

What guides the rocket? (Mission Statement)

What powers the rocket? (Needs)

Launch Pad

CHAPTER FIFTEEN

Tough Questions

W*hat should I do if I don't know a person who really wants to be on my leadership core team?*

You should follow two rules of thumb when people volunteer their services. First, don't assume that the job for which they are volunteering is the best or only one for them. We can easily set people up for failure by giving them a responsibility that is not appropriate. Enthusiasm and a good heart will not make up the difference.

Second, allow people opportunities to succeed in smaller responsibilities before they're given the larger tasks. (If a person refuses to be interested in a smaller task and is holding out for the "important" jobs, then you should wonder if their motivation is sound.) Giving people small doses of responsibility does two things: it gets them involved, and it gives you an opportunity to get to know them and watch them work.

The other alternative is to invite this individual to be a part of a leadership development group (see chapter 5). We made it a strong recommendation for anyone who wanted to be involved in our singles ministry. The payoffs were wonderful. The groups allowed us to get to know a handful of people, even if they didn't "take a position." It also gave us a better picture of the kind of niche that would be appropriate for those who "volunteered."

What should I do when my senior pastor puts the pressure on me for spending time with a few people? He thinks I'm away from the office a lot.

Don't be shocked. It's not uncommon to receive pressure (or at least some skepticism) when you practice relational ministry. To be proactive, you should not only communicate with those around you, but also with those above you (senior staff, church board, etc.). Talk about your philosophy of ministry (see chapter 7) in a face-to-face meeting with the senior staff member. Make it clear that you are not managing an adult-baby-sitting service. Tell the senior staff person the names of the people with whom you want to spend time and a little about their stories and their vision for the singles ministry.

In addition to face-to-face communi-cation, we advocate continual memos about updates in the ministry to the senior staff member. Monthly memos need only be one page, mentioning names and stories about how the singles ministry is affecting people's lives. This non-antagonistic vehicle lets the senior pastor know the benefits of your philosophy of spending time with a few.

As an unpaid volunteer in a smaller church, I am swamped with a job as well as other church commitments. How do I find time to develop leaders and give the ministry away?

Shed a few of your responsibilities. Take a vacation. Relax. It's okay to do only what you can do. It's not the end of the world if you can't compete with large churches with endless programming. Ironically, giving the ministry away is the answer to your problem. In the long run, it relieves you because you aren't needed to lead every meeting or set up chairs for every activity. Take on only one small task. The foundation you build is most important.

> *Talk about your philosophy of ministry in a face-to-face meeting with the senior staff member. Make it clear that you are not managing an adult-baby-sitting service.*

What should I do about church members who don't take singles ministry seriously (Singles aren't "real" adults yet) or who view our singles ministry with suspicion?

There will always be people in the church who either don't understand or, because of their fear, will be gossips and doomsayers. Given that reality, we can too easily take such pronouncements personally. We need reminders that such notions are almost always reflections of the individual's uneasiness, not any failure on our part. We should not try to change such people, but begin the process of reeducation. Invite suspicious and vocal opponents to singles functions. Allow single adults to be "living witnesses" during church services. Offer to teach other Christian education classes where you can talk about what it means to be a single adult in the church.

Can I "Rocket plan" for more than a year, making even longer-range goals—two or three years?

Can you Rocket plan for more than a year? Yes. Is it wise? No. As Terry said in the first chapter, expect transition, especially among single persons. You may be wasting your time to plan two and three years ahead, because your entire single adult ministry may look different then. Part of the Rocket process is to reevaluate every six months. You can look ahead during this evaluation time.

You talk about one-year commitments with a six-month evaluation. What happens when leaders serve two to three years or more?

Nothing is wrong with a person serving that long, but it generally makes it difficult for new people to become involved. In this case, the ministry can become owned by a few who take everything personally. The longer a person serves, the greater the chance his or her creativity will become stifled. If someone wants to serve longer, give him or her other areas of service. Don't reenlist people for their previous positions.

Glossary

Addiction. An obsession with a substance or behavior that people internalize as essential to their identity. Because of a tenuous and insecure core identity, people cling precariously to this substance or behavior, which offers promises of relief, fulfillment, or happiness. (See chapter 3.)

Codependency. A condition in which people feel their identity is contingent on being responsible for the health and well-being of other people. In this state, people serve others out of wrong motives, do not give responsibility away, have no time for personal renewal, and feel unappreciated for all the work that they do for other people. (See chapter 3.)

Community. A group of persons who provide support and encouragement, allowing for doubt, frustration, and grief. No one particular form of community exists. For some, community may be an organized small group—a regular weekly meeting. For others, connections with the persons who make up this community may be more spontaneous and irregular. (See chapter 10.)

Destination Language. This language implies the word *should* (for example, *grow up, settle down, get married*). It leaves you feeling that you're never far enough along. It doesn't allow you to embrace or enjoy where you are today. It makes you feel guilty because you haven't tried hard enough. (See chapter 3.)

Dream Session. This is the time to be creative—to sit back and let yourself imagine. This is where you and your team members look within each target area and try to picture: "In terms of this target, if nothing were impossible, what would I like to see happen?" All dreams are written down. Don't stop to discuss or rationalize. After you take a night or longer to pray about them, you choose three to five dreams on which you want to work. (See chapter 9.)

Empower. Giving others power, responsibility, and ownership for dreams, ideas, tasks, and input. Giving people the ability to lead or to make choices—the power to make choices. Permitting and enabling them to take responsibility. (See chapter 4.)

Goals. Goals are the "feet" that carry out a mission statement. Goals are specific enough to accomplish. In the Rocket process, you and your team members establish goals for three-, six-, nine-, and twelve-month phases. (See chapter 9.)

Hierarchical Ministry. This type of ministry states that power is limited and must be divided. Assumes that only a certain amount of power exists, consequently, power must be allocated—most recognizably through an organizational chart. The person at the top of the chart is given the greatest percentage of power, while the remainder is divided among the "lower" boxes. (See chapter 5.)

Job Description. Specific written outline of what is expected of persons holding certain positions. A job description normally states the position title, position purpose, specific responsibilities, who the team member reports to and from whom he or she receives information, required gifts or skills, expectations, length of term, goals, and evaluation date. (See chapter 6.)

Journey Language. This type of language recognizes that where you are has value. It leaves you with a feeling of hope. It gives you a sense of encouragement for taking the next step. It allows you to enjoy or embrace where you are today. (See chapter 3.)

Mission Statement. This is the ministry's purpose. It tells people where you are headed and keeps you from becoming tempted away from the target by seemingly urgent distractions. It is one of the first steps you take when working through the Rocket planning process. Here is a sample mission statement: "We intend to give singles the opportunity to gain a world view and to respond to the world's needs in experiences that foster relationships with each other and with those to whom they go. It is our goal to share the gospel and ourselves in ministry." (See chapter 9.)

Personal Boundaries. The ability to say no. Learning your limits. Knowing you can't do everything. (See chapter 11.)

Philosophy of Ministry. This answers the question, "Why are we doing things the way we are?" The same "sheet of music" off which your leadership core team plays. Teams operate best when they know why they are in existence. An example of one philosophy: "The starting point of our ministry is God. The guide for our ministry is the Bible. The focus of our ministry is people, not programs. The environment of our ministry is teamwork, not individualism." (See chapter 7.)

Relational Leadership/Ministry. This type of ministry concentrates on building people, not just starting a program, creating an environment of nurture where others are empowered, avoiding hierarchical or autocratic leadership. The ministry is owned by the people. Power is limitless. Every person has potential ownership and therefore power, or the capacity to effect change. Each has the power to make decisions, have choices, give input, solve problems, plan for the future, and take responsibilities. (See chapters 2 and 5.)

Sabbath. A period of rest in which we quiet the internal noise and take the time necessary to separate ourselves from the people who cling to us and the routines to which we cling. (See chapter 11.)

Self-Nurture. To practice personal boundaries. (See chapters 4 and 11.)

Self-Responsibility. Personal development, self-care, self-nurture. (See chapters 4 and 11.)

Small Group. A group of three to twelve people who intentionally come together to study, pray, and share their lives. Called *covenant groups, discipleship groups, support groups*, or *small groups*, they share the same purpose: To help members grow in Christ and in Christian community. In the process, we find family, a place where we belong in the Christian community. (See chapter 10.)

Targets. The ministry's objectives. These help you and your team members focus, and not try to hit everything. Targets for a single adult ministry could be: classes for different age groups (twenties, thirties, forties-plus); divorce recovery workshops; missions; and a resource center for single parents. Targets are established in the Rocket planning process. (See chapter 9.)

Notes

HOW TO USE THIS BOOK

1. Terry Hershey, *Young Adult Ministry* (Loveland, CO: Group, 1986), pages 15-16.

CHAPTER 1: FACTS AND MYTHS ABOUT SINGLE ADULTS

1. Barna Research Group, "America 2000: What the Trends Mean for Christianity," as reported in *Single Adult Ministries Journal*, no. 67, October 1989, page 1.

CHAPTER 2: LEADERSHIP: A NEW DEFINITION

1. George Barna, *America 2000: What the Trends Mean for Christianity* (Glendale, CA: Barna Research Group, 1989), page 34.
2. Howard Butt, *The Velvet Covered Brick* (San Francisco: Harper & Row, 1973), page 112.
3. Eugene H. Peterson, *Working the Angles: A Trigonometry for Pastoral Work* (Grand Rapids, MI: Eerdmans, 1987), page 1.
4. Anne Wilson Schaef and Diane Fassel, *The Addictive Organization* (San Francisco: Harper & Row, 1990), page 38.

CHAPTER 3: OBSTACLES TO EFFECTIVE LEADERSHIP

1. Reprinted by permission of UFS, Inc.

CHAPTER 4: A THEOLOGY OF BEING EMPOWERED

1. Henri Nouwen, *In the Name of Jesus: Reflections on Christian Leadership in the Future* (New York: Crossroad, 1989), page 37.

2. Henri Nouwen, *The Wounded Healer: Ministry in Contemporary Society* (Garden City, NY: Image Books, 1979), pages 81-82.
3. Gordon Dahl, *Work, Play, and Worship in a Leisure-Oriented Society* (Minneapolis, MN: Augsburg, 1972), page 12.

CHAPTER 5: TEAM SELECTION

1. John Naisbitt and Patricia Aburdene, *Megatrends 2000: Ten New Directions for the 1990's* (New York: Morrow, 1990), pages 218-219, 226.
2. Peter F. Drucker, *The New Realities: In Government and Politics, In Economics and Business, In Society and World View* (New York: Harper & Row, 1989), page 203.

CHAPTER 7: TEAM COMMUNICATION

1. Bruce Larson, *Setting Men Free* (Grand Rapids, MI: Zondervan, 1967), pages 113-116.
2. Alan Loy McGinnis, Lecture at SALT III, Arrow Head Springs, May 7-10, 1985.

CHAPTER 8: TEAM ROLES

1. Richard C. Halverson, *How I Changed My Thinking About the Church* (Grand Rapids, MI: Zondervan, 1972), pages 73-74.

CHAPTER 10: SMALL GROUPS: BEING IN COMMUNITY

1. Keith Miller, *Taste of New Wine* (New York: Bantam Books, 1973), page 22.
2. Jennifer James, "Compare Turtles to Heroes of Yore," *Seattle Times*, November 11, 1990, page L-3.

CHAPTER 11: LEARNING TO SAY NO

1. Schaef and Fassel, page 221.
2. Henri Nouwen, *Lifesigns* (Garden City, NY: Doubleday, 1986), page 49.
3. Keith Clark, *Make Space Make Symbols: A Personal Journey Into Prayer* (Notre Dame, IN: Ave Maria Press, 1979), page 11.
4. Andrew Greeley, *Confessions of a Parish Priest* (New York: Simon and Schuster, 1986), page 225.
5. Frederick Buechner, *Telling the Truth: The Gospel as Tragedy, Comedy, & Fairy Tale* (San Francisco: Harper & Row, 1977), page 66.
6. C. S. Lewis, *Letters to an American Lady* (Grand Rapids, MI: Eerdmans, 1975), page 73.
7. Clark, page 31.
8. Luke 10:41, MLB.

Bibliography

Beattie, Melody, *Codependent No More* (Harper, 1987).

Bradley, John, and Carty, Jay, *Unlocking Your Sixth Suitcase* (NavPress, 1991).

Bradshaw, John, *The Family* (Health Communications, 1988).

Bradshaw, John, *Healing the Shame That Binds You* (Health Communications, 1988).

Carnes, Patrick, *Contrary to Love* (Comp Care, 1989).

Carnes, Patrick, *Out of the Shadows: The Sexual Addiction* (Comp Care, 1983).

Cermak, Timmon, *A Time to Heal* (Tarcher, 1988).

Conroy, Pat, *The Great Santini* (Bantam, 1976).

Conroy, Pat, *Prince of Tides* (Bantam, 1987).

Eaton, Chris, and Hurst, Kim, *Vacations with a Purpose* (Singles Ministry Resources/NavPress, 1991).

Fagerstrom, Douglas L., *Singles Ministry Handbook* (Victor Books, 1988).

Flanagan, Bill, *Developing a Divorce Recovery Ministry* (Singles Ministry Resources/NavPress, 1991).

Fossum, Merle A., and Mason, Marilyn J., *Facing Shame* (W.W. Norton, 1986).

Griffin, Em, *Getting Together: A Guide for Good Groups* (InterVarsity Press, 1982).

Groom, Nancy, *From Bondage to Bonding* (NavPress, 1991).

Halpern, Howard, *How to Break Your Addiction to a Person* (McGraw Hill, 1982).

Hershey, Terry, *Beginning Again: Life After a Relationship Ends* (Nelson, 1986).

Hershey, Terry, *Clear-Headed Choices in a Sexually Confused World* (Group, 1988).

Hershey, Terry, *Go Away . . . Come Closer* (Word, 1990).

Hershey, Terry, *Intimacy: The Longing of Every Human Heart* (Harvest House, 1984).

Hershey, Terry, *Young Adult Ministry* (Group, 1986).

Hestenes, Roberta, *Turning Committees Into Communities* (NavPress, 1991).

Hestenes, Roberta, *Using the Bible in Groups* (Westminster Press, 1985).

Howatch, Susan, *Glittering Images* (Fawcett, 1988).

Jones, Jerry, ed., *Single Adult Ministry* (Singles Ministry Resources/NavPress, 1991).

Jones, Jerry, ed., *The Idea Catalog for Single Adult Ministry* (Singles Ministry Resources/NavPress, 1991).

Kasl, Charlotte Davis, *Women, Sex and Addiction* (Ticker and Fields, 1989).

Kennedy, Eugene, *The Trouble With Being Human* (Image Books, 1986).

Kiersey, David, and Marilyn Bates, *Please Understand Me*—Meyers/Briggs Type
    Indicator (Prometheus, 1984).
Lee, John, *Flying Boy: Healing the Wounded Man* (Health Communications, 1987).
Lenters, William, *The Freedom We Crave* (Eerdmans, 1985).
Mallison, John, *Building Small Groups in the Christian Community* (Australia: Renewal
    Publications, 1978).
Malone, Thomas, and Malone, Patrick, *The Art of Intimacy* (Prentice Hall, 1987).
McBride, Neal F., *How to Lead Small Groups* (NavPress, 1990).
Miller, Alice, *The Drama of the Gifted Child* (Basic Books, 1981).
National Association of Single Adult Leaders, P.O. Box 1600, Grand Rapids, MI 49501.
National Single Adult Ministries Resource Directory (Singles Ministry
    Resources/NavPress, 1991).
Peck, M. Scott, *The Road Less Traveled* (Touchstone, 1978).
Schaef, Anne Wilson, *Co-Dependence* (Harper, 1986).
Schaef, Anne Wilson, *Escape From Intimacy* (Harper, 1989).
Shain, Merle, *When Lovers Are Friends* (Bantam, 1978).
Single Adult Ministries Journal, P.O. Box 60430, Colorado Springs, CO 80960-0430.
Singles Ministry Resources Leadership Training Group, P.O. Box 2658, Woodinville,
    WA 98072.
Viorst, Judith, *Necessary Losses* (Simon and Schuster, 1986).

For a complete catalog of resources for your ministry with single adults, write
SINGLES MINISTRY RESOURCES, P.O. Box 62056, Colorado Springs, CO 80962-2056.
Or call (800) 487-4SAM.

For a catalog of Terry Hershey resources, write Christian Focus, P.O. Box 2658,
Woodinville, WA 98072.

More Resources for Your Ministry with Single Adults

Contact SINGLES MINISTRY RESOURCES
for a FREE catalog of all the best resources available
to help you build an effective ministry
with single adults in your church
and community.

Singles Ministry Resources
P.O. Box 62056
Colorado Springs, Colorado 80962-2056

Or call (800) 487-4SAM
or (719) 488-2610